To Trish

11/21/95

Happy
Birthday

Love
Dad

The New York Times

New England
Heritage Cookbook

The New York Times

New England Heritage Cookbook

Jean Hewitt

CASTLE

Drawings by Ray Skibinski

Arrangement has been made to publish this edition by Castle,
a division of Book Sales Inc. of Secaucus, New Jersey

87   9

ISBN No.: 0-89009-444-6

Printed in the United States of America

The CASTLE trademark is registered in
the U.S. Patent and Trademark Office.

Contents

Introduction

In connection with my search over the past ten years for authentic regional recipes, I've traveled in most of the fifty states. Aside from the warmth and friendliness of the people, who were willing to share their cooking secrets, the biggest bonus was seeing the incredible natural beauty this country has to offer. From the majesty of Bryce and Zion canyons in Utah to mountain-ringed Diamond Lake in Oregon, from the Grand Tetons seen from Jackson Hole, Wyoming, to the picturesque island of Chincoteague in Virginia and the bluegrass country of Kentucky, the variety of scenery is enormous and the expanse of land to be explored staggering.

But New England is home.

I spend every weekend, year round, in a little house with a big kitchen, near the ocean in Rhode Island. Here the traces of my British accent do not sound strange, and my heritage is similar to, even though more recent than, that of many of my Yankee neighbors.

I am very familiar with the New England states of Connecticut, Rhode Island, Massachusetts, New Hampshire, Vermont and Maine. I have driven from Greenwich, Connecticut, to Aroostook County, Maine, and from Portsmouth, New Hampshire, to Bennington, Vermont, and points in between. Four of the states boldly face the sea, while a small stretch of New Hampshire just edges the Atlantic. Their intriguing coastlines, sand- and rock-covered beaches and quaint fishing villages have a special appeal for me as places to enjoy and as sources of glorious seafood, one of the important ingredients in New England cooking.

There is no better way to savor the bounty from the sea than at an old-fashioned clambake. But it's becoming harder to find a bakemaster who will supervise the digging of the pit and the gathering of the flat stones and rockweed to re-create the way the Indians ate their shellfish. However, steamer clams, lobsters, fish, sausage, sweet potatoes and corn, pulled from a bake-in-a-barrel and eaten alfresco, taste equally good. Fish fillets wrapped around sausages and enclosed in parchment for cooking are a Rhode Island clambake specialty, and in this state the chicken is often left out.

One thing common to all New England clambakes is chowder . . . and rarely with tomatoes. In South, or Washington, County of Rhode Island no milk or cream is added either. The liquid is clam broth and water and the solids tried-out, or fried, salt pork pieces, a little onion, diced potatoes and chopped quahogs or hard-shelled clams. There may be clam cakes or clam fritters to go with the chowder, and if so, don't pass them up. They're great eating.

Soft steamer clams come next, and the neophyte should know that the small tender clams are plucked from the shell by the dark neck, dipped first in fragrant clam broth to remove any trace of sand and then in melted butter. To eat the neck or not is a personal choice, one that depends on how tender they are, but there is no question that the broth is downed, too.

Tackling boiled, or steamed, lobsters for the first time is a formidable task, but the morsels of tender, sweet meat, drenched in melted butter, are worth all the effort of cracking and picking. In New Hampshire and Maine the shore dinner is a popular alternative to the clambake, and it too begins with clam or fish chowder and progresses through steamers and fried clams to lobsters and corn on the cob.

Salmon is not as plentiful in New England waters as it once was, but poached with egg sauce and served with new potatoes and fresh peas, it is still the traditional fare for the Fourth of July. Egg sauce is also the accompaniment for Cape Cod Turkey, which translates to poached cod or haddock.

Thrifty New England settlers learned to dry cod after good catches to see them through the winter months when the fishing boats could not go out. This also allowed the fish to be shipped to inland areas, and even today dried codfish cakes with bacon are as popular for breakfast in Vermont as they are in Massachusetts. Mackerel and alewives have a dedicated following among New England fish eaters and should not be overlooked. The glories of striped bass, bluefish, pollock, fluke, swordfish and Connecticut River shad do not have to be extolled. Broiled, grilled, baked or fried, they all are superb, provided they are not overcooked.

8

The kitchen is the heart of a New England home, and cooking tends to be simple, honest and frugal. It is based on the natural bounty of the region just as it was when the first settlers landed in Plymouth and learned to cook with corn, cranberries, squash and beans. Add to these free-for-the-gathering wild berries, beach plums, rose hips, dandelions, fiddlehead greens and maple syrup for a variety of unique taste experiences and recipe variations.

The early settlers in New England discovered that flour made from corn was not a substitute for wheat flour in bread baking, but their experiments taught them that corn meal mixed with boiling water in varying proportions made a "hasty pudding," or mush, that was good as porridge or chilled, sliced and fried. With more liquid added, and cooked on a griddle, the mush became johnny cakes to serve with melted butter or creamed dried beef or to carry on a journey. In many books they are referred to as journey cakes.

Stretching their precious rye and whole wheat flour by adding corn meal, sweetening it with molasses brought from the West Indies, the settlers made steamed brown bread and baked anadama bread. The story goes that a Gloucester fisherman couldn't get his wife to bake bread so he mixed up a batch himself while muttering "Anna-damn-'er."

The aroma of baked beans slowly simmering with molasses, onion and salt pork permeates New England homes on a Saturday because supper is traditionally baked beans and brown bread, piccalilli, or mustard pickles, and catchup with ham added in good times. Custard pie is a favorite for dessert. There are enough leftover beans for Sunday's breakfast and to put between slices of bread for Monday's lunch. Succotash is another popular New England bean dish. In some areas meat is an important ingredient, and in others succotash is fresh beans and corn, plus the ubiquitous salt pork, milk, butter and sugar.

Salt pork adds flavor and fat to chowders, boiled dinners and vegetables and in lean times is served fried or roasted as the *pièce de résistance*. New Englanders preserved it in brine for year-round use just as they corned beef at slaughtering time. Corned beef has nothing to do with corn but got the name from the "corns," or grains, of saltpeter or gunpowder used in the curing. Thursday is the night for boiled dinner in New England when the juicy red corned beef is served nestled in a ring of cabbage, carrots, turnips, parsnips and beets. Leftover meat is chopped, not ground, and mixed with beets to make red flannel hash.

New Englanders do not live by bread and meat alone, and no meal is complete without a baked dessert: a lucious wild blueberry grunt or slump

9

with dumplings made from biscuit dough cooked on top of the fruit mixture; a pandowdy or cobbler with biscuit crust baked on top of the apples, peaches or berries. Many of the desserts and vegetable mixtures are sweetened and flavored with maple syrup, and the ultimate treat is maple sugar-in-snow, with sour pickles, offered outside the sugarhouse in early spring.

Cranberry pies, breads, muffins, puddings and relishes were sweetened with maple syrup or molasses in colonial times, but modern cooks tend to use sugar for the tart, bright-red berries that are an important crop in Massachusetts. Try mixing cranberries and nuts into an apple pie filling, and you have a whole new dessert treat. They freeze easily with no preparation and make a delectable and pretty sherbert.

Squash in its myriad forms is a staple throughout New England. Squash and pumpkin are ingredients in pies, cakes, quick breads and muffins, too, and they are cooked, mashed and pressure canned, or frozen, for year-round use. The hard winter varieties, including butternut, acorn and hubbard, keep well in a dry cellar and are excellent cut into pieces of manageable size and baked with salt, butter and a smidgen of brown sugar, until tender.

If I have given the impression that New Englanders are a homogeneous group, this is far from true. As in the rest of the United States, there are many ethnic groups that have enhanced the region with their culture and cuisines. The Portuguese tended to migrate to the fishing villages in Massachusetts and Rhode Island, and they have added Iberian-style fish stews, fish with vinegar and salt cod dishes, spicy sausages and the famous Portuguese sweet bread to New England's culinary triumphs.

The Irish are synonymous with Boston, and there's many a loaf of soda bread and pot of lamb stew still made according to recipes brought from the old country. Italians came to New England to use their talents in quarrying granite, cutting stone, creating magnificent estates and many other ways. Today Italian families still gather around a kitchen table to make a hundred pounds of homemade sausage—some to eat fresh and the remainder to dry in a well-ventilated attic.

Pickling and canning peppers, eggplant, tomatoes and cucumbers and curing olives are other family-oriented tasks. In one small Rhode Island resort town the residents of Italian descent wait until the summer people leave, and then cousins, aunts, grandmothers and neighbors move into the kitchen of the local restaurant to whip up caldrons of steaming relishes, tomato sauce and pickled peppers. Even the children pitch in and help wash bottles and fill jars. To keep up their strength, the workers feast on mountains of homemade sausage and peppers, ravioli with meat sauce, stuffed shells and sugar-dusted fried pastries.

New England cooking is plain compared with the intricacies of French and Chinese cuisines, but it is hearty, healthful and appealing—and this book offers a generous sampler for your pleasure.

JEAN D. HEWITT

Westerly, Rhode Island

The New York Times
New England Heritage
Cookbook

Appetizers
and Soups

Cheese Crisps
CONNECTICUT

1 cup flour	¼ teaspoon salt
¼ cup butter	Dash freshly ground black
⅓ cup finely grated Cheddar	pepper
cheese	2 egg yolks, lightly beaten.

1. Preheat the oven to 400 degrees

2. Place the flour in a bowl and, with the finger tips or a pastry blender, work in the butter until the mixture resembles coarse oatmeal.

3. Stir in the cheese, salt and pepper and enough of the egg yolk mixture to make a dough which will cling together.

4. Turn out onto a lightly floured board. Roll out half the dough to one-quarter-inch thickness and cut with a small round cutter. Place on a lightly greased baking sheet. Bake ten minutes, or until golden. Cool on a rack.

Yield: About two dozen crisps.

Cheese-Stuffed Celery Appetizer

VERMONT

½ cup crumbled blue cheese
⅓ cup finely chopped water
   cress leaves

2 tablespoons soft butter
   Celery ribs, cut into two-
   inch lengths.

Blend the cheese, water cress and soft butter together in an electric blender or in a bowl with a wooden spoon. Fill the celery pieces and chill.
Yield: Six servings.

Chicken Liver Pâté

CONNECTICUT

   Gizzards and hearts from
   six to eight chickens
   Chicken broth
2 onions, finely chopped
⅓ cup butter, approximately
6 to eight chicken livers
2 tablespoons cognac

2 hard-cooked eggs, finely
   chopped
   Salt and freshly ground
   black pepper to taste
1 teaspoon thyme
½ teaspoon marjoram
   Toast triangles.

1. Cover the gizzards and hearts with broth. Bring to a boil, cover and simmer until tender, about twenty-five minutes. Drain. Chop finely or grind through a meat chopper or an electric blender.

2. Sauté the onions in one-third cup butter in a heavy skillet. Add the livers and cook over high heat, stirring frequently, until the livers are brown outside but still pink inside, adding butter if necessary.

3. Chop finely and add to the giblet mixture.

4. Add the cognac, eggs, salt, pepper, thyme and marjoram. Mix well. Pile into a crock and chill well. Serve with toast triangles.
Yield: Ten servings.

Baked Stuffed Clams

MASSACHUSETTS

12	medium-size cherrystone clams, well scrubbed
2	tablespoons water
	Rock salt (optional)
2	tablespoons butter
2	shallots, finely chopped
2	cloves garlic, finely chopped
2	cups soft bread crumbs
¼	cup finely chopped celery
2	tablespoons chopped parsley
½	teaspoon basil
½	teaspoon oregano
2	tablespoons freshly grated Parmesan cheese
1	tablespoon olive oil
1	tablespoon dry white wine
	Freshly ground black pepper to taste
8	slices bacon, cut into thirds.

1. Preheat the oven to 350 degrees.
2. Place the clams and water in a pan. Cover and steam until the clams just open, about eight minutes. Reserve the broth. Remove the clams from the shells and chop finely. Wash all shell halves and set in a shallow baking pan. Bury in rock salt if it is available.
3. Melt the butter in a skillet and sauté the shallots and garlic in it until tender but not browned. Stir in the bread crumbs, celery, parsley, basil, oregano, cheese, oil, wine and pepper. Mix well.
4. Stir in enough of the reserved clam broth to moisten the stuffing but not make it soggy.
5. Distribute the chopped clams among the twenty-four shells. Top with bread crumb mixture and then a piece of bacon. Bake ten minutes and then brown under the broiler.

Yield: Four servings.

Codfish Balls

MASSACHUSETTS

1½	cups salt cod pieces
2½	cups peeled, cubed potatoes
2	tablespoons butter
1	egg, beaten
	Pepper to taste
	Deep oil for frying.

1. Soak the codfish in water to cover for twelve to sixteen hours, changing water three to four times. Drain.

17

2. Place the drained fish in a saucepan, cover with water, bring to a boil and simmer partially covered until the fish flakes easily, about twenty minutes. Drain and flake the fish.

3. Cook the potatoes in boiling water (without salt) until soft, about twenty minutes. Drain and dry over low heat for a minute or two.

4. Pass the potatoes through a potato ricer or mash well. Combine with the fish, butter, egg and pepper and beat until smooth.

5. Drop teaspoonfuls of the mixture (four or five at a time) into deep oil heated to 375 degrees and fry until golden, about four minutes. Drain and keep warm while frying the rest of the mixture.

Yield: Four to six servings.

Curried Flan Appetizer

CONNECTICUT

½	onion, finely chopped	1	cup mayonnaise
1	rib celery, finely chopped	4	hard-cooked eggs, chopped
1½	tablespoons butter	¼	cup chopped salted almonds
2	to three teaspoons curry powder, or to taste		(optional)
5	teaspoons unflavored gelat-in	2	tablespoons chopped parsley (optional)
2¼	cups chicken broth		Pumpernickel or crackers.

1. Sauté the onion and celery in the butter until tender. Sprinkle with the curry powder and cook, stirring, one minute.

2. Soak the gelatin in one-quarter cup of the broth. Heat the remaining broth to boiling, add softened gelatin and stir into the curry mixture. Bring to a boil, stirring.

3. Cool and chill the mixture until it begins to thicken. Blend in the mayonnaise, eggs, almonds and parsley if desired. Pour mixture into a cold wet mold and chill until firm. Unmold and serve as spread with pumpernickel or crackers

Yield: About one dozen to twenty servings.

Ham Mousse

VERMONT

1	envelope unflavored gelatin	2	tablespoons chopped stuffed green olives (optional)
¼	cup cold water		
1	cup boiling chicken broth	½	cup mayonnaise
2	teaspoons Worcestershire sauce	1	small onion, finely grated
1	teaspoon celery salt		Lettuce leaves
2	teaspoons dry mustard		Sour pickles.
2	cups finely ground cooked ham		

1. Soak the gelatin in the cold water for five minutes. Stir in the boiling broth until the gelatin dissolves. Add the Worcestershire, celery salt and mustard.

2. Combine the ham, olives if used, mayonnaise and onion in a bowl. Stir in the hot gelatin mixture. Pour into a mold or two miniature loaf pans. Chill several hours or overnight.

3. Unmold, slice and serve on lettuce with sour pickles.

Yield: Six servings.

Lobster Canapés

RHODE ISLAND

3	tablespoons butter	1½	cups cooked lobster meat, finely chopped
½	cup freshly grated Parmesan cheese		
1	egg yolk	48	one-and-one-half-inch to two-inch rounds toasted bread.
3	tablespoons dry sherry		
⅛	teaspoon cayenne pepper		
½	teaspoon Worcestershire sauce		

1. Preheat the oven to 425 degrees.

2. Cream the butter and cheese together. Stir in the egg yolk, sherry, cayenne and Worcestershire. Add the lobster and mix well.

3. Place a spoonful of the lobster mixture on each toast round. Place on a baking sheet and bake five minutes.

Yield: Four dozen.

Pickled Mackerel
RHODE ISLAND

4	small mackerel, cleaned	12	peppercorns
4	cups water	1	small hot red pepper
½	cup cider vinegar		Lemon wedges
¼	cup salt		Buttered thinly sliced
4	bay leaves		brown bread.

1. Preheat the oven to 250 degrees.
2. Place the mackerel in a shallow baking dish.
3. Combine the remaining ingredients and pour over fish. Bake forty-five minutes. Allow to cool in the liquid.
4. To serve, remove fish from bones and skin. Serve fish with lemon wedges and brown bread.

Yield: Eight servings.

Onions with Blue Cheese
CONNECTICUT

2	tablespoons lemon juice	1	clove garlic, crushed
½	cup salad oil	¼	cup crumbled blue cheese
1	teaspoon Worcestershire sauce	2	cups sliced red or sweet yellow onions, separated into rings
⅛	teaspoon freshly ground black pepper		Buttered pumpernickel.

1. Combine the lemon juice, oil, Worcestershire, pepper and garlic in a bowl. Beat to mix. Add the cheese and onions. Stir to mix.
2. Cover and chill overnight or up to forty-eight hours. Remove the garlic clove and serve with buttered pumpernickel.

Yield: Six servings.

Creamed Oysters
RHODE ISLAND

24	oysters	1	cup freshly grated Parmesan cheese
	Rock salt		
1	cup heavy cream	½	cup melted butter.

1. Open the oysters and remove from the shell. Wash twenty-four half shells and place an oyster in each. Set in a shallow baking pan filled with rock salt.

2. Pour two teaspoons of the cream over each oyster. Sprinkle each with two teaspoons of the cheese and one teaspoon of the melted butter. Broil under a preheated broiler just until the oyster edges curl and the cheese is lightly browned.

Yield: Six servings.

Baked Oysters with Bacon
MASSACHUSETTS

2 dozen oysters	Lemon wedges
Rock salt	Parsley sprigs.
6 slices bacon, cut in quarters crosswise	

1. Preheat the oven to 375 degrees.

2. Open the oysters and leave on the half shell. Set the oysters in the shell on rock salt (to steady them) in a shallow metal baking dish.

3. Place a piece of bacon on top of each oyster. Bake until the oysters curl, about five minutes. Serve garnished with lemon wedges and parsley sprigs.

Yield: Four to six servings.

Oyster and Sweetbread-Filled Patty Shells
MASSACHUSETTS

2 pounds sweetbreads	1 teaspoon Worcestershire sauce
Cold water	Freshly ground black pepper to taste
Cider vinegar	
Salt	
Boiling salted water	⅛ teaspoon cayenne pepper
5 tablespoons butter	¼ teaspoon paprika
3 tablespoons flour	¼ teaspoon nutmeg
1 cup milk	8 hot cooked puff paste shells.
1 pint shucked oysters with liquor	

1. Early in the day, soak the sweetbreads about two hours in cold water to which one tablespoon vinegar and one teaspoon salt have been added. Change the water, adding more vinegar and salt, two or three times, removing the membrane as it loosens.

2. Drain the sweetbreads, cover with boiling salted water and simmer gently twenty minutes, or until tender. Plunge immediately into cold water.

3. Remove the remaining membrane and stems. Place the sweetbreads under weights for two hours to remove excess water, draining occasionally.

4. Close to serving time, melt three tablespoons of the butter in a heavy skillet and sauté the sweetbreads in it five minutes on each side. Remove the sweetbreads and slice. Reserve in a warm place.

5. Add the remaining butter to the skillet. Blend in the flour and gradually stir in the milk. Bring to a boil, stirring.

6. Stir in the oysters with liquor, stirring constantly. Season with the Worcestershire, one-half teaspoon salt, the pepper, cayenne, paprika and nutmeg.

7. Return the sweetbreads to the mixture and heat through. Serve in the patty shells.

Yield: Eight servings.

Sardines with Sour Cream

MAINE

½	cucumber, peeled, halved, seeded and chopped	1	tablespoon lemon juice
5	radishes, finely chopped		Salt and freshly ground black pepper to taste
2	scallions, finely chopped	3	four-ounce cans Maine sardines
1	cup sour cream		
1	teaspoon Worcestershire sauce		Boston lettuce leaves
	Few drops Tabasco		Lemon wedges.

1. Place the cucumber in a piece of paper towel and squeeze out excess moisture. Place in a small bowl. Add the radishes, scallions, sour cream, Worcestershire, Tabasco and lemon juice. Mix well and season with salt and pepper. Chill.

2. Drain the sardines. To serve, place lettuce leaves in six chilled

cocktail or sherbet glasses. Spoon in a tablespoon of the sour cream-vegetable mixture. Top with the sardines, dividing the number equally among the glasses.

3. Top with the remaining sour cream-vegetable mixture.
4. Serve garnished with lemon wedges.

Yield: Six servings.

Skewered Scallops
MASSACHUSETTS

2	tablespoons finely grated onion	8	slices bacon, cut in half crosswise
2	tablespoons lemon juice	8	mushroom caps
	Salt and freshly ground black pepper to taste	3	tablespoons melted butter
1	pound sea scallops, cut in half if very large		Lemon wedges.

1. Combine the onion, lemon juice, salt and pepper in a bowl. Pick over, rinse and dry the scallops. Add to the bowl, stir, cover and allow to marinate twenty minutes at room temperature or up to two hours in the refrigerator.

2. Thread scallops alternately with the bacon and mushrooms on eight individual skewers. Broil, brushing the scallops and mushrooms with the butter, eight to ten minutes, or until the bacon is crisp and the scallops are opaque and firm, turning frequently. Serve with lemon wedges.

Yield: Four servings.

Scallops Mayonnaise
MASSACHUSETTS

1	pound scallops	3	tablespoons finely chopped scallions, including green part
	Salt to taste		
¾	cup mayonnaise		
½	cup sour cream	2	tablespoons finely chopped stuffed green olives
1	tablespoon horseradish, or to taste		Tabasco to taste.
1	teaspoon mustard, preferably Dijon or Düsseldorf		

23

1. If bay scallops are used, leave them whole; if sea scallops are used, cut them in half. Place in a saucepan with water to barely cover. Add salt. Bring to a boil and simmer three to five minutes. Do not overcook or scallops will toughen. Drain and chill well.

2. Combine the remaining ingredients. Serve scallops with mayonnaise dressing.

Yield: Four servings.

Marinated Maine Sardines

3	three-and-three-quarter-ounce to four-ounce cans sardines	½	teaspoon horseradish
¾	cup sour cream	½	teaspoon salt
¼	cup light cream	½	cup onion, thinly sliced, separated into rings
¼	cup tarragon vinegar	1	cup thinly sliced peeled cucumber
2	tablespoons lemon juice		Boston lettuce cups.
2	tablespoons dry white wine		
1	clove garlic, crushed		

1. Day before, drain the sardines and arrange in a single layer in a shallow baking dish. Combine the sour cream, light cream, vinegar, lemon juice, wine, garlic, horseradish and salt.

2. Mix together cream mixture, the onion and cucumber and spread over sardines. Chill overnight. Next day, arrange in lettuce cups.

Yield: Six servings.

Cold Shrimp Appetizer

MAINE

1	cup homemade mayonnaise	1	tablespoon cognac
1	teaspoon finely grated onion	1	cup cooked, shelled and deveined shrimp
1	clove garlic, crushed		Lettuce cups.
1	tablespoon catchup		

Combine the mayonnaise, onion, garlic, catchup and cognac in a bowl. Add the shrimp, toss and chill. Remove garlic. Serve in lettuce cups.

Yield: Three servings.

Cy's Fried Steamers

RHODE ISLAND

2 dozen freshly opened
steamer clams (with necks);
save the juice for chowder
Unflavored dry bread crumbs

Clarified butter
Lemon wedges
Tartar sauce.

1. Place the steamer clams between sheets of wax paper and flatten the bodies with a mallet or rolling pin. Collect the juice to use in chowder.

2. Coat the clams with bread crumbs, cover and chill an hour or longer.

3. Heat a large heavy skillet; add two tablespoons butter and a single layer of breaded clams, leaving room in between so that they brown on all sides. Cook over medium heat until golden; turn and cook until golden. Keep warm until all are cooked. Serve with lemon wedges and tartar sauce.

Yield: Eight servings.

Stuffed Zucchini

VERMONT

1 large zucchini
2 tablespoons olive oil
1 medium-size onion, finely
chopped
½ clove garlic, finely chopped
½ tablespoon wine vinegar

Salt and freshly ground
black pepper to taste
½ teaspoon chervil
½ teaspoon tarragon
1 tablespoon chopped parsley
Toast triangles.

1. Halve the zucchini lengthwise and scoop out the flesh, leaving a one-quarter-inch shell. Chop the flesh.

2. Heat the oil and sauté the onion, garlic and chopped zucchini in it until tender. Increase the heat to evaporate any excess moisture.

3. Add the vinegar, salt, pepper, chervil, tarragon and parsley. Pile into the zucchini shells and serve warm or cold, with toast triangles.

Yield: About four servings.

Beef and Barley Soup

MAINE

1	pound beef shin or soup beef, cubed	3 sprigs parsley
1	tablespoon bacon drippings	1 onion, sliced
1	large cracked beef or veal knuckle bone	1 bay leaf
8	cups cold water	¼ cup pearl barley
1½	teaspoons salt	¼ cup brown rice
1	teaspoon freshly ground black pepper	½ cup chopped celery
		2 cups stewed tomatoes
		2 tablespoons chopped parsley.

1. Day before, sauté the meat cubes in the bacon drippings until sealed but not browned. Add the bone, water, salt, pepper, parsley sprigs, onion and bay leaf. Bring to a boil and boil vigorously while skimming the surface of scum. Cover and cook gently two hours.

2. Add the barley and rice and cook one hour longer.

3. Cool and chill overnight. Next day, remove surface fat, bones and parsley sprigs. Add the remaining ingredients. Check seasoning and simmer forty-five minutes.

Yield: Eight servings.

Baked Bean Soup

MASSACHUSETTS

2	cups cold baked beans	2 cups canned tomatoes
2	medium-size onions, minced	2 tablespoons flour
½	clove garlic, finely chopped	2 tablespoons butter
4	cups cold water	Salt and freshly ground black pepper to taste.

1. Place the beans, onions, garlic and water in a saucepan and simmer about thrity minutes.

2. Heat the tomatoes, put through an electric blender or food mill and add to the bean mixture.

3. Mix the flour and butter together and add a little of the hot soup. Return all to the pan and cook, stirring, until soup thickens. Season with salt and pepper.

Yield: Six servings.

Black Bean Soup
MASSACHUSETTS

2	cups black beans (one pound dried)	1	tablespoon lemon juice
2	onions, sliced	¼	cup dry sherry
1	clove garlic, finely chopped	1	hard-cooked egg, finely chopped
1½	teaspoons salt	6	slices lemon
¼	teaspoon freshly ground black pepper	1	tablespoon chopped parsley.
⅛	teaspoon dry mustard		

1. Pick over and wash the beans. Place in a bowl, cover with cold water and soak overnight. Drain the beans and place in a kettle with six cups water, the onions, garlic, salt and pepper. Bring to a boil, cover and simmer two hours, or until beans are very soft.

2. Press the bean mixture through a food mill or blend in an electric blender and return to the clean kettle. Add the mustard, lemon juice, sherry and hard-cooked egg, bring to a boil and, if necessary, add water to thin to suitable consistency. Serve each portion garnished with a lemon slice sprinkled with parsley.

Yield: Six servings.

Yankee Bean Chowder
MASSACHUSETTS

1	cup dried pea beans or navy beans	1	teaspoon salt
1	onion, finely chopped	½	teaspoon freshly ground black pepper
1	cup diced carrots	1	cup diced potatoes
1	green pepper, diced	2	cups milk.
1½	cups canned tomatoes		

1. Day before, pick over and wash the beans. Cover with cold water and let soak overnight.

2. Next day, drain the beans and place in a kettle with one and one-half quarts fresh cold water.

3. Add the onion and bring to a boil. Cover and simmer until beans are barely tender, about thirty minutes. Add the carrots, green pepper, to-

matoes, salt and black pepper and cook ten minutes. If desired, soup can be put through an electric blender or food mill at this point.

4. Add the potatoes and milk and cook fifteen minutes longer, or until the potatoes are tender. Check seasoning.

Yield: Six servings.

Cabbage Soup

NEW HAMPSHIRE

3	tablespoons butter	Salt and freshly ground
1	small onion, chopped	black pepper to taste
1	medium-size head green	3 cups milk, scalded
	cabbage, coarsely shredded	1 cup heavy cream, scalded
1½	cups water	Croutons.

1. Heat the butter in a large heavy saucepan and sauté the onion until golden. Add the cabbage and cook, stirring, until wilted.

2. Pour in the water, salt and pepper, bring to a boil, cover and cook fifteen minutes.

3. Add the milk and cream and bring to a boil. Taste for seasoning; add salt and pepper if needed. Serve with croutons.

Yield: Six servings.

Cheese Soup

VERMONT

¼	cup butter	4 cups chicken broth
¼	cup chopped white part of	2 tablespoons butter
	the leek or onion	2 tablespoons flour
¼	cup finely chopped carrot	1 cup milk
¼	cup finely chopped celery	6 ounces grated Cheddar
	heart with leaves	cheese
	Grated rind of one lemon	1½ teaspoons Worcestershire
½	bay leaf	sauce
¼	teaspoon white pepper	Tabasco to taste.
½	teaspoon dry mustard	

28

1. Melt the one-quarter cup butter in a heavy saucepan and sauté the leek or onion, carrots and celery until tender but not browned.

2. Add the lemon rind, bay leaf, pepper, mustard and broth, bring to a boil, cover and simmer twenty minutes, or until the vegetables are tender.

3. Melt the two tablespoons butter in a small pan, blend in the flour and gradually stir in the milk. Bring to a boil, stirring, until the mixture thickens and boils.

4. Remove from heat and stir in the cheese. Continue to stir until the cheese is melted. Gradually whisk the chicken broth mixture into the cheese sauce. Reheat but do not boil. Add the Worcestershire and Tabasco. Serve immediately.

Yield: Six servings.

Chicken Chowder
RHODE ISLAND

¼ cup diced salt pork
1 onion, sliced
1 rib celery, finely chopped
2 cups peeled, cubed potato
3 cups chicken broth
1½ to two cups cooked, cubed chicken (one large whole chicken breast, poached)

1 cup milk
1 cup heavy or light cream
Salt and freshly ground black pepper to taste
2 tablespoons chopped parsley.

1. Sauté the salt pork in a large heavy saucepan until the fat is rendered and the pork pieces are crisp. Remove the pork pieces and reserve.

2. Add the onion and celery to the pan and sauté until golden. Add the potatoes and cook, stirring, three minutes.

3. Pour in the broth, bring to a boil, cover and cook until the potatoes are tender, about twenty minutes. Add the chicken, milk, cream and reserved pork bits and bring to a boil. Season to taste with salt and pepper. Sprinkle with the parsley and serve immediately.

Yield: Four servings.

Creamed Chicken Soup
NEW HAMPSHIRE

1	three-and-one-half-pound chicken, cut into serving pieces	½	teaspoon freshly ground black pepper
6	cups water	¼	cup butter
2	ribs celery with leaves, diced	2	onions, thinly sliced
1	bay leaf	4	baking potatoes, peeled and thinly sliced or diced
2	sprigs parsley	1	cup light cream
1¾	teaspoons salt	¼	cup chopped parsley.

1. Place the chicken pieces in a heavy casserole or kettle. Add the water, celery, bay leaf, parsley sprigs, one teaspoon of the salt and one-quarter teaspoon of the pepper. Bring to a boil, cover and simmer gently until the chicken is tender, about fifty minutes. Remove the chicken pieces from the broth. Strain the broth into a kettle and remove the surface fat.

2. Take the chicken meat from the bones and skin and cut the meat into large slivers. Set aside.

3. Heat the butter in a skillet and sauté the onions in it until transparent but not browned. Add the potatoes, toss and cook two to three minutes without browning.

4. Add the vegetables to the broth in the kettle. Add the remaining salt and pepper. Cover, bring to a boil and simmer forty-five minutes, or until the potatoes are very tender.

5. Pass the mixture through a sieve or puree in an electric blender. Return to the kettle. Stir in the cream and reserved chicken. Reheat, but do not boil. Serve garnished with the chopped parsley.

Yield: Eight servings.

Cape Cod Clam Chowder
MASSACHUSETTS

¼	pound bacon, finely diced	¼	teaspoon basil
2	medium-size onions, finely chopped	2	cups boiling water
3	cups diced potatoes	24	chowder clams (preferably large quahogs), ground, liquor and all, through medium blade of food grinder.
2	teaspoons salt		
½	teaspoon oregano		

1. Sauté the bacon and onions in a large kettle until onions are tender and golden. Pour off excess fat.

2. To the kettle, add the potatoes, salt, oregano, basil and water and let simmer until potatoes are tender, about fifteen minutes.

3. Add the clams. This is the base. (See note to prepare chowder.) *Yield:* About one quart of base.

Note: Next day, add to base one quart of milk, two tablespoons butter and salt and freshly ground black pepper to taste. Heat.

Old-Fashioned Clam Chowder
MASSACHUSETTS

60	to seventy-two chowder clams, scrubbed until water runs clear	1	bay leaf
		3	large potatoes, peeled and diced
½	pound salt pork, diced		Salt and freshly ground black pepper to taste
6	large onions, sliced		
4	to six leeks, cleaned and sliced	2	tablespoons flour
		2	tablespoons butter
3	tomatoes, peeled and chopped	2	large pilot crackers, crumbled
2	cups canned tomatoes	1	teaspoon Worcestershire sauce
3	ribs celery, diced		
1	tablespoon chopped parsley	2	to four drops Tabasco.
1	teaspoon thyme		

1. Place the clams in a large kettle or clam steamer with one-half cup water. Steam the clams until they open, about ten minutes, depending on the size.

2. Reserve the broth. Remove clams from shells and remove the long necks and coarse membrane. Chop half the clams, leaving remaining clams whole. Reserve.

3. Cook salt pork in a heavy kettle until golden. Add onions and leeks and sauté until tender.

4. Measure the reserved broth and add water to make up to two quarts and add to the kettle. Add the chopped tomatoes, canned tomatoes, celery, parsley, thyme, bay leaf, potatoes, salt and pepper. Bring to a boil and simmer, covered, about thirty to forty minutes.

5. Blend the flour with the butter and, while stirring, add a little at a

time to the hot soup. Add the crackers, Worcestershire, Tabasco and reserved clams. Reheat and test for seasoning.

Yield: About five quarts; fifteen to twenty servings.

Corn Chowder
NEW HAMPSHIRE

¼	pound salt pork	1	teaspoon salt
	Boiling water	½	teaspoon freshly ground
1	large onion, thinly sliced		white pepper
2	potatoes, peeled and cubed	2	cups light cream.
2	cups chicken broth		
1½	cups corn kernels freshly		
	cut from the cob		

1. Place the salt pork in a bowl and pour boiling water over. Let stand five minutes. Drain. Dice the pork.

2. Cook the pork pieces in a kettle until crisp. Remove the pieces and reserve. Sauté the onion in the fat remaining until it is tender.

3. Add the potatoes and broth. Cover and simmer until the potatoes are barely tender, about fifteen minutes. Add the corn, salt and pepper and cook two minutes longer.

4. Stir in the cream and heat to boiling. Sprinkle the top with reserved pork pieces before serving.

Yield: Four to six servings.

Egg Chowder
MAINE

¾	cup diced salt pork		Freshly ground black pepper to taste
1	onion, thinly sliced		
3	potatoes, peeled and sliced	4	eggs
4	cups milk, scalded		Pilot crackers.

1. Cook the salt pork until it releases some of the fat, but do not allow to become crisp.

2. Add the onion and potatoes and cook, stirring occasionally, ten minutes. Add the milk and pepper and cook gently until potatoes are tender.

32

3. Break eggs into simmering mixture and cook three minutes. Serve with crackers.

Yield: Four servings.

Rhode Island Fish Chowder

1 pound salt pork, cut into strips, soaked in boiling water five minutes and drained	3 tablespoon chopped parsley
	⅛ teaspoon cayenne pepper
4 pounds cod or sea bass fillets, cut into four-inch squares	Split pilot crackers, cream crackers or ship biscuits or any plain, unsalted crackers that have not been oil-dipped
3 cups finely chopped onions	3 tablespoons butter
1 tablespoon chopped fresh summer savory or one teaspoon dried savory	1 tablespoon flour.

1. Make a layer of the salt pork in the bottom of a chowder kettle. Top with a layer of the fish, then the onions and season with some of the savory, parsley and cayenne.

2. Make a layer of the crackers. Repeat layers until all ingredients are used, ending with crackers that have been spread with two tablespoons of the butter.

3. Pour water down the side of the kettle until water almost covers top layer of crackers. Bring to a boil, cover and simmer one hour. Replenish water level with boiling water if level sinks too low.

4. Decant the liquid into a saucepan. Blend together the remaining butter and the flour and gradually whisk the mixture into the simmering liquid.

5. Transfer solid part of chowder to a tureen or soup bowls and pour thickened liquid over.

Yield: Eight to ten servings.

33

Down-East Haddock Chowder

MAINE

⅓ cup diced salt pork
1 onion, finely chopped
3 potatoes, peeled and cubed
2 pounds haddock fillets, cut
into strips or cubes
1 quart water
1 rib celery with leaves,
chopped

Salt and freshly ground
black pepper to taste
⅛ teaspoon mace
3 cups milk
3 large pilot crackers, crumbled.

1. Cook the salt pork in a kettle until crisp. Remove the pieces and reserve.

2. In the fat remaining in the kettle, sauté the onion until tender but not browned. Add the potatoes, fish, water, celery, salt, pepper and mace. Bring to a boil, cover and simmer gently until potatoes are tender, about fifteen minutes.

3. Stir in the milk, crackers and reserved pork pieces and heat to boiling.

Yield: About six servings.

Note: This chowder can be made with smoked haddock or smoked cod fillets, provided three tablespoons of butter are substituted for the salt pork.

Kettle Stock

VERMONT

4 pounds, more or less, fresh
or cooked chicken car-
casses, beef bones or veal
bones
3 pounds chicken wings
1 veal knuckle
2 beef marrow bones
2 large onions, each studded
with four whole cloves
3 cloves garlic
6 carrots
4 leeks, trimmed, split in half
and well washed

3 white turnips, peeled
3 bay leaves
6 tablespoons coarse salt
16 peppercorns
6 sprigs parsley
Top leaves and outside ribs
of six celery stalks
3 pounds brisket of beef
1 four-pound to five-pound
chicken.

1. Place the carcasses or bones, wings, veal knuckle, marrow bones, onions, garlic, carrots, leeks, turnips, bay leaves, salt, peppercorns, parsley and celery in an eight-quart to ten-quart kettle. Add cold water to within two inches of the kettle rim. Bring slowly to a boil and skim frequently as necessary. Let simmer so that the broth barely bubbles two to two and a half hours. Add the brisket and cook two hours longer.

2. Add the chicken and cook about one hour longer or until the brisket and chicken are done and tender. Remove the chicken and brisket, which may be served at this point, using as much broth as necessary.

3. Strain all the broth and store in pint and quart containers. Refrigerate overnight. Skim off all fat; then freeze the stock.

Yield: Five quarts to six quarts strained broth.

Lobster Chowder
MAINE

⅓ cup diced salt pork	Dash cayenne pepper
1 small onion, finely chopped	2 cups cubed, cooked lobster
2 cups peeled, cubed potato	3 cups light cream or milk
1½ cups water	2 tablespoons dry sherry
Salt and freshly ground black pepper to taste	1 egg yolk, lightly beaten.

1. Render the salt pork in a heavy kettle until all the fat is removed and the pieces are crisp. Remove the pieces and reserve.

2. Add the onion to the fat in the kettle and cook slowly until the onion is transparent. Add the potatoes and cook, stirring, five minutes. Add the water, salt, pepper and cayenne, bring to a boil, cover and simmer twenty minutes, or until the potatoes are tender.

3. Add the lobster. Combine the cream or milk, sherry and egg yolk in a small bowl. Add some of the hot chowder to the cream mixture while stirring. Return to the kettle and heat, stirring, until mixture thickens slightly and lobster is heated through. Do not allow to boil.

Yield: Four servings.

Cape Cod Lobster Soup

MASSACHUSETTS

2 one-pound to one-and-one-half-pound live lobsters
5 tablespoons butter
3 large ship biscuits or pilot crackers

4 cups milk, scalded
Salt and freshly ground black pepper to taste
1 cup diced cooked lobster meat.

1. Plunge a knife into the thorax of the lobsters where body and head join, to kill them. Discard head and thorax, but retain tomalley and coral. With a cleaver or large chef's knife, cut tail and claws into small sections.

2. Heat two tablespoons of the butter in a heavy saucepan. Add lobster sections and cook, stirring, until pieces turn pink.

3. Crush the biscuits or crackers and mix to a paste with remaining butter. Mix in milk and pour over the lobster in the pan. Season with salt and pepper. Bring to a boil, stirring. Grate in the coral and add tomalley.

4. Add the cooked lobster meat and serve.

Yield: Four servings.

Oxtail Soup

VERMONT

1 oxtail, cut into eight to ten pieces
6 cups water
1½ teaspoons salt
¼ teaspoon freshly ground black pepper
1 onion, sliced
2 whole cloves
2 tablespoons butter

1 carrot, sliced
1 white turnip, cubed
2 ribs celery, diced
¼ head cabbage, shredded
¼ teaspoon thyme
1 bay leaf
Lemon juice to taste
Salt and freshly ground black pepper to taste.

1. Place the oxtail in a heavy kettle. Cover with the water and bring to a boil. Skim as necessary. Add the salt, pepper, onion and cloves and simmer, covered, two hours, or until the meat is tender.

2. Remove the oxtail and remove excess fat. Reserve the broth.

3. Melt the butter in a clean kettle, add the carrot, turnip, celery and

cabbage and cook, stirring, until golden. Add the reserved broth, thyme and bay leaf, bring to a boil, cover and simmer twenty-five minutes. Add the oxtail, reheat, add lemon juice, salt and pepper to taste.

Yield: Six servings.

Cream of Oyster Soup
MASSACHUSETTS

¼ cup butter
1 small onion, finely chopped
3 tablespoons flour
⅛ teaspoon freshly ground black pepper
¼ cup finely chopped celery
¼ teaspoon celery salt

1 cup boiling chicken broth or water
½ cup sliced mushrooms
3 cups milk
1 pint picked-over oysters with liquor
   Salt to taste.

1. Melt the butter in a heavy saucepan and sauté the onion until golden. Stir in the flour, pepper, celery and celery salt.

2. Stir in the broth or water and mushrooms, bring to a boil and simmer five minutes. Add the milk and oysters and bring to a boil. Add salt if needed and serve immediately.

Yield: Four servings.

Oyster Stew
RHODE ISLAND

2 cups oysters
4 cups milk, scalded
¼ cup butter

1½ teaspoons salt
¼ teaspoon freshly ground black pepper.

1. Strain the liquor from the oysters through cheesecloth into a saucepan. Pick over the oysters for shell or grit and clean if necessary.

2. Bring the oyster liquor to a boil. Add the oysters, bring to a boil and simmer just until the edges curl, about four minutes. Remove the oysters with a slotted spoon. If they are very large, quarter them.

3. Add the milk and butter to the oyster liquor. Season with the salt and pepper and return the oysters. Reheat and serve immediately.

Yield: Four servings.

Parsnip Chowder

VERMONT

⅓	cup diced salt pork	4	cups milk, scalded
2	onions, thinly sliced	3	tablespoons butter
2½	cups peeled, cubed parsnips		Salt and freshly ground
1	cup peeled cubed potatoes		black pepper to taste
2	cups chicken broth	⅓	cup rolled cracker crumbs.

1. Sauté the salt pork in a large heavy saucepan until the fat is rendered and the pork pieces are crisp. Remove the pieces and reserve.

2. Add the onions and sauté until golden.

3. Add the parsnips and potatoes and cook, stirring, three minutes. Add the broth, bring to a boil, cover and cook over low heat until the vegetables are tender, about twenty-five minutes.

4. Add the milk, butter, salt and pepper and bring to a boil. Stir in the cracker crumbs and reserved pork pieces.

Yield: Eight servings.

Parsnip Soup

MASSACHUSETTS

½	cup diced salt pork	4	cups half-and-half, scalded
1	onion, finely chopped	2	tablespoons flour
2	cups peeled, cubed parsnips	¼	cup butter
2	cups peeled, cubed potatoes	2	tablespoons chopped pars-
2	cups water		ley.
	Salt and freshly ground		
	black pepper to taste		

1. Cook the salt pork until it is crisp. Remove pieces and reserve. In the fat remaining, sauté the onion until tender but not browned. Add the parsnips, potatoes, water, salt and pepper.

2. Simmer, covered, until vegetables are tender, about twenty minutes. Stir in the half-and-half.

3. Blend together the flour and butter and whisk, bit by bit, into the simmering soup. Sprinkle with the parsley and reserved pork pieces.

Yield: Eight servings.

Midsummer Eve Soup of Fresh Green Peas

CONNECTICUT

1½	cups fresh peas and a few tender young pods broken into bits		centrated, boiling chicken broth
	Boiling salted water	1	tablespoon butter
	Chopped fresh tarragon	1	tablespoon flour
	Chopped fresh mint	½	cup heavy cream
2½	cups well-seasoned, con-	1	cup champagne.

1. Cook the peas and pods in boiling salted water until just tender. Drain and place in an electric blender.

2. Add three-quarters teaspoon each tarragon and mint, the broth, butter and flour and blend one minute. Pour into a saucepan, bring to a boil and simmer five minutes or until thick. Chill.

3. Just before serving, stir in the cream and champagne. Garnish with additional mint and tarragon.

Yield: Four servings.

Fresh Pea Soup

MAINE

3	leeks, finely chopped	2	cups shelled fresh peas (about two pounds)
1	onion, finely chopped		Salt and freshly ground black pepper to taste
¼	cup butter		
2	tablespoons flour		
6	cups chicken broth	1	cup heavy or light cream.
1	sprig mint		

1. Sauté the leeks and onion in the butter in a heavy saucepan until tender. Sprinkle with the flour and stir to mix.

2. Stir in the broth, bring to a boil and add the mint and peas. Cook, covered, until the peas are tender, about fifteen minutes. Remove the mint sprig.

3. Puree the mixture through a food mill or in batches in an electric blender. Return to the clean pan. Bring to a boil and add salt and pepper and the cream. Reheat. If too thick, add a little milk.

Yield: Six servings.

Note: This soup is also delicious when chilled.

Split Pea Soup
NEW HAMPSHIRE

2	cups dried yellow split peas	1	carrot, quartered
	Cold water		Salt and freshly ground
1	ham bone		black pepper to taste
2	ribs celery, chopped	1	large potato, diced
1	onion, studded with two		Boiling water, if necessary.
	whole cloves		

1. Day before, pick over and wash the peas. Cover with cold water and let soak overnight.

2. Next day, drain the peas and place in a kettle with fresh water to cover. Add the ham bone, celery, onion studded with cloves, carrot, salt and pepper. Bring to a boil, cover and simmer two hours, or until peas are tender. Add the potato and cook thirty minutes longer.

3. Rub the soup through a sieve or pass through an electric blender. Adjust consistency with boiling water if soup is too thick. Check seasoning.

Yield: Eight servings.

Portuguese Soup
MASSACHUSETTS

1	pound chorizo, linquica or smoked garlic sausages		imported plum tomatoes, drained and chopped
¼	cup olive oil	1	one-pound can white beans,
1	onion, finely chopped		rinsed in cold water and
1	clove garlic, finely chopped		drained
3	medium-size potatoes, peeled and sliced one-quarter-inch thick	½	pound kale or spinach, tough center stems removed, shredded
6	cups chicken broth		Salt and freshly ground
1	two-pound-three-ounce can		black pepper to taste.

1. Prick the sausages several times. Place in a saucepan with water to cover, bring to a boil and simmer, uncovered, fifteen minutes. Drain and slice.

2. Heat the oil in a heavy kettle and sauté the onion and garlic until tender but not browned. Add the potatoes and cook, stirring, three minutes. Pour in the broth, bring to a boil, cover and cook twenty minutes, or until the potatoes are done.

3. With a potato masher mash the potatoes into the broth, add the tomatoes and beans, bring to a boil and cook, covered, twenty minutes.

4. Add the kale or spinach and cook until wilted, about five minutes. Add the reserved sausage slices and reheat. Add salt and pepper to taste.

Yield: Six servings.

Pumpkin Soup
MASSACHUSETTS

1 onion, finely chopped	8 cups chicken broth
1 bunch scallions with some of the green part, finely chopped	Salt and freshly ground black pepper to taste
¼ cup plus three tablespoons butter	3 tablespoons flour
	2 cups light cream
1 two-pound-thirteen-ounce can pumpkin puree	2 cups crisp croutons.

1. Sauté the onion and scallions in one-quarter cup of the butter until tender but not browned.

2. Add the pumpkin puree and cook gently five minutes.

3. Stir in the broth and cook, stirring, ten minutes. Season with salt and pepper.

4. Blend together the remaining butter and the flour and whisk into the simmering soup. Stir in the cream and reheat just before serving. Serve sprinkled with the croutons.

Yield: About eight to ten servings.

Salt Pork Chowder
VERMONT

⅓ cup diced salt pork
3 carrots, sliced
3 onions, chopped
6 medium-size potatoes,
   peeled and cubed

6 cups boiling water
Salt and freshly ground
black pepper to taste.

1. Sauté the salt pork in a large heavy saucepan until the fat is rendered and the pork is crisp. Remove the pork pieces and reserve.
2. Add the carrots and onions to the pan and cook, stirring, until golden. Add the potatoes, boiling water, salt and pepper. Bring to a boil, return the pork pieces, cover and simmer one hour or longer.
  Yield: Six servings.
  Note: True Yankees like to refrigerate this overnight and reheat to serve the next day.

Scallop Stew
MASSACHUSETTS

¼ cup butter
4 cups sea scallops
1 tablespoon flour
4 cups milk

½ teaspoon salt
⅛ teaspoon freshly ground
white pepper.

1. Melt two tablespoons of the butter in a skillet. Add the scallops and sauté three minutes.
2. In a small saucepan, melt remaining butter and blend in the flour. Gradually stir in the milk and bring to a boil, stirring.
3. Add the salt and pepper. Add the scallop-and-butter mixture.
4. Transfer the stew to the top of a double boiler set over low heat to keep the water in the bottom of the boiler hot but not boiling. Let the stew set about ten minutes.
  Yield: Four servings.

Sorrel Soup
NEW HAMPSHIRE

¼ cup butter
½ onion, finely chopped
1 cup finely chopped sorrel or spinach leaves, coarse center ribs removed

2 tablespoons flour
⅛ teaspoon nutmeg
   Salt and pepper to taste
2 cups chicken broth
1 cup heavy or light cream.

1. Melt the butter in a heavy saucepan and sauté the onion until golden. Add the sorrel or spinach and cook, stirring, until wilted. Sprinkle with the flour and stir.

2. Add the nutmeg, salt, pepper and broth, bring to a boil and simmer fifteen minutes. Puree in two batches in an electric blender and return to a clean pan.

3. Bring to a boil, add the cream and reheat but do not boil. Check the seasoning and add salt and pepper if necessary.

Yield: Four servings.

Tomato and Clam Broth
MASSACHUSETTS

1½ cups fresh or bottled clam broth
1½ cups tomato juice
    Juice of half a lemon
    Freshly ground black pepper to taste

1 teaspoon Worcestershire sauce
4 tablespoons whipped cream
2 teaspoons chopped fresh parsley or chives.

1. Combine the broth and tomato juice in a saucepan and bring just to a simmer. Add the lemon juice, pepper and Worcestershire.

2. Pour the broth into four hot cups and top each serving with whipped cream. Garnish the cream with the parsley or chives.

Yield: Four servings.

Tomato Soup
CONNECTICUT

¾ cup butter
2 tablespoons olive oil
1 large onion, thinly sliced
2 teaspoons chopped fresh
   thyme or one-half teaspoon
   dried thyme
2 tablespoons chopped fresh
   basil or one teaspoon dried
   basil

Salt and freshly ground
black pepper to taste
3 pounds ripe tomatoes, seeded and quartered
3 tablespoons tomato paste
¼ cup flour
4 cups chicken broth
1 teaspoon sugar
1 cup heavy cream.

1. Heat one-half cup of the butter and the oil in a heavy kettle. Add the onion and cook until tender but not browned.

2. Add the thyme, basil, salt, pepper, tomatoes and tomato paste. Simmer ten minutes.

3. Mix the flour with six tablespoons of the broth and stir into the tomato mixture. Add the remaining broth and cook thirty minutes, stirring frequently.

4. Pass the mixture through the finest blade of a food mill or through a fine sieve. Reheat and stir in the sugar and cream. Do not boil. Swirl in the remaining butter.

Yield: About eight servings.

Vegetable Soup
NEW HAMPSHIRE

¼ cup butter
4 ribs celery, diced
3 onions, chopped
1 green pepper, seeded and
   chopped
1 zucchini, washed and diced
1 dozen large ripe tomatoes,
   peeled, seeded and chopped

4 cups chicken broth, vegetable broth or water
   Salt and freshly ground
   black pepper to taste
2 teaspoons basil
1 bay leaf.

44

1. Melt the butter in a large heavy saucepan, add the celery, onions, green pepper and zucchini and cook, stirring, until golden.

2. Add the tomatoes, broth or water, salt, pepper, basil and bay leaf. Bring to a boil, cover and simmer forty-five minutes. The soup can be served immediately or pureed in a blender and reheated.

Yield: Four servings.

Rockport Whiting Chowder

MASSACHUSETTS

4	one-pound whiting	½	cup diced salt pork
1	bay leaf	1	onion, chopped
2	sprigs parsley	4	potatoes, peeled and diced
	Salt and freshly ground black pepper to taste	4	cups milk, scalded.

1. Wash the whiting and place in a kettle with water barely to cover. Add the bay leaf, parsley, salt and pepper. Bring to a boil, cover and simmer gently about ten minutes, or until the fish flakes easily.

2. When the whiting are cool enough to handle, skin and bone them and cut into chunks. Strain the stock in which the fish was cooked and reserve.

3. Cook the salt pork until crisp, remove the pieces and reserve. In the fat remaining, sauté the onion until tender. Add the potatoes, salt, pepper and reserved fish stock and pork pieces. Simmer fifteen minutes.

4. Add the fish pieces and the milk. Reheat, but do not boil.

Yield: Four servings.

Fish
and Shellfish

Striped Bass with Minced Clam Stuffing
MASSACHUSETTS

1	four-pound to six-pound striped bass, cleaned	¼	cup chopped onion
	Salt and freshly ground	¼	cup chopped celery
	black pepper to taste	½	cup butter, melted
2	five-ounce cans minced clams	4	cups soft bread crumbs
		2	tablespoons lemon juice.

1. Preheat the oven to 400 degrees.

2. Wipe the fish with a damp paper towel. Sprinkle cavity with salt and pepper. Drain the clams, reserving the liquor.

3. Cook the onion and celery in half the butter until tender. Stir in the bread crumbs until butter is absorbed. Toss crumbs until they brown slightly. Stir in the lemon juice, clams and enough clam liquor to moisten. Season with salt and pepper.

4. Spoon stuffing into cavity of fish. Close with skewers or lace with string. Brush fish with remaining butter. Bake in pan lined with aluminum foil fifty to seventy minutes, or until fish flakes easily when tested with a fork.

Yield: Six to eight servings.

Shrimp-Stuffed Striped Bass
RHODE ISLAND

1	four-pound striped bass	½	cup fine soft bread crumbs
¼	cup diced salt pork or butter	1	tablespoon chopped parsley
2	tablespoons finely chopped shallots	¼	teaspoon thyme
½	cup sliced mushrooms		Salt and freshly ground black pepper to taste
1	pound shrimp, shelled, deveined and roughly chopped	2	tablespoons melted butter
		2	tablespoons lemon juice.

1. Clean the fish, but leave the head on.
2. Preheat the oven to 400 degrees.
3. Cook the salt pork, if used, in a skillet until the pieces are crisp. Remove the salt pork pieces and reserve. Add the shallots to the drippings or to the butter, if used, and cook until tender but not browned.
4. Add the mushrooms and shrimp and cook quickly until the shrimp turn pink and the mushrooms wilt, about five minutes. Add the bread crumbs, parsley, thyme, salt, pepper and reserved pork pieces. Stuff the fish with the mixture and secure with skewers or sew to close.
5. Place the fish in a greased baking dish. Brush with the melted butter, season with salt and pepper and sprinkle the lemon juice over all.
6. Bake about thirty-five minutes, or until the fish flakes easily.
Yield: Four servings.

Boston Bluefish Florentine
MASSACHUSETTS

1½	pounds spinach, washed and chopped	1	teaspoon Worcestershire sauce
¼	cup butter	⅓	cup grated Gruyère cheese
2	shallots, finely chopped	2	pounds Boston bluefish (American pollock) fillets, skinned and cut into six serving pieces
¼	cup flour		
1½	cups milk or light cream		
	Salt and freshly ground black pepper to taste		
¼	teaspoon nutmeg	¼	cup freshly grated Parmesan cheese.

1. Preheat the oven to 350 degrees.

2. In a large pan, put the spinach with just the water that clings to it. Cover tightly and cook until spinach wilts. Drain well in a sieve, pressing out excess moisture.

3. Melt the butter and sauté the shallots in it until tender. Stir in the flour; then gradually stir in the milk or cream.

4. Bring the sauce to a boil, stirring, and simmer two minutes. Season with salt and pepper. Add the nutmeg, Worcestershire and Gruyère cheese. Stir until cheese has melted.

5. Mix drained spinach with half the sauce and spread in the bottom of a shallow heatproof dish. Arrange the fish fillet pieces over the top.

6. Pour remaining sauce over all, sprinkle with the Parmesan and bake about twenty minutes, or until fish flakes easily. Dish can be glazed under the broiler if desired.

Yield: Six servings.

Baked Stuffed Bluefish
MASSACHUSETTS

1	four-pound bluefish	3	small strips salt pork
1½	teaspoons salt	2	tablespoons melted butter
1	recipe oyster stuffing (see Broiled Stuffed Lobster, page 70)	1	tablespoon lemon juice.

1. Preheat the oven to 350 degrees.

2. Wash and dry the fish and sprinkle with salt inside and outside. Stuff the cavity loosely with the oyster stuffing and close by sewing or with skewers.

3. Make three diagonal slashes in the flesh of the fish and insert the salt pork. Place fish in a greased baking dish.

4. Pour the butter and lemon juice over fish and bake about forty minutes, or until the fish flakes easily.

Yield: Six servings.

Baked Bluefish

RHODE ISLAND

1	four-pound bluefish	½	cup butter
	Salt and freshly ground	1	tablespoon wine vinegar
	black pepper		Lemon slices
1	teaspoon chopped fresh		Boiled potatoes.
	rosemary		

1. Preheat the oven to 400 degrees.
2. Thoroughly clean and scale the fish, but leave the head and tail intact. Rinse the fish under cold water and pat dry with paper towels. Sprinkle the fish inside and outside with salt and pepper.
3. Place the fish in a baking dish and sprinkle the rosemary around the fish. Dot the fish generously with the butter.
4. Bake the fish about thirty minutes, basting every five minutes or so. When the fish flakes easily, transfer to a hot serving platter.
5. Add the vinegar to the baking dish, heat thoroughly and pour the pan drippings over the fish. Garnish with lemon slices and serve with boiled potatoes.

Yield: Six servings.

Creamed Cod

NEW HAMPSHIRE

1½	pounds salt codfish	2	eggs, lightly beaten
½	cup butter		Boiled potatoes
1½	tablespoons flour		Pickled beets.
2	cups light cream		

1. Soak the codfish several hours in water to cover, changing the water frequently. Drain codfish and place in a saucepan with fresh water to cover. Bring to a boil and simmer gently ten minutes. Drain and flake the fish.
2. Melt the butter and blend in the flour. Gradually stir in the cream and bring to a boil, stirring until mixture thickens. Cook three minutes. Add the codfish and cook five minutes longer.
3. Add a little hot sauce to the eggs, return all to the pan and reheat, but do not boil. Serve with boiled potatoes and pickled beets.

Yield: Six servings.

Codfish Pie

½ pound salt codfish, cut into pieces
¼ pound salt pork, diced
1 medium-size onion, finely chopped
3 tablespoons flour
⅛ teaspoon freshly ground black pepper
2½ cups milk
1 cup diced cooked potatoes
Biscuit dough made from one and one-half cups flour (page 173)

1. Soak the codfish two hours in water to cover, changing the water three times. Drain codfish and place in a kettle with fresh water to cover. Bring to a boil and simmer, covered, until tender, about ten minutes. Drain and flake the fish.

2. Preheat the oven to 450 degrees.

3. Cook the salt pork in a skillet until pieces are crisp. Remove salt pork pieces and reserve. Remove all but three tablespoons fat from the skillet.

4. Sauté the onion in the fat in the skillet until tender. Blend in the flour and pepper. Gradually stir in the milk and cook, stirring, until mixture thickens. Stir in codfish, reserved pork pieces and the potatoes.

5. Turn into a deep baking dish. Drop the biscuit dough mixture on top of the hot cod mixture and bake fifteen minutes, or until biscuit topping is browned and cooked.

Yield: Four servings.

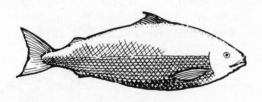

Fresh Cod Maître d'Hôtel
MASSACHUSETTS

1	six-pound codfish, boned and skinned	5	tablespoons butter
1	clove garlic, thinly sliced	¼	cup flour
3	sprigs fresh thyme or one-half teaspoon dried thyme	1	cup heavy cream
		1	tablespoon finely chopped parsley
1	onion, sliced	¼	teaspoon cayenne pepper
15	peppercorns	1	tablespoon finely chopped chives
½	bay leaf		
2	sprigs parsley		Coarse salt (Maldon or kosher salt)
	Salt to taste		
6	medium-size unpeeled potatoes		Freshly ground black pepper.

1. It is best to have the fish boned and skinned by the fish man. Be certain, however, to remove all small bones he may have overlooked.

2. Place the filleted fish in one layer in a large skillet. Add the garlic, thyme, onion, peppercorns, bay leaf, parsley sprigs, salt and water to cover. Bring to a boil and simmer ten minutes. Turn off heat and let fish stand in stock until ready to serve.

3. Meanwhile, place the potatoes in a large saucepan and add salt and water to cover. Cook until tender.

4. Melt three tablespoons of the butter and stir in the flour, using a wire whisk. Carefully pour off and strain two cups fish stock and add it, stirring. When the mixture is thickened and smooth, simmer twenty minutes, stirring occasionally. Add the cream and simmer twenty minute minutes longer, stirring occasionally. Add the chopped parsley, cayenne and chives. Remove the sauce from the heat and swirl in the remaining butter.

5. Carefully transfer the fish from the stock to a warm serving platter. Peel the potatoes and slice them around the fish. Pour the hot sauce over all and serve immediately. Serve with coarse salt and black pepper on the side.

Yield: Six servings.

Rhode Island Clam Cakes

2 eggs, lightly beaten
1 cup clams, drained and
  chopped
1 teaspoon salt
⅛ teaspoon freshly ground
  black pepper

1 cup milk
2 cups flour
3 teaspoons baking powder
  Fat or oil for deep-frying.

1. Combine the eggs, clams, salt, pepper, milk, flour and baking powder.

2. Form into small cakes and fry, a few at a time, in a frying basket in fat or oil heated to 360 degrees. Drain on paper towels.

Yield: Four servings.

Clam Cakes

MASSACHUSETTS

2 tablespoons butter
2 tablespoons finely minced
  shallot
1¼ cups soft bread crumbs
2 eggs, lightly beaten
½ cup heavy cream
2 seven-ounce cans minced
  clams, drained
½ cup finely minced celery

1 tablespoon lemon juice
2 tablespoons chopped parsley
½ teaspoon salt
⅛ teaspoon white pepper
1 egg, beaten and diluted
  with one tablespoon water
  Fat for deep-frying.

1. Melt the butter in a saucepan and sauté the shallot in the butter until soft but not browned.

2. Add one-half cup of the bread crumbs, the lightly beaten eggs, the cream, clams, celery, lemon juice, parsley, salt and pepper. Chill the mixture at least two hours.

3. Shape into eight two-inch cakes. Dip the cakes into the remaining crumbs and then into the remaining egg. Coat the cakes with crumbs a second time. Allow the cakes to dry out for fifteen minutes.

4. Fry the cakes, a few at a time, until golden brown in deep fat heated to 375 degrees. Drain.

Yield: Six servings.

Clam and Corn Casserole

MAINE

2 cups freshly shucked lit-
tlenecks with liquor
1 cup cracker crumbs
2 tablespoons very finely
chopped onion
3 eggs, lightly beaten

½ cup milk
1 cup cream-style corn
2 tablespoons melted butter
Salt and freshly ground
black pepper to taste.

1. Preheat the oven to 350 degrees.
2. Combine all the ingredients in a large bowl, mix lightly and pour into a buttered casserole. Bake forty-five minutes.
Yield: Four servings.

Clam Soufflé

MASSACHUSETTS

6 tablespoons butter
6 tablespoons flour
1 cup clam juice
1 cup heavy cream
1½ cups minced canned clams
8 egg yolks

¼ cup freshly chopped parsley
Salt and freshly ground
white pepper to taste
Grated nutmeg to taste
12 egg whites.

1. Preheat the oven to 375 degrees.
2. Melt the butter and blend in the flour. Mix the clam juice and cream and slowly add to the butter-flour mixture, stirring constantly. Cook, stirring, until thickened. Add the minced clams and remove from the heat to cool slightly.
3. Beat the egg yolks thoroughly and add to the sauce. Stir in the parsley and season with salt, pepper and nutmeg.
4. Beat the egg whites until firm. Fold them thoroughly into the sauce. Pour into two buttered two-quart soufflé dishes and bake thirty-five minutes.
Yield: Ten to one dozen servings.

Clam Pie
MASSACHUSETTS

4 cups ground clams with
   their liquor
1 egg, lightly beaten
1 cup cracker crumbs
⅛ teaspoon marjoram
⅛ teaspoon thyme

Salt and freshly ground
   black pepper to taste
½ cup milk
Pastry for a two-crust ten-
   inch pie
2 tablespoons butter.

1. Preheat the oven to 425 degrees.

2. In a bowl, mix together the clams, egg, crumbs, marjoram, thyme, salt, pepper and milk.

3. Line a ten-inch pie plate with the pastry. Pour in the clam filling, dot with the butter and top with remaining pastry. Make a steam hole and bake fifteen minutes. Reduce oven heat to 350 degrees and continue baking forty-five minutes longer.

Yield: Six servings.

Mushroom-Stuffed Clams
MASSACHUSETTS

24 fresh cherrystone or littleneck clams (see note)
¼ cup water
3 slices bacon, cut into small
   cubes
½ pound mushrooms, caps
   and all, finely minced
1½ tablespoons finely chopped
   shallots
⅛ pound Gruyère cheese,
   Swiss cheese or Fontina
   cheese
2 tablespoons finely chopped
   parsley

1 small clove garlic, finely
   minced
¾ cup fine soft bread crumbs
½ cup finely minced heart of
   celery
3 tablespoons dry white wine
1 egg yolk
Salt and freshly ground
   black pepper to taste
½ cup freshly grated Parmesan cheese.

1. Preheat the oven to 400 degrees.

2. Wash the clams well and place in a kettle. Add the water, cover and steam until the clams open. Remove the clams and let them cool. Take the clams from the shells and chop them on a flat surface. There should be about two-thirds cup chopped clams. Set aside. Reserve twenty-four shells for filling.

3. Cook the bacon in a large saucepan until the bits are crisp. Do not burn. Remove the bacon bits and reserve. Pour off all but two tablespoons fat from the saucepan. Add the mushrooms to the fat in the saucepan. Add the shallots and cook, stirring, until the mushrooms are wilted. Let cool.

4. Chop the Gruyère, Swiss or Fontina cheese into tiny cubes. Add with the parsley, garlic, bread crumbs, celery, wine and egg yolk to the mushroom mixture. Add salt, pepper and the reserved clams.

5. Fill the reserved clam shells with the mixture and sprinkle with the Parmesan cheese and reserved bacon bits. Bake ten minutes or longer, or until the filling is bubbly and golden brown. Serve hot.

Yield: Six servings.

Note: Canned clams may also be used in this recipe. To do this, drain the clams and measure out approximately two-thirds cup. Proceed with the recipe, starting with step 3. In lieu of the reserved clam shells, spoon the mixture into scallop shells or small ramekins and bake.

Cape Cod Deep-Dish Clam Pie
MASSACHUSETTS

8	cups soft-shelled clams	3	tablespoons butter
2	cups cold water	3	tablespoons flour
2	cups cubed potatoes	1	cup milk
1	onion, finely chopped		Pastry made from one and
1	cup salted water		one-half cups flour.
1	teaspoon sugar		
	Freshly ground black pepper to taste		

1. Wash the clams in several changes of lukewarm water.

2. Drain the clams and place in a kettle. Add the cold water and bring slowly to a boil. When the clams have opened, remove from the heat. Strain the clam broth through a double thickness of cheesecloth. Reserve broth.

3. Remove clams from shells. Dip each clam into the broth. Snip off and discard the dark heads. Strain the broth again. Chop the clams to any size desired.

4. Preheat the oven to 400 degrees.

5. Place the potato cubes and onion in a saucepan and add the salted water. Bring to a boil, cover and simmer until potatoes are tender. Add the sugar, pepper, chopped clams and the strained clam broth. Bring to a boil.

6. Blend the butter and flour, using the fingers. Stir, bit by bit, into the simmering stew. Bring the milk to a boil and add it to the stew. Remove from the heat.

7. Butter a one-and-one-half-quart pie dish or casserole generously and pour in the clam mixture. Cover with rolled-out pastry and prick the top with a fork or make small slashes with a knife. Bake thirty minutes, or until pastry is golden brown. Serve piping hot.

Yield: Six to eight servings.

Double Crust Clam Pie
MASSACHUSETTS

2¼	cups flour	
1	teaspoon salt	
¾	cup shortening	
6	tablespoons water, approximately	
3	cups ground clams, preferably quahogs	
½	cup finely chopped onion	

¾ cup fresh cracker crumbs, preferably made from pilot crackers
   Freshly ground black pepper to taste
¼ teaspoon thyme
¾ cup light cream.

1. Preheat the oven to 375 degrees.

2. Combine the flour and salt in a mixing bowl. With a pastry blender or two knives, cut in the shortening until the mixture looks like coarse corn meal.

3. Sprinkle the water over the mixture, one tablespoon at a time, and mix lightly with a fork until all flour is moist.

4. With the hands, gather the dough into a ball and divide it in half. On a lightly floured board, roll out each half in a circle one-eighth-inch thick and about one and one-half inches larger in diameter than the pie plate used. Line a nine-inch pie plate with one circle of dough, leaving one-half inch overhanging.

5. Combine the clams, onion, crumbs, pepper, thyme and all but one tablespoon of the cream in a mixing bowl. Pour the filling into the pie plate. Cover with the remaining circle of dough and neatly trim the edges. Fold the edge of the top pastry under the edge of the lower pastry and seal by pressing together. Flute the edges, if desired. Brush the top of the pie with the remaining cream, prick the top of the pie and bake forty minutes, or until golden brown and baked through.

Yield: Six to eight servings.

Fried Clams

MASSACHUSETTS

1	egg, separated	½	cup flour
½	cup milk	24	clams, shucked and drained
1	tablespoon butter		of liquor
¼	teaspoon salt		Fat or oil for deep-frying.

1. Beat the egg yolk with one-quarter cup of the milk. Stir in the butter, salt and flour and beat until smooth. Gradually beat in remaining milk.

2. Beat the egg white until stiff but not dry. Fold into the batter. Dip each clam into the batter. Fry clams, a few at a time, in fat or oil heated to 375 degrees. Drain on paper towels.

Yield: Three or four servings.

Clam Fritters

RHODE ISLAND

2	cups clams	2	eggs, lightly beaten
1¾	cups flour	1	cup milk
1	tablespoon baking powder	2	teaspoons grated onion
½	teaspoon nutmeg	1	tablespoon butter, melted
1½	teaspoons salt		Fat or oil for deep-frying.

1. Drain the clams and chop them.

2. Place the flour, baking powder, nutmeg and salt in a bowl. In a second bowl, mix together the eggs, milk, onion, butter and clams. Pour clam mixture into dry ingredients and stir until smooth.

3. Drop batter by teaspoonfuls into fat or oil heated to 360 degrees. Fry until golden. Drain on paper towels.
Yield: Four servings.

Clam Sauce with Spaghetti
MASSACHUSETTS

⅓ cup olive oil
2 cloves garlic, halved and flattened
1 quart cherrystone clams, shucked, chopped, and liquor reserved
   Bottled clam juice

3 tablespoons chopped Italian parsley
   Salt and freshly ground black pepper to taste
½ teaspoon oregano
1 pound spaghetti, cooked al dente, drained.

1. Heat the oil in a heavy saucepan and sauté the garlic in it until lightly browned. Remove the garlic.
2. Measure the reserved clam liquor and make up to one cup with bottled clam juice. Add with the chopped clams and the parsley to the oil, bring to a simmer and cook about two minutes.
3. Season with salt and pepper and add the oregano. Pour over the spaghetti.
Yield: Four servings.

Sister Lisset's Shaker Fish Balls
MASSACHUSETTS

2 cups leftover cooked fish, bones removed and fish flaked
4 cups chopped cooked potatoes
2 egg yolks, beaten

1 tablespoon minced parsley
   Salt and freshly ground black pepper to taste
   Lard or fat for deep-frying
   Salt pork-and-milk gravy (recipe below).

1. Put the fish in a wooden chopping bowl and add the potatoes. Chop together until very fine.
2. Add the egg yolks, parsley, salt and pepper. Form into balls the

59

size of a goose egg. Deep-fry in lard or fat until golden brown. Serve with gravy.

Yield: Six servings.

Hancock Shaker Village Salt Pork-and-Milk Gravy
MASSACHUSETTS

¼   pound salt pork, cut into
     cubes
¼   cup flour
3   cups milk
     Salt and freshly ground
     black pepper to taste.

1. Place the salt pork cubes in a saucepan and cook, stirring, until they start to become crisp. Remove cubes from the saucepan and set aside.

2. Add the flour to saucepan and cook briefly, stirring, without burning. Add the milk, stirring rapidly. When mixture thickens and is smooth, add salt and pepper. Simmer ten minutes, stirring.

3. Chop salt pork cubes and add to sauce. Serve with fish balls.

Yield: Three cups.

Martha's Vineyard Stonewall Bouillabaisse

MASSACHUSETTS

3 pounds fresh fluke or
flounder with bones, heads
and tails

3 pounds black bass, sea bass
or striped bass with bones,
heads and tails

2 pounds scrod with bones,
heads and tails

1 whole eel

80 mussels, scrubbed and
cleaned

80 littleneck or cherrystone
clams, the smaller the better
Salted water

½ cup olive oil

2 medium-size onions, finely
chopped

6 shallots, finely minced

2 cloves garlic, finely minced

1 bay leaf

¼ teaspoon chopped fresh
thyme or dried thyme

¼ teaspoon crushed fennel
seeds
Salt to taste

½ teaspoon freshly ground
black pepper

¼ teaspoon leaf saffron,
crushed
Cayenne pepper to taste

1 two-inch piece fresh orange
rind

½ gallon dry white wine

3 cups heavy cream

6 one-pound to one-and-one-
half-pound lobsters,
steamed (page 69)
Crusty French bread
Chilled white wine.

1. Have the fluke, black bass, scrod or whatever fish are used cut into fillets, but reserve the bones, heads and tails. Cut the fillets into serving pieces and set aside.

2. Have the eel skinned and cleaned. Set aside.

3. Toss the mussels and clams into separate basins of plain water to which salt has been added. Drain and set aside.

4. Heat the oil in a large steamer or kettle and cook the onions, shallots and garlic in it, stirring, until onions are wilted. Add the bay leaf, thyme, fennel seeds, salt, black pepper, saffron, cayenne, orange rind and wine. Add the reserved eel and the fish bones, heads and tails. Cover and simmer, stirring occasionally, about twenty minutes. Drain in a colander, pressing with a wooden spoon to extract most of the liquid. Rinse out the kettle. Discard the solids in the colander.

5. Add the liquid to the kettle. Bring to a boil and add the reserved pieces of fish fillets. Cook gently five minutes, or until fish flakes easily. Do not overcook. Using a slotted spoon or other skimmer, carefully remove

61

the fish from the kettle. Cover fish with aluminum foil or plastic wrap to keep warm.

6. Add the mussels and clams to the kettle and cover. Simmer until shells open, eight to ten minutes. Add the cream and bring just to a boil, but do not boil. If desired, add salt and pepper to taste.

7. Pour the contents of the kettle into a very large, hot serving bowl. Add the reserved fish fillets. Garnish the bowl with the lobster meat and lobster claws stuck upright into the mussels and clams. Serve immediately in hot soup bowls, with crusty French bread and a chilled white wine.

Yield: Fourteen servings.

New England Fish Stew
MASSACHUSETTS

⅓ cup butter	1 pound whiting fillets, cut into two-inch slices
¾ cup finely chopped onions	1 pound cod fillets, cut into two-inch pieces
1 clove garlic, finely chopped	1 pound scallops, halved if large
¾ cup diced celery	16 cherrystone or littleneck clams in shells, scrubbed and rinsed under cold water
2 cups fresh or bottled clam juice	
1 cup water	
2 one-pound cans tomatoes	2 small cooked lobsters or two cups cooked lobster meat.
½ teaspoon thyme	
1 bay leaf, crumbled	
¼ teaspoon saffron	
Salt and freshly ground black pepper to taste	

1. Melt the butter and sauté the onions and garlic in it until tender

2. Add the celery, clam juice, water, tomatoes, thyme, bay leaf, saffron, salt and pepper. Bring to a boil and simmer ten minutes.

3. Add the whiting, cod, scallops and clams and cook eight minutes, or until fish flakes easily. Remove the lobster meat from cooked lobsters, if used. Add lobster meat to stew.

Yield: Eight servings.

Block Island Stew

RHODE ISLAND

3   cloves garlic, finely minced
3   shallots, finely minced
½   cup olive oil
½   teaspoon chopped thyme
¼   cup chopped parsley
1   bay leaf
1½ cups dry white wine
3   ripe tomatoes, peeled, seeded and coarsely chopped (two and one-half cups to three cups)

Salt and freshly ground black pepper to taste
1   large or two small cleaned squid
1½ pounds cod fillets
1½ pounds striped bass fillets
12 littleneck clams, scrubbed and rinsed under cold water.

1. In a Dutch oven, cook the garlic and shallots in the oil briefly without browning. Add the thyme, parsley, bay leaf and wine and bring to a boil. Simmer, partially covered, about ten minutes. Add the tomatoes, salt and pepper and simmer ten minutes longer, stirring occasionally.

2. Lay the squid lengthwise on the sauce; then add the cod and bass fillets. Sprinkle with salt and pepper. Cover and simmer ten minutes. Add the clams and cover. Simmer just until the clams open and give up their juices. Serve piping hot.

Yield: Six servings.

Baked Haddock

MAINE

4   thin slices salt pork
1   onion, sliced
2½ pounds haddock fillets (see note)
3   tablespoons melted butter
2   tablespoons flour

1   cup milk
1   bay leaf
Salt and freshly ground black pepper to taste
¼   cup lemon juice.

Sauce:

2   egg yolks
½   cup heavy cream
¼   teaspoon salt
½   cup boiling water

2   tablespoons lemon juice
½   cup finely chopped cooked lobster meat or cooked shrimp.

63

1. Preheat the oven to 350 degrees.

2. Place the salt pork in the bottom of a shallow baking dish.

3. Sprinkle with half the onion slices. Arrange the fish fillets over the onion and salt pork. Sprinkle with remainder of the onion slices.

4. Spoon the butter over all and sprinkle with the flour. Pour the milk over the fish. Add the bay leaf, salt, pepper and lemon juice. Cover and bake twenty minutes. Remove cover and bake twenty minutes longer.

5. Meanwhile, prepare the sauce. Combine the egg yolks and cream and beat very well. Beat in the salt and boiling water and place in the top of a double boiler over hot water. Cook, stirring, three minutes, or until thickened. Add the lemon juice and lobster or shrimp. Serve separately with the fish.

Yield: Six servings.

Note: Cod fillets may be substituted for the haddock fillets.

Smoked Haddock Flan

MAINE

Pastry shell:

1	cup flour		1	egg yolk
¼	teaspoon salt			Ice water.
⅓	cup butter or shortening			

Fish:

1½	pounds smoked haddock with bones (see note), if salty, soaked thirty minutes in cold water		1	cup milk, approximately.

Filling:

2	tablespoons butter			Freshly ground black pepper to taste
½	cup finely chopped leeks			
2	tablespoons chopped parsley		2	hard-cooked eggs, halved.

Sauce:

2	tablespoons butter			Salt and freshly ground black pepper to taste.
2	tablespoons flour			

Potato mixture:

3 medium-size baking potatoes, boiled, peeled and riced or sieved

2 egg yolks

Salt and freshly ground black pepper to taste

6 tablespoons finely grated Gruyère cheese.

1. To prepare pastry, place the flour and salt in a bowl. With the finger tips or a pastry blender, blend in the butter or shortening until mixture resembles coarse oatmeal. With a fork, stir in the egg yolk and enough ice water to make a dough.

2. Roll out the dough on a lightly floured board or pastry cloth and use to line an eight-inch or nine-inch scalloped pie pan or pie plate. Chill well.

3. Preheat the oven to 425 degrees.

4. Line the chilled shell with aluminum foil and fill with dried beans or uncooked rice. Bake eight minutes, or until shell is set. Remove foil and beans or rice and bake shell three to five minutes longer, or until done and lightly browned.

5. Meanwhile, place the fish in a large skillet. Pour in milk until fish is three-quarters submerged.

6. Bring to a simmer, cover and simmer eight to ten minutes, or until the fish flakes easily. Remove the fish, strain the liquid and reserve one cup for the sauce. Remove the skin and bones from the fish and flake it. There should be about two cups. Reserve.

7. To prepare filling, melt the butter in a skillet and sauté the leeks in it until tender but not browned. Stir in the reserved fish and the parsley, season with pepper and keep warm. Reserve the hard-cooked egg halves.

8. To prepare sauce, melt the butter in a small pan, blend in the flour and gradually stir in the reserved cup fish stock. Season with salt and pepper.

9. Bring to a boil, stirring until sauce thickens. Hold over hot water until needed.

10. To prepare potato mixture, place the hot riced or sieved potatoes in a bowl and beat in the egg yolks, salt, pepper and four tablespoons of the cheese.

11. Place the filling in the bottom of the baked pie shell and embed the hard-cooked egg pieces in the filling in a pattern like spokes in a wheel. Pour the sauce over all.

12. Fit a pastry bag with a star tube. Pipe the potato mixture through the pastry bag around the flan and make a wheel pattern.

13. Sprinkle with the remaining cheese and brown under the broiler.

Yield: Four servings.

Note: Any good fish store can order smoked haddock.

This recipe may be made ahead through step 12 and held refrigerated. Reheat in a preheated 375-degree oven until bubbly, about twenty to thirty minutes. Proceed with step 13.

One pound boneless smoked cod may be substituted for the haddock. If salty, it too should be soaked thirty minutes in cold water.

Abigail's Biscuit-Topped Haddock Pie

MASSACHUSETTS

4	boiled potatoes, sliced	¼	cup fish stock or potato water
3	onions, thinly sliced	1	teaspoon catchup
3	cups cooked haddock, roughly flaked	1	teaspoon prepared mustard
4	hard-cooked eggs, sliced	2	tablespoons butter
	Salt and freshly ground black pepper to taste	1	recipe biscuit dough (page 173).

1. Preheat the oven to 450 degrees.

2. In a buttered shallow baking dish, make alternate layers of the potatoes, onions, fish and eggs, seasoning each layer with salt and pepper.

3. Combine the stock or potato water, catchup and mustard and pour over. Dot with the butter and top with the biscuits. Bake twenty minutes, or until biscuits are done and mixture is bubbling hot.

Yield: Six servings.

Note: Cooked cod may be substituted for the cooked haddock.

Cape Cod Lobster Roll

MASSACHUSETTS

8 frankfurter buns	1 tablespoon finely chopped
¼ cup butter, melted	parsley
3 cups (about one and one-half pounds to two pounds) cooked lobster meat, cut into bite-size pieces	¼ cup finely chopped scallions, including green part
	Tabasco to taste
1 cup mayonnaise	Lemon juice to taste
½ cup minced heart of celery	Salt and freshly ground black pepper to taste
1 small clove garlic, finely minced	Stuffed olives, parsley sprigs or lobster claws for garnish.
2 tablespoons chopped fresh basil or one-half teaspoon dried basil	

1. Preheat the oven to 400 degrees.

2. Split the buns and arrange them, split side up, on a baking dish. Brush them with the butter and bake until lightly browned. Remove from the oven and set aside.

3. Combine the lobster, mayonnaise, celery, garlic, basil, parsley, scallions, Tabasco, lemon juice, salt and pepper. Blend well.

4. Spoon equal parts of the filling onto each of the split buns and serve garnished with stuffed olives, parsley sprigs or lobster claws.

Yield: Eight servings.

Lobster Alexander

MASSACHUSETTS

1 large or two small lobsters, steamed and chilled	2 hard-cooked egg yolks
	Salt and freshly ground black pepper to taste
½ teaspoon finely chopped fresh tarragon	1 teaspoon Dijon mustard
½ teaspoon finely chopped fresh parsley	1 tablespoon wine vinegar
	¼ teaspoon Worcestershire sauce, or more to taste
½ teaspoon finely chopped fresh chives	½ cup olive oil
½ teaspoon finely chopped fresh chervil (optional)	½ teaspoon Madeira wine.

67

1. Remove the lobster meat from the tail and claws. Slice the tail meat and arrange it on a platter. Add the claw meat left whole.

2. Blend the the tarragon, parsley, chives and chervil if desired in a mixing bowl. Add the egg yolks and mash them thoroughly with a fork. Add salt, pepper, the mustard, vinegar and Worcestershire. Blend thoroughly with a wire whisk.

3. While beating with a whisk, gradually add the oil to the sauce. Stir constantly until the sauce is like a mayonnaise. Add the Madeira and spoon a little sauce onto each piece of lobster.

Yield: Four to six servings.

Creamed Lobster

MAINE

5 one-and-one-half-pound lobsters	1 teaspoon thyme
	1 bay leaf
12 tablespoons butter	¼ cup chopped shallots
Salt and freshly ground	1 cup dry sherry
black pepper to taste	2 cups finely chopped mush-
1 teaspoon paprika	rooms
¾ cup chopped onions	4 cups heavy cream, scalded
1 cup finely diced carrots	2 tablespoons flour
1 cup chopped celery	Boiled rice.

1. Plunge a knife into the thorax or center portion of each lobster where the body and tail meet, to kill the lobster.

2. For each lobster, break off the large claws and sever body and tail. Crack the claws and cut the tail section in two crosswise. Split the body lengthwise and remove and discard the tough "sac" near the eyes. Remove the coral and tomalley, or liver.

3. Place all corals and livers in a mixing bowl and add three tablespoons of the butter. Set aside.

4. Melt three tablespoons of the remaining butter in each of two heavy skillets large enough to accommodate the lobster pieces and claws (can be done in one pan if a large enough one is available). Dividing the ingredients between the pans, sprinkle lobster with salt, pepper and the paprika and stir. Add the onions, carrots, celery, thyme, bay leaf and shallots and cook, stirring, over relatively high heat until lobster turns pink.

5. Add the sherry, stirring. Add the mushrooms. Simmer, covered, ten minutes.

6. Add two cups of the cream to each of the pans.

7. Remove the lobster from the skillets. Discard body pieces. If desired, the lobster meat may be removed from the shell. Or the meat may be served in the shell. In any event, keep the lobster covered and warm until ready to serve.

8. Combine the two pans of sauce and simmer, uncovered, fifteen minutes. Strain and press as much liquid from the solids as possible.

9. Using the fingers, blend the butter with the livers and corals. Turn off the heat from the sauce and stir in the mixture. Knead the remaining butter with the flour to make a beurre manié and with a wire whisk incorporate into the sauce. Heat to thicken and add the lobster. Cook without boiling until lobster is heated through. Serve piping hot, with boiled rice.

Yield: Six servings.

Lobster Thermidor
MAINE

¼	cup butter	1	cup heavy cream, scalded
2	cubed cooked lobster meat	3	egg yolks, beaten
2	tablespoons cognac		Salt and freshly ground black pepper to taste
3	tablespoons dry sherry	⅛	teaspoon cayenne pepper.

1. Melt the butter, add the lobster meat and cook three minutes. Shake the pan or stir while cooking.

2. Add the cognac and sherry.

3. Pour the cream over the egg yolks and add to lobster mixture. Reheat, stirring, until mixture thickens, but do not allow to boil.

4. Season with salt, pepper and cayenne.

Yield: Two servings.

Steamed Lobster
RHODE ISLAND

Use a kettle large enough to hold all the lobsters to be cooked. Add one inch of water to the bottom of the kettle and bring to a rolling boil. Add the lobsters, head down, and cover closely. Cook twelve minutes for one-and-one-quarter-pound to one-and-one-half-pound lobsters; fifteen minutes for two-pound lobsters; twenty minutes for three-pound lobsters, and so on.

Baked Lobster
MASSACHUSETTS

1 one-and-one-half-pound live lobster Salt and freshly ground black pepper to taste	¼ cup butter Lemon wedges Melted butter (optional).

1. Preheat the oven to 350 degrees.
2. Plunge a heavy butcher knife into the thorax or center of the lobster where the body and tail meet, to kill the lobster. Quickly cut the body in half lengthwise. Break the lobster in half and remove the tough "sac."
3. Sprinkle the lobster with salt and pepper and dot the cut portions generously with the butter. Place, cut side up, on a baking dish and bake exactly twenty minutes.
4. Serve with lemon wedges and, if desired, melted butter.

Yield: One or two servings.

Note: This method for baking lobster is better than broiled. The lobster is more moist and tender.

Broiled Stuffed Lobster
CONNECTICUT

Oyster stuffing:

¼ cup butter	1 teaspoon salt
½ cup chopped onion	¼ teaspoon freshly ground
½ cup chopped celery	black pepper
4 mushrooms, chopped	½ teaspoon thyme
1 pint oysters with liquor	¼ teaspoon marjoram.
4 cups dry bread crumbs	
2 tablespoons chopped parsley	

Lobsters:

4 one-pound to one-and-one-half-pound lobsters	Melted butter Lemon wedges.

1. To prepare stuffing, melt the butter in a skillet and sauté the onion and celery in it until tender. Add the mushrooms and cook two minutes longer.
2. Drain the oysters, reserving liquor. Chop the oysters and add to the mushroom mixture.

3. Add the bread crumbs, parsley, salt, pepper, thyme, marjoram and enough of the reserved oyster liquor to moisten.

4. Plunge a heavy butcher knife into the thorax or center of the lobsters where the body and tail meet, to kill the lobsters. Split the lobsters lengthwise and remove the dark vein down the center and the "sac" behind the eyes. Crack the claws.

5. Place the lobsters shell side up over hot coals on a barbecue grill or shell side down under a preheated broiler and broil five minutes.

6. Fill the body cavity with the oyster stuffing and wrap in a heavy-duty aluminum foil to grill shell side down on charcoal grill or shell side up under a broiler. Broil about fifteen minutes. Serve with melted butter and lemon wedges.

Yield: Four servings.

Broiled Live Maine Lobster

1	two-pound to two-and-one-half-pound lobster		Salt and freshly ground black pepper to taste
½	cup cracker crumbs	¼	cup melted butter

1. Plunge a knife into the thorax or center of lobster between the head and tail, to kill the lobster. Cut the entire length of lobster from between the eyes to end of the tail. Remove the "sac" behind the eyes.

2. Remove the tomalley, or liver, and mix with the cracker crumbs, salt, pepper and butter.

3. Broil lobster, shell side up, six minutes. Turn, spread with the cracker mixture and broil six minutes on flesh side.

Yield: One serving.

Broiled Mackerel

RHODE ISLAND

3	one-pound to one-and-one-half-pound mackerel, slit down along the backbone to butterfly	2	tablespoons soft butter
1	tablespoon oil	2	tablespoons finely chopped parsley
	Salt and freshly ground black pepper to taste	2	tablespoons lemon juice
1	tablespoon Dijon-style mustard	6	ripe tomatoes, cut in half crosswise
		3	tablespoons seasoned bread crumbs.

1. Place the fish on the oiled rack of the broiler pan and broil four to six inches from a preheated broiler until brown, about four to six minutes. Turn the fish and broil four minutes longer. Mix the oil, salt and pepper and brush over.

2. Combine the mustard, butter, parsley and lemon juice and spread over the inside of the fish. Broil one minute longer. Transfer the fish to a warm platter and keep warm.

3. Sprinkle the cut surfaces of the tomatoes with the crumbs and broil until bubbly. Use to garnish the fish platter.

Yield: Six servings.

Baked Stuffed Mackerel

MASSACHUSETTS

1	three-and-one-half-pound to four-pound mackerel	2	tablespoons finely chopped parsley
	Salt and freshly ground black pepper	¼	cup fresh bread crumbs
4½	tablespoons butter	⅛	teaspoon thyme
1	small onion, finely chopped	⅛	teaspoon summer savory or chervil
¼	pound mushrooms, thinly sliced	1	lemon, cut in half.

1. Preheat the oven to 350 degrees.

2. Wash and split the mackerel and dry with paper towels. Season the inside and out with salt and pepper. Place the fish on buttered foil on a baking dish.

3. Melt three tablespoons of the butter in a small skillet and sauté the onion until transparent. Add the mushrooms and cook three minutes longer. Mix in the parsley, bread crumbs, thyme and savory or chervil.

4. Use the mixture to stuff the mackerel. Close the opening by sewing or toothpicks. Dot with the remaining butter, squeeze half the lemon over fish and make three gashes in fish. Draw aluminum foil around the fish, but do not completely cover. Bake forty minutes, or until the fish flakes easily.

5. Cut the remaining lemon half into wedges and serve with the fish.

Yield: Four servings.

Mussels in Wine

MASSACHUSETTS

24 mussels, well scrubbed and
   beards removed
½ cup dry white wine
1 bay leaf
¼ teaspoon thyme
½ onion, chopped

1 clove garlic, chopped
   Salt and freshly ground
   black pepper to taste
2 tablespoons chopped parsley.

1. Place the mussels in a kettle with the remaining ingredients. Cover tightly and bring to a boil.

2. Cook about eight minutes, or until the mussels open. Serve with broth.

Yield: Four servings.

Breaded Oysters

MASSACHUSETTS

2 twelve-ounce containers
   oysters with liquor (about
   thirty-six shucked fresh
   oysters with liquor)
1½ cups dry bread crumbs
1½ cups flour
¼ cup milk

2 eggs, lightly beaten
1 teaspoon salt
⅛ teaspoon freshly ground
   black pepper
   Fat or oil for deep-frying
   Lemon wedges or tartar
   sauce.

1. Drain the oysters.

2. Combine the bread crumbs and flour.

3. Combine the milk, eggs, salt and pepper.

4. Roll the oysters in the crumb mixture, then in the egg mixture and again in the crumb mixture.

5. Fry, a few at a time, two to three minutes, or until they are golden, in a fry basket, in fat or oil heated to 350 degrees. Drain on paper towels. Serve with lemon wedges or tartar sauce.

Yield: Six servings.

73

Poached Pollock with Crab Sauce

MASSACHUSETTS

2 pounds pollock fillets, cut into six serving pieces
6 tablespoons butter
2 tablespoons lemon juice
Salt and freshly ground black pepper to taste
2 tablespoons chopped scallions, including green part
¼ cup flour
½ cup fish stock or light cream

1 cup milk
2 tablespoons dry sherry
Few drops Tabasco, or to taste
½ pound flaked and picked-over crab meat, preferably fresh
¼ cup buttered soft bread crumbs.

1. Preheat the oven to 350 degrees.
2. Place the fillets in a single layer in a buttered baking dish. Melt two tablespoons of the butter and mix with the lemon juice, salt and pepper and pour over the fish. Bake until it flakes easily, about twenty minutes.
3. Meanwhile, melt the remaining butter and sauté the scallions in it until tender. Stir in the flour; then gradually stir in the fish stock or cream and the milk. Bring to a boil, stirring, and cook two minutes.
4. Stir in the sherry, Tabasco and crab meat. Season with salt and pepper.
5. Pour the crab sauce over the cooked fish. Sprinkle with the bread crumbs and glaze under the broiler.
Yield: Six servings.

Fourth of July Boiled Salmon, Peas and Egg Sauce

MAINE

Salmon:

2 tablespoons butter
1 small onion, chopped
1 rib celery, chopped
2 sprigs parsley
1 tablespoon salt
1 bay leaf

3 whole cloves
2 cups dry white wine
2 quarts boiling water
1 four-pound to six-pound piece fresh salmon.

74

Sauce:

½ cup butter	2 hard-cooked eggs, chopped
2 tablespoons flour	3 cups cooked fresh peas.
½ teaspoon salt	
¼ teaspoon freshly ground black pepper	

1. To prepare salmon, melt the butter and sauté the onion and celery in it until tender. Add the parsley, salt, bay leaf, cloves, wine and water. Simmer ten minutes.

2. Wrap the salmon in double thickness of muslin and lower into the simmering stock. Cover and simmer very gently about thirty-five to forty-five minutes, or until fish flakes easily.

3. Remove fish by lifting muslin and unwrap onto a warm platter. Remove skin and keep fish warm. Strain fish stock and reserve two cups.

4. To prepare sauce, melt one-quarter cup of the butter in a saucepan and blend in the flour. Gradually stir in the reserved fish stock, the salt and pepper. Bring to a boil, stirring until mixture thickens.

5. Stir in the eggs and remaining butter.

6. Arrange the peas around the salmon and pour the egg sauce over the fish.

Yield: Eight to ten servings.

Broiled Scrod

MASSACHUSETTS

2 pounds scrod fillets (small cod or haddock)	1 tablespoon Dijon or Düsseldorf mustard
Salt and freshly ground black pepper	1˙ teaspoon Worcestershire sauce
½ cup butter, melted	Few drops Tabasco
2 cups fine soft bread crumbs	3 tablespoons lemon juice
¼ cup chopped green pepper	2 tablespoons freshly grated Parmesan cheese.
¼ cup finely chopped onion	

1. Cut the fish into four portions. Season with salt and pepper.

2. Combine one-third cup of the butter, the bread crumbs, green pepper, onion, mustard, Worcestershire, Tabasco and lemon juice.

3. Place the fish on a broiler tray. Brush with remaining butter and

broil five minutes. Turn fish pieces. Top with bread crumb mixture and sprinkle with the Parmesan. Broil about seven minutes, or until fish flakes easily and surface is lightly browned.

Yield: Four servings.

Broiled Shad Roe
CONNECTICUT

1	pair shad roe	2	tablespoons melted butter
4	slices bacon		Lemon wedges.

1. Wrap the roe in the bacon slices and broil five minutes on each side, or until bacon and roe are done. Do not overcook.

2. Pour the butter over and serve with lemon wedges.

Yield: One serving.

Smelts with Anchovy Spaghetti
MAINE

1	cup dry bread crumbs	12	anchovy fillets
½	cup freshly grated Parmesan cheese	1	clove garlic, crushed
½	teaspoon salt	¼	cup soft butter
2	pounds pan-dressed smelts	2	tablespoons olive oil
2	eggs, lightly beaten	⅛	teaspoon cayenne pepper
	Vegetable oil for frying	8	ounces spaghetti, cooked al dente, drained.

1. Combine the bread crumbs, cheese and salt. Wash and dry fish. Dip into the eggs and then into the bread crumb mixture. Set the fish on a rack and let stand about fifteen minutes to allow the coating to dry.

2. Pour the vegetable oil into a heavy skillet to a depth of one and one-half inches. Heat to about 360 degrees. Add the smelts and fry four to five minutes on each side, or until fish flakes easily. Drain on paper towels.

3. Mash the anchovies and garlic together with a fork. Gradually work in the butter, olive oil and cayenne. Add to the hot cooked spaghetti and toss. Serve the smelts with the spaghetti.

Yield: Four servings.

76

Chilmark Scallops
MASSACHUSETTS

2 pounds bay scallops
½ cup flour
¼ cup soft bread crumbs
  Cayenne pepper to taste
½ teaspoon paprika

  Salt and freshly ground
  black pepper to taste
  Juice of one lemon
¼ pound butter, melted.

1. Preheat the broiler.
2. Drain the scallops and set aside.
3. Combine the flour, bread crumbs, cayenne, paprika,. salt and pepper. Dredge the scallops lightly in the mixture and arrange them in one layer in a baking dish. Sprinkle the lemon juice over all and then pour the butter over.
4. Broil until golden on one side; then turn and cook until golden on the other. Do not overcook. Serve hot.
Yield: Four servings.

Sautéed Shrimp
MASSACHUSETTS

4 tablespoons olive oil
2 pounds large shrimp,
  shelled and deveined with
  the tails left on
2 tablespoons finely chopped
  shallots
1 large clove garlic, finely
  chopped
2 ten-ounce packages frozen
  artichoke hearts, cooked

  until just thawed, then
  drained
½ pound mushrooms, sliced
  Salt and freshly ground
  black pepper to taste
½ teaspoon thyme
1 tablespoon chopped parsley
2 to three tablespoons lemon
  juice, or to taste.

1. Heat the oil in a large heavy skillet. Add the shrimp and sauté quickly, stirring frequently, until pink.
2. Add the shallots and garlic and cook two minutes.
3. Add the artichoke hearts, mushrooms, salt, pepper, thyme, parsley and lemon juice. Cook, stirring, until the mushrooms and shrimp are tender, about three minutes.
Yield: Six servings.

Rhode Island Steamer Clambake

6	cups water	6	ears corn in husks,
	Seaweed or wet celery,		soaked in salted water
	lettuce and/or spinach		one hour
3	broiler-fryer chickens,	48	small clams
	split	4	to six one-pound
6	unpeeled medium-size		lobsters
	baking potatoes		Melted butter.
6	unpeeled medium-size		
	onions		

1. Place the water in bottom of a twenty-quart steamer. Cover with upper section and place a generous layer of wet, well-rinsed seaweed or greens in the bottom.

2. Wrap the chicken pieces in cheesecloth, tie corners and place on top of seaweed or greens. Wrap five of the potatoes similarly and place on chicken. Wrap the onions and place on chicken.

3. Wrap the ears of corn in cheesecloth and place on top of potatoes, and then the clams wrapped in four bundles of a dozen each, and last, the lobsters in cheesecloth.

4. Top ingredients with more seaweed or wet greens. Place remaining potato in middle and cover.

5. Steam until potato on top is cooked, about one and one-half hours; that means the bake is ready to pull. Serve with melted butter.

Yield: Six servings.

Tuna-Stuffed Peppers à la Sarda
CONNECTICUT

8	large green peppers	1	cup peeled, seeded,
4	cloves garlic		chopped tomatoes
	Olive oil	½	cup capers, drained
1	can anchovy fillets,	¼	cup finely chopped parsley
	chopped	1	teaspoon chopped fresh ba-
1½	cups soft bread crumbs		sil
2	seven-ounce cans tuna fish,	¼	cup pignoli (pine nuts)
	flaked	½	cup currants.

1. Preheat the oven to 375 degrees.

2. Cut a slice off the stem end of each pepper and remove core and seeds. Set peppers in a baking dish.

3. Sauté the garlic in one-half cup oil until brown. Remove garlic and discard.

4. Add the anchovies and bread crumbs to the oil and sauté briefly.

5. Add the remaining ingredients. Mix well and use to fill the peppers. Spoon a little oil over each one. Bake, uncovered, about one hour, or until tender.

Yield: Four servings.

Point Judith Tuna

RHODE ISLAND

2	pounds fresh tuna fish	¼	cup tomato sauce
	Cold salted water	¼	teaspoon oregano
¼	cup olive oil	¼	teaspoon thyme
½	cup finely chopped onion	1	bay leaf
½	cup finely diced carrot		Salt and freshly ground
½	cup finely diced celery		black pepper to taste
1	cup sliced mushrooms	¾	cup dry white wine
6	anchovy fillets, finely	¼	cup fish stock or clam juice
	chopped	2	egg yolks
8	cherrystone clams, well		Juice of one lemon
	scrubbed		Chopped parsley.

1. Soak the tuna overnight in cold salted water, draining and replacing the water as often as practical.

2. Next day, heat the oil in a large heavy saucepan and sauté the onion, carrot, celery and mushrooms in it until lightly browned. Beat in the anchovies until well blended.

3. Towel-dry the tuna and brown on both sides in the pan.

4. Add the clams in their shells, the tomato sauce, oregano, thyme, bay leaf, salt and pepper. Stir. Add the wine and stock or clam juice.

5. Bring to a boil, cover and simmer slowly about fifteen minutes, or until the fish flakes easily. Remove the fish to a warm platter. Strain the stock remaining and return to the pan.

6. Mix the egg yolks with the lemon juice. Add a little of the hot

stock to the mixture, return to the pan and stir until the sauce thickens slightly. Do not boil. Pour over the fish. Garnish with chopped parsley.

Yield: Four servings.

Whiting with Mushrooms

MAINE

4	eight-ounce whiting		Salt and freshly ground
½	cup milk		black pepper to taste
¼	cup flour	⅛	teaspoon nutmeg
9	tablespoons butter		Juice of one lemon
1	onion, finely chopped	1	tablespoon chopped pars-
½	pound mushrooms, chopped		ley.

1. Wash and pat the fish dry. Dip the fish in the milk and then coat it with the flour. Heat three tablespoons of the butter in a large heavy skillet. Sauté the fish over moderate heat until browned on both sides, turning once. Transfer to a heatproof platter and keep warm.

2. Wipe the skillet clean, add three more tablespoons butter and sauté the onion until transparent. Add the mushrooms and cook until most of the liquid has evaporated. Season with salt, pepper and the nutmeg and spread over the fish.

3. Heat the remaining butter in the skillet until brown, but do not allow to scorch. Stir in the lemon juice. Add the parsley and pour over fish.

Yield: Four servings.

Meat, Poultry, Game and Other Main Dishes

Beef Pudding

VERMONT

½	cup flour
1¼	teaspoons salt
½	teaspoon freshly ground black pepper
2	pounds boneless beef chuck, cubed
6	tablespoons oil
5	medium-size onions, chopped
2	cloves garlic, finely chopped

1¼	cups beer
1	bay leaf
½	teaspoon thyme
¼	teaspoon basil
2	cups two-inch pieces carrots
4	cups hot seasoned, creamy mashed potatoes
2	tablespoons butter.

1. Mix the flour with three-quarters teaspoon of the salt and one-quarter teaspoon of the pepper and dredge the meat in the mixture. Heat the

81

oil in a heavy skillet and brown the meat in it very well. Transfer meat to a heavy Dutch oven.

2. Add the onions and garlic to the drippings left in the skillet and sauté until tender but not brown. Transfer onions and garlic to Dutch oven.

3. Add the beer to the skillet and bring to a boil, stirring to remove all browned-on bits. Pour into Dutch oven and add remaining salt and pepper, the thyme and basil. Bring to a boil, cover and simmer one and one-half hours, or until tender. Add the carrots. Cook twenty minutes longer.

4. Preheat the oven to 400 degrees.

5. Transfer meat mixture to an oblong casserole and top with potatoes. Swirl a fork, or the bowl of a spoon, over the potato mixture to make a decorative pattern. Dot with the butter and bake until lightly browned, about fifteen minutes.

Yield: Eight servings.

Paprika Beef

NEW HAMPSHIRE

4	pounds beef chuck or round, cut into one-inch cubes	2	tablespoons brown sugar
	Flour	2	teaspoons dry mustard
¼	cup meat or bacon drippings	½	cup cider vinegar
		1⅓	cups beef broth
2	tablespoons paprika	8	large onions, sliced
2	teaspoons salt		Buttered spaetzle or noodles.
½	teaspoon freshly ground black pepper		

1. Dredge the meat in flour and brown, a small quantity at a time, in the drippings in a heavy Dutch oven or large skillet.

2. Return all meat to skillet. Add the paprika, salt, pepper, sugar, mustard, vinegar, one cup of the broth and the onions. Bring to a boil, cover and simmer two hours, or until meat is tender.

3. Measure the liquid in the meat mixture. For every cup liquid, measure out one and one-half tablespoons flour and add to the remaining broth. Add to the meat mixture and cook, stirring, until the gravy thickens. Check seasoning and serve over hot buttered spaetzle or noodles.

Yield: Eight servings.

Monday's Bean Pot Stew
CONNECTICUT

2 tablespoons bacon drippings

1 pound top round beef, cut into cubes

2 onions, sliced

3 carrots, sliced

1 white turnip, diced

¼ yellow turnip, diced

2 ribs celery, diced

Salt and freshly ground black pepper to taste

¼ cup old-fashioned oats

Boiling water

3 potatoes, cubed.

1. Preheat the oven to 350 degrees.

2. Heat the bacon drippings in a skillet, add the beef cubes and brown on all sides. Add the onions, carrots, white turnip, yellow turnip, celery, salt and pepper. Turn into a bean pot.

3. Stir in the oats and enough boiling water barely to cover. Bake two hours, replenishing water as needed. Add the potatoes and cook one hour longer.

Yield: Four servings.

Spicy New England Pot Roast
NEW HAMPSHIRE

3 tablespoons flour

2 teaspoons salt

¼ teaspoon freshly ground black pepper

1 four-pound boned and rolled beef arm or blade or bottom round pot roast of beef

3 tablespoons bacon drippings or oil

½ cup freshly grated horserad-ish or prepared drained horseradish (four-ounce jar, see note)

1 cup whole cranberry sauce

1 stick cinnamon, broken in two

4 whole cloves

1 cup beef broth

16 small white onions

1 bunch carrots, cut into three-inch lengths.

1. Mix the flour with the salt and pepper and dredge the meat in the mixture. Rub the mixture into all the surfaces.

2. Heat the bacon drippings or oil in a heavy Dutch oven or casserole

and brown the meat in it on all sides very well over high heat. Pour off the drippings into a skillet and reserve.

3. Mix together the horseradish, cranberry sauce, cinnamon, cloves and broth and add to the meat.

4. Bring the mixture to a boil, cover tightly and simmer gently about two hours, or until the meat is barely tender.

5. Meanwhile, brown the onions in the reserved drippings in the skillet. Add the carrots and cook two minutes longer. Drain from the fat and add to the meat broth. Cover and cook about twenty-five minutes longer, or until vegetables and meat are tender.

Yield: Eight servings.

Note: The quantity of horseradish is correct—it loses its pungency as it cooks.

The gravy is delicious over noodles.

Family-Style Meat Balls
VERMONT

3	pounds ground beef chuck	3 Italian hot sausages, ground
2	cups soft bread crumbs	2 onions, ground
2	teaspoons salt	1 clove garlic, ground
½	teaspoon freshly ground black pepper	1 green pepper, ground
2	tablespoons oregano	2 eggs
⅓	cup freshly grated Parmesan cheese	Milk
		4 cups homemade tomato sauce (page 273).

1. Mix all ingredients together except the milk and tomato sauce. Add enough milk to make a stiff mixture that can be molded into meat balls.

2. Form into one-inch balls and simmer in the tomato sauce thirty minutes.

Yield: Ten servings.

Note: The meat mixture can be shaped into hamburgers or cooked as meat loaf.

Polenta Ring with Meat Sauce

CONNECTICUT

1 cup yellow corn meal	1 clove garlic, finely minced
3½ cups water	¼ cup chopped green pepper
2 teaspoons salt	½ pound ground round steak
1 cup grated sharp Cheddar cheese	2½ cups Italian plum tomatoes
2 tablespoons peanut oil	½ teaspoon thyme
1 cup finely chopped onions	½ bay leaf

1. Blend the corn meal with one cup of the water.

2. Add one teaspoon of the salt to remaining water and bring to a boil. Add the corn meal mixture, stirring constantly. Cook, stirring frequently, until thickened. Continue cooking over low heat ten minutes, stirring frequently. Add the cheese and stir until melted. Grease an eight-inch ring mold and add the polenta mixture. Keep warm while preparing meat sauce.

3. Heat the oil in a skillet and add the onions, garlic and green pepper. Cook until onions are wilted. Add the ground round steak. Stir to break up the meat and continue cooking until meat loses its red color. Add the tomatoes, thyme, bay leaf and remaining salt and simmer about thirty minutes.

4. Unmold the polenta ring onto a serving dish and pour the sauce in the center. Serve immediately.

Yield: Six to eight servings.

Beef 'n' Rice Casserole

NEW HAMPSHIRE

1½ cups uncooked rice
3 tablespoons olive oil
1 bay leaf, crumbled
¾ pound ground beef round
¼ pound Italian sausage, diced
1 small onion, finely chopped
1 clove garlic, finely chopped
1 small green pepper, finely chopped
½ rib celery, finely chopped
2½ cups water, beef broth or chicken broth

1 eight-ounce can tomato sauce
3 medium-size or two extra-large eggs, lightly beaten
2 tablespoons tomato paste
3 tablespoons grated Romano cheese
2 teaspoons salt
½ teaspoon freshly ground black pepper
½ teaspoon sugar
6 slices mozzarella cheese (optional).

1. Soak the rice in water to cover fifteen minutes. Drain the rice and place in a one-and-three-quarters-quart casserole.

2. Place the oil, bay leaf, ground beef, sausage, onion, garlic, green pepper and celery in a skillet and cook until the meat loses its redness and the vegetables are tender. Cool ten minutes.

3. Preheat the oven to 350 degrees.

4. Add the water or broth, the tomato sauce, eggs and tomato paste to the rice and mix well. Add the cooled meat mixture, grated cheese, salt, black pepper and sugar. Stir to mix well. Bake two hours, or until the rice is tender.

5. Place the mozzarella cheese, if desired, on top during the last ten minutes of cooking.

Yield: Four servings.

Lamb Meat Balls

MASSACHUSETTS

½ pound stale white, Italian or French bread slices
1½ pounds ground lean chuck
1½ pounds ground lean lamb
2 large onions, finely chopped
½ cup finely chopped fresh mint leaves
2 eggs, lightly beaten
2 tablespoons grated Romano cheese
1 tomato, peeled and chopped
Salt and freshly ground black pepper to taste
Flour
Oil and melted butter for frying.

1. Pull the bread into pieces and place in a bowl. Cover with water and let stand five minutes. Squeeze out excess moisture from the bread.

2. Put the chuck and lamb in a large bowl and add the bread. Add the onions, mint, eggs, cheese, tomato, salt and pepper. Mix well with the hands. If the mixture is too stiff, add a little water. Let the mixture stand several hours to blend flavors before shaping.

3. Shape the meat into two-inch balls for luncheon size or one-inch balls for appetizers and flatten slightly on the top. Dredge well in flour to give a good coating.

4. Heat enough oil and melted butter in a large heavy skillet just to cover the bottom depth of one-eighth inch. Add the meat balls and fry on all sides over medium heat until browned. The meat balls should have a crusty brown outside.

Yield: Ten luncheon servings or two dozen appetizer servings.

Stuffed Meat Loaf

VERMONT

Mushroom tomato sauce:
2 tablespoons olive oil
1 tablespoon butter
1 medium-size onion, finely chopped
1 clove garlic, finely chopped
2 cups mushrooms, sliced
1 one-pound-twelve-ounce can Italian plum tomatoes packed in puree
1 six-ounce can tomato paste
1½ cups water
1½ teaspoons salt
½ teaspoon freshly ground black pepper
1 teaspoon basil, pulverized
¼ cup to one-third cup dry red wine.

Meat loaf:

2 pounds ground lean beef chuck
2 eggs
1 small green pepper, diced
⅓ cup chopped parsley
1 onion, finely chopped
3 slices stale bread, soaked in water and then excess moisture squeezed out
½ teaspoon salt
½ teaspoon freshly ground black pepper
¾ cup Italian plum tomatoes.

Filling:

3 hard-cooked eggs, chopped
½ cup julienne strips Genoa salami
¼ cup freshly grated Romano and/or Parmesan cheese
⅓ cup julienne strips pimento
½ cup finely chopped parsley
½ cup soft bread crumbs
1 tablespoon mayonnaise
½ teaspoon thyme
Freshly ground black pepper to taste.

1. To prepare mushroom tomato sauce, heat the oil and butter in a heavy three-quart to four-quart saucepan. Add the onion and garlic and sauté until tender. Add the mushrooms and cook three minutes longer.

2. Add the tomatoes, tomato paste, water, salt and pepper. Stir to mix and bring to a boil, stirring.

3. Simmer the sauce, partially covered with a lid, thirty to thirty-five minutes (the lid prevents spattering but allows some evaporation), stirring occasionally to prevent sticking. Stir in the basil and wine and cook five minutes longer.

4. Meanwhile, combine the meat loaf ingredients in a large bowl and mix thoroughly with the hands.

5. Preheat the oven to 375 degrees.

6. Combine the filling ingredients in another bowl and mix well.

7. On a double thickness of aluminum foil, pat out the meat loaf mixture into a rectangle about 12-by-9 inches. Place the filling in a long sausage shape atop meat about two inches from a long side.

8. Gradually roll the meat loaf mixture around the filling like a jellyroll using the foil as a guide to the rolling. Remove the foil and place the stuffed meat roll in a baking pan. Bake forty-five minutes, or until done. Serve in slices, with the sauce served separately.

Yield: Eight to ten servings.

Meat Balls with Brown Beans
VERMONT

Brown beans:

2	cups dried pinto beans	2	teaspoons salt
2½	quarts water	¼	cup maple syrup.
¼	cup cider vinegar		

Meat balls:

1	cup fine dry bread crumbs	3	eggs, lightly beaten
1	cup milk	2	teaspoons salt
3	tablespoons bacon drippings	½	teaspoon freshly ground black pepper
¼	cup chopped onion	½	teaspoon ground allspice
1	pound ground beef chuck	1	teaspoon nutmeg
1	pound ground lean pork	1	cup water, approximately.

1. To prepare brown beans, wash the pinto beans and soak in the water overnight. Next day, place beans and soaking liquid in a kettle and bring to a boil. Cover and simmer until tender, about one and one-half hours. Add the vinegar, salt and syrup and mix well. Cook thirty minutes longer.

2. To prepare meat balls, soak the bread crumbs in the milk for fifteen minutes. Melt two tablespoons of the drippings and sauté the onion in them until tender.

3. Combine soaked bread crumbs, the onion, beef, pork, eggs, salt, pepper, allspice and nutmeg. Mix well. Shape into one-inch balls.

4. Melt remaining bacon drippings in a heavy skillet. Add the meat balls and brown on all sides. Add one-third cup of the water and simmer, covered, until meat balls are tender and cooked through, about forty-five minutes. Add more of the water as necessary during cooking.

5. Serve the meat balls over, or in the middle of a circle of, the brown beans.

Yield: Six to eight servings.

Ravioli à la Romana
CONNECTICUT

1	large Bermuda onion, finely chopped	1	three-pound beef pot roast, braised with onion and red wine, put through the finest blade of a meat grinder
3	tablespoons olive oil		
2	pounds fresh spinach, chopped, or two packages frozen chopped spinach		Salt and freshly ground black pepper to taste
½	cup pignoli (pine nuts) (optional)	1	recipe pasta (recipe below), thinly rolled
½	pound ricotta cheese		Boiling salted water
1	egg	4	cups homemade tomato sauce (page 273).
	Freshly grated Parmesan cheese		

1. Sauté the onion in the oil until tender and golden. Add the spinach and cook until spinach is cooked and mixture is dry. Pass through the finest blade of the meat grinder, with nuts if used.

2. Mix together the ricotta, egg and one-quarter cup Parmesan. In a large bowl, combine the meat, spinach mixture and cheese mixture and mix well. Season with salt and pepper. Form into tiny one-inch balls.

3. Line a ravioli tin with pasta dough. Place a meat ball in each depression. Cover with dough, roll to cut and set ravioli to dry. Repeat until all dough and filling are used.

4. Preheat the oven to 375 degrees.

5. Cook the ravioli, in small batches, in large kettle of boiling salted water about ten minutes. Drain and arrange in a shallow casserole. Spoon the sauce over. If desired, sprinkle with three-quarters cup Parmesan. Bake about fifteen minutes.

Yield: Six dozen ravioli; nine to ten servings.

Note: The uncooked ravioli can be frozen after thirty minutes' drying time.

Pasta
CONNECTICUT

6 cups flour
1 tablespoon salt

6 eggs.

1. Place the flour and salt in a bowl. Make a well in the center and add the eggs. Beat with a wooden spoon, gradually incorporating the flour.
2. Add water to make a fairly stiff dough. Knead the dough until it is elastic and smooth, about ten minutes.
3. Pass one-sixth of the dough through pasta machine at the widest setting several times, folding dough in thirds as it lengthens for successive rollings. Set the machine at number two or three for the final rolling to make ravioli.
Yield: Enough for six dozen ravioli.

Vermont Boiled Dinner

4 pounds corned beef
3 large yellow turnips, peeled and cut into one-half-inch slices
6 large carrots or about twenty small carrots
6 medium-size potatoes, peeled and halved
10 to twelve beets, freshly cooked and peeled

2 to four heads cabbage, quartered and freshly cooked
Melted butter
Chopped parsley
Mustard (optional)
Horseradish (optional).

1. Place the corned beef in a large kettle and add water to cover. Simmer three hours, or until tender when pierced with a fork. Meanwhile, one hour before meat is done, add the turnips. Thirty minutes before meat is done, add the carrots and potatoes.
2. When meat and vegetables are tender, slice the meat and place it on a warm large serving platter. Surround the meat with turnip slices, carrots, potatoes, the beets and cabbage. Pour melted butter over the vegetables and sprinkle potatoes with parsley.
3. Serve with mustard and horseradish if desired.
Yield: Ten to one dozen servings.

Red Flannel Hash

VERMONT

2 cups chopped cooked
corned beef
3 cups diced cooked potatoes
1½ cups diced cooked beets
2 tablespoons grated onion
1 teaspoon Worcestershire
sauce

Salt to taste
¼ teaspoon freshly ground
black pepper
2 tablespoons bacon drip-
pings.

1. In a bowl, combine the corned beef, potatoes, beets, onion, Worcestershire, salt and pepper.

2. Heat the bacon drippings in a heavy skillet and spread the corned beef mixture over bottom of skillet. Cook over medium-high heat until underside of hash is browned. Turn and brown the other side.

Yield: Four servings.

Corned Beef Hash

MASSACHUSETTS

3 cups finely diced cooked
corned beef
2 cups finely diced cooked
potatoes
3 tablespoons butter
¾ cup finely chopped onions

1 tablespoon Worcestershire
sauce
Salt and freshly ground
black pepper to taste
Peanut oil
Catchup (optional).

1. Combine the corned beef and potatoes in a mixing bowl.

2. Melt the butter and cook the onions in it until thoroughly wilted. Add onions to the corned beef mixture. Add the Worcestershire, salt and pepper and blend lightly.

3. Brush a skillet with oil and spoon the corned beef mixture into the skillet, pressing down to cover the bottom fully. Cook over moderate heat until well browned on the bottom.

4. Serve with catchup if desired.

Yield: About four servings.

Joe Booker Stew

MAINE

¼	pound salt pork, diced	2	cups sliced carrots
1½	pounds lean boneless beef chuck or veal, cut into one-inch cubes	2	cups diced potatoes
			Salt and freshly ground black pepper to taste
6	cups water	2	tablespoons chopped parsley
2	cups diced white or yellow turnips	1	recipe dumplings for soup (page 286).
2	cups sliced onions		

1. Render the salt pork in a large heavy Dutch kettle or casserole until the pieces are crisp. Remove the pieces and reserve.

2. Add the meat to the fat remaining and cook, stirring, until browned on all sides. Add the water, bring to a boil, cover and simmer one and one-half hours, or until the meat is almost tender.

3. Add the turnips, onions, carrots, potatoes, salt and pepper, bring to a boil, cover and cook thirty minutes, or until the vegetables are tender. Sprinkle with the parsley.

4. Add more liquid if necessary to make the level of the liquid one-inch above the stew. Drop in the dumplings and cook according to directions.

Yield: Eight servings.

Frizzled Chipped Beef

RHODE ISLAND

¼	pound dried beef, torn into bite-size pieces	1	cup heavy cream
	Boiling water		Freshly ground black pepper to taste
4	tablespoons butter	½	teaspoon lemon juice
¼	pound mushrooms, sliced		Milk
1	egg		Toast triangles or johnnycakes (page 171).
1	egg yolk		

1. Place the beef in a small bowl, cover with boiling water and let stand two minutes. Drain and pat the beef pieces dry with a paper towel.

2. Melt two tablespoons of the butter in a heavy skillet and cook the

mushrooms quickly until the liquid has evaporated. Remove the mushrooms and reserve.

3. Melt the remaining butter in the skillet. Beat together the egg, egg yolk and cream and pour into the skillet. Heat, stirring, until the mixture thickens, but do not allow to boil.

4. Add the beef, reserved mushrooms, pepper and lemon juice. If the mixture is too thick, thin with milk. Reheat, but do not allow to boil. Serve over toast triangles or johnnycakes.

Yield: Four servings.

Ham Loaf

VERMONT

1	pound smoked, cooked ham, ground	⅛	teaspoon freshly ground black pepper
1	pound ground lean pork	¾	cup light brown sugar
2	eggs, lightly beaten	2	teaspoons dry mustard
½	cup milk	⅓	cup cider vinegar
½	cup cracker crumbs	⅓	cup water.
1	teaspoon salt		

1. Preheat the oven to 350 degrees.

2. Combine the ham, pork, eggs, milk, cracker crumbs, salt and pepper and pack into a loaf pan.

3. Bake forty-five minutes.

4. Meanwhile, combine the remaining ingredients in a saucepan, bring to a boil and boil five minutes.

5. Bake the ham loaf forty-five minutes longer, basting frequently with the sauce.

Yield: Eight servings.

Ham Mousse

MASSACHUSETTS

3½	cups finely ground cooked ham (see step 1)	¼	cup cold water
1⅓	cups chicken broth	2	eggs, separated
1	envelope unflavored gelatin	1	cup heavy cream
		¼	cup dry sherry.

1. The ham must be ground as fine as possible. Refrigerate.
2. Bring the broth to a boil.
3. Soak the gelatin in the water and stir into the hot broth. Stir to dissolve gelatin.
4. Beat the egg yolks lightly; add a little of the hot mixture to the yolks; then add yolks to the broth, stirring constantly. Cook over low heat, stirring with a wooden spoon, just until sauce coats the spoon. Do not overcook or sauce may curdle. Cool sauce, but do not chill.
5. Beat the egg whites until stiff. Beat the cream until stiff. Blend the two; then fold in the sauce, ham and sherry. Pour the mixture into a one-and-one-half-quart mold and chill. Unmold onto a platter before serving.

Yield: Six servings.

Baked Ham with Maple Glaze
VERMONT

½ five-pound to seven-pound ready-to-eat ham
2 dozen whole cloves
½ cup maple syrup
¼ teaspoon dry mustard
1 cup unsweetened pineapple juice

½ cup dry bread crumbs
2 tablespoons light brown sugar
Pinch cinnamon.

1. Preheat the oven to 325 degrees.
2. Remove any brown part of the fat from the ham and score the fat into a diamond pattern. Place a whole clove in the middle of each diamond. Place on rack in roasting pan.
3. Combine the maple syrup, mustard and pineapple juice and pour over the ham. Bake one hour, basting with juices from pan several times.
4. Combine the bread crumbs, sugar and cinnamon and pat over the surface of the ham, return to the oven and bake twenty to thirty minutes longer, or until browned, basting twice with juices.

Yield: About eight servings.

Apple Glazed Vermont Ham

1 twelve-pound Vermont ham   ½ cup apple syrup.
½ cup Vermont apple jelly

1. Preheat the oven to 325 degrees.
2. Place a whole Vermont ham, uncovered, on a rack in a shallow roasting pan. Bake the ham twenty-five minutes to the pound, or, if a meat thermometer is used, until it registers 160 degrees. Just before the ham is to be done, remove it from the oven and trim off most of the rind, leaving a collar of rind around the shank. Score the fat side of the ham in diamond shapes. Combine the apple jelly and syrup and spread on the ham.
3. Increase the oven heat to 450 degrees. Return the ham to the oven and bake until glazed, five to fifteen minutes.
Yield: Sixteen to eighteen servings.

Eggplant and Macaroni Casserole
MASSACHUSETTS

⅓ cup olive oil	1 teaspoon oregano
1 large eggplant, peeled and cubed (about two quarts)	¼ teaspoon cinnamon
½ cup diced celery	1 recipe homemade tomato sauce (page 273)
8 ounces elbow macaroni, cooked al dente, drained	8 ounces mozzarella cheese, thickly sliced.
1 pound ground lamb Salt and freshly ground black pepper to taste	

1. Preheat the oven to 375 degrees.
2. Heat the oil in a large skillet. Add the eggplant and sauté until lightly browned. Combine the eggplant, celery and macaroni in a large bowl.
3. Cook the lamb in a skillet until lightly browned, breaking up the lumps as meat cooks. Season with salt, pepper, oregano and cinnamon. Add to the macaroni mixture.
4. Stir in the tomato sauce and check the seasoning. Turn into a two-and-one-half-quart to three-quart deep casserole. Top with the mozzarella and bake thirty minutes, or until the casserole is bubbly hot and the cheese is melted and lightly browned.
Yield: Four servings.

Stuffed Crown Roast of Lamb
MASSACHUSETTS

¼ cup soft bread crumbs
½ recipe eggplant and macaroni casserole (recipe above), using only enough tomato sauce to moisten and omitting the mozzarella cheese

1 crown roast of lamb, made from sixteen rib chops
2 tablespoons lemon juice
Salt and freshly ground black pepper to taste
3 tablespoons freshly grated Parmesan cheese.

1. Preheat the oven to 350 degrees.
2. Mix the bread crumbs into the casserole mixture.
3. Rub the crown roast all over with the lemon juice and season with salt and pepper. Stuff with the eggplant mixture, piling it up and placing any extra in a small baking dish. Sprinkle with the cheese.
4. Place the roast on a rack in a shallow pan and roast one hour and twenty minutes, or until the roast reaches the desired degree of doneness. Cook the extra dish of stuffing for the last twenty minutes of roasting time.
   Yield: Eight servings.

Baked Lamb Ring with Mashed Potatoes
VERMONT

2 tablespoons oil
2 tablespoons chopped onion
1 clove garlic, finely chopped
4 mushrooms, finely chopped
2 pounds ground lean lamb
2 eggs, lightly beaten
½ cup chopped green pepper
1½ cups soft bread crumbs
1 teaspoon salt

¼ teaspoon freshly ground black pepper
1 tablespoon chopped parsley
1 teaspoon rosemary
12 piped rosettes made from three cups seasoned mashed potatoes mixed with two egg yolks
2 tablespoons melted butter.

1. Preheat the oven to 350 degrees.
2. Heat the oil in a small skillet and sauté the onion and garlic in it until lightly browned. Add the mushrooms and cook until the extra liquid has been evaporated.
3. Place the onion mixture in a bowl and mix with the lamb, eggs, green pepper, bread crumbs, salt, pepper, parsley and rosemary. Pack into a greased eight-inch ring mold.

4. Bake one hour. Set in a warm place.

5. Increase the oven heat to 375 degrees. Place the potato rosettes on a greased baking sheet, sprinkle with the butter and bake until lightly browned, about ten minutes.

6. Unmold the lamb ring onto a hot platter and pile the rosetttes in the middle or around.

Yield: Six servings.

Lamb on a Spit
CONNECTICUT

½ cup plus two tablespoons olive oil	2 whole cloves
1 large carrot, finely chopped	1 clove garlic, crushed
1 large onion, finely chopped	6 cups dry red wine or dry white wine
2 shallots, finely minced	2 cups wine vinegar
½ cup finely minced celery	2 teaspoons thyme
Salt	1 six-pound leg of lamb, boned and tied
½ teaspoon peppercorns	Freshly ground black pepper.
4 bay leaves	
6 sprigs parsley	

1. Heat one-half cup of the oil and add the carrot, onion, shallots and celery. Cook, stirring, until onion is wilted.

2. Add one tablespoon salt, the peppercorns, bay leaves, parsley, cloves, garlic, wine, wine vinegar and one teaspoon of the thyme. Simmer slowly thirty minutes. Cool thoroughly.

3. Pour the marinade over the meat. Let stand three days in refrigerator, turning occasionally.

4. When ready to roast, drain the meat one hour before cooking, reserving marinade. Rub meat with remaining oil, remaining thyme and salt and pepper to taste.

5. If the spit is used, roast the lamb to the desired degree of doneness, basting occasionally with a little of the marinade. The time will depend on the intensity of the heat and proximity to the fire. If the meat is to be roasted in the oven, preheat the oven to 350 degrees. Place the lamb in a roasting pan and roast, basting occasionally with a little of the marinade, fifteen to twenty minutes a pound.

6. When the meat is cooked, a sauce may be made with the drip-

pings. To do this, pour off the fat and stir into the drippings, bit by bit, butter kneaded with equal parts of flour. The sauce should be thin.

Yield: Ten servings.

Leg of Lamb with Saffron-and-Caper Sauce
CONNECTICUT

6 tablespoons butter	of spring lamb, boned and
2 cloves garlic, mashed	tied, with bones reserved
1 teaspoon monosodium glutamate (optional)	1 tablespoon cornstarch
	½ cup heavy cream
1 teaspoon salt	¾ teaspoon leaf saffron
1 teaspoon cayenne pepper	1 bottle capers, drained.
1 five-pound to six-pound leg	

1. Night before, cream together the butter, garlic, monosodium glutamate if desired, salt and cayenne and spread all over the roast. Double-wrap the lamb and bones in heavy-duty aluminum foil and refrigerate overnight.

2. Next day, remove meat package from refrigerator two hours before cooking.

3. Preheat the oven to 375 degrees.

4. Place the meat package in a roasting pan and roast thirty-five minutes a pound for medium degree of doneness and forty-five minutes a pound for well done.

5. Combine the cornstarch and three tablespoons water. Open the foil and pour off the juices from the roast. Add to the juices the cornstarch mixture, cream and saffron. Measure liquid. It should measure two and one-half cups. Add water to make up quantity if necessary.

6. Bring the mixture to a boil, stirring, and cook five minutes. Sauce should be the consistency of light cream. Add water if necessary. Add the capers.

7. Discard the bones and carve the roast. Serve hot with the sauce served separately. Or, to serve cold, arrange lamb slices in a serving dish, pour sauce over and chill.

Yield: About ten servings.

Baked Breast of Lamb

CONNECTICUT

3	pounds breast of lamb, cut into two-inch pieces	¼	cup water
	Salt and freshly ground black pepper to taste	¼	cup currant jelly
		2	tablespoons chopped parsley
1	cup dry red wine	1	teaspoon marjoram.

1. Preheat the oven to 375 degrees.
2. Place the meat, fat side down, in a large open roasting pan. Season with salt and pepper. Bake one hour, or until barely tender.
3. Combine the remaining ingredients in a small saucepan and bring to a boil.
4. Pour off the accumulated drippings and fat from the roasting pan. Pour the wine mixture over lamb and bake, basting frequently, thirty minutes longer, or until the lamb is glazed and tender.

Yield: Six servings.

Lamb and Sausage Stew

VERMONT

2	links pork sausage	1	teaspoon paprika
¼	cup olive oil		Salt and freshly ground black pepper to taste
2	or three cloves garlic, finely minced	1½	cups fresh or canned beef broth
2	pounds lamb, cut into one-inch cubes	1½	cups homemade (page 273) or canned tomato sauce
2	carrots, diced		Cooked rice or noodles.
3	ribs celery, finely chopped		
½	teaspoon ground rosemary		

1. Place the sausage in a skillet and cook until done. Drain the sausage; then cut into thin slices.
2. Heat the oil and add the garlic. Cook over moderate heat until the garlic starts to brown; then remove the garlic and discard. Brown the lamb in the oil remaining in the pan. Add the vegetables, sausage and seasonings.
3. Add the broth and tomato sauce and bring to a boil. Simmer one

and one-half hours, or until the meat is fork-tender. Serve with rice or noodles.

Yield: Four to six servings.

Breast of Lamb with Dill Sauce
CONNECTICUT

3	pounds breast of lamb	1	tablespoon cider vinegar
	Salt and freshly ground	1	teaspoon sugar
	black pepper to taste	½	cup heavy cream
1	large carrot, sliced	2	egg yolks
1	medium-size onion, diced	¾	cup freshly snipped dill
½	cup diced celery		weed, or more to taste
1	to two tablespoons flour,		Boiled potatoes
	depending on desired thickness of sauce		Cucumber salad.

1. Trim the lamb of excess fat. Cut the meat into two-inch cubes. Sprinkle with salt and pepper. Place in a deep kettle. Add the carrot, onion, celery and water to cover. Simmer, covered, over low heat about one to one and one-quarter hours, or until the meat is tender, skimming as necessary and stirring occasionally.

2. Drain the cooking liquid into a saucepan and cook down to one and one-half cups. Mix the flour with a little water and stir into the liquid. Cook, stirring constantly, until smooth and thickened. Stir in the vinegar and sugar.

3. Beat together the cream and egg yolks. Stir into the sauce. Pour the sauce over the meat and heat thoroughly. Sprinkle with the dill before serving. Serve with boiled potatoes and cucumber salad.

Yield: Four to six servings.

Connecticut Bean Pot

1	pound Italian hot sausages, sliced	½	teaspoon basil
1	pound Italian sweet sausages, sliced	2	bay leaves
1	kielbasa (Polish sausage), sliced	¾	cup dry sherry
3	onions, sliced and separated into rings	3	one-pound cans pork and beans
½	teaspoon thyme	1	eight-ounce can tomato sauce
			Whole or sliced frankfurters (optional).

1. Preheat the oven to 350 degrees.

2. Place the sausages and onions in a heavy Dutch oven or casserole and cook gently until sausages are done.

3. Add the remaining ingredients and bring to a boil. Cover and bake one and one-half hours. If desired, frankfurters, whole or sliced, may be added during the last twenty minutes of baking.

Yield: Ten to one dozen servings.

Pork Chops with Onions

NEW HAMPSHIRE

¼	cup bacon drippings	¾	cup dry white wine
1	to two cloves garlic, finely minced	¾	cup freshly squeezed orange juice
6	thick pork chops	1½	cups thinly sliced onions
2	teaspoons dry mustard Salt and freshly ground black pepper	2	green peppers, cored, seeded and cut into strips Cooked rice.

1. Heat the bacon drippings and add the garlic. Cook, stirring, but do not brown.

2. Smear the pork chops with the mustard and sprinkle with salt and pepper. Brown on both sides in the bacon drippings and add the wine and orange juice. Cook over low heat until the sauce is slightly reduced. Add the onions and green peppers. Cover the pan.

3. Continue cooking over low heat until the chops are tender, one to one and one-half hours. If desired, add more salt and pepper to taste and serve hot with rice.

Yield: Six servings.

Cranberry Pork Chops
MASSACHUSETTS

6 rib or loin pork chops, each three-quarters-inch to one-inch thick
1 tablespoon butter
1 teaspoon salt
⅛ teaspoon freshly ground black pepper

1 cup fresh cranberries
¼ cup brown sugar
2 teaspoons cornstarch
⅔ cup water
1 large orange, peeled and cut into one-quarter-inch slices.

1. Brown the chops on both sides in the butter in a heavy skillet or Dutch oven. Pour off excess drippings. Season chops with the salt and pepper.

2. Add the cranberries and brown sugar, cover tightly and simmer forty-five minutes, or until the chops are thoroughly cooked.

3. Remove the chops to a heated platter. Combine the cornstarch with the water and add to the liquid in skillet. Cook, stirring, until the sauce is thickened. Add the orange slices and reheat. Pour the sauce over the chops.

Yield: Six servings.

Pork Chop Casserole
MAINE

6 shoulder pork chops (about one and one-half pounds to two pounds)
2 tablespoons shortening
   Salt and freshly ground black pepper
½ cup finely chopped leeks
1 cup uncooked rice

2½ cups chicken broth
1 cup drained canned tomatoes
½ teaspoon thyme
½ teaspoon sage
¼ teaspoon marjoram
2 tablespoon chopped parsley
1 bay leaf.

1. Preheat the oven to 350 degrees.

2. Brown the chops on both sides in the shortening in a large skillet. Remove the chops, season lightly with salt and pepper and keep warm. Add the leeks to the fat remaining in the skillet and sauté slowly until tender.

3. Add the rice and cook, stirring, five minutes. Add the broth, to-

103

matoes, thyme, sage, marjoram, parsley, bay leaf, one and one-half tea-spoons salt and one-quarter teaspoon pepper and bring to a boil.

4. Place the rice mixture in the bottom of a heavy three-quart cas-serole. Top with the chops. Cover and bake one hour. Remove the bay leaf before serving.

Yield: Six servings.

Galatoise Polonaise
CONNECTICUT

½	pound thin-sliced lean ba-con, cooked until crisp	1	pound sauerkraut, rinsed and drained
1	pound fresh lean boneless pork, cut into thin slices	2	juicy apples, peeled, cored and sliced
½	pound cooked smoked ham, sliced	4	white onions, thinly sliced
½	pound frankfurters, sliced	1	small head cabbage, sliced, parboiled in salt water five
1	pound mushrooms, sliced		minutes
1	eight-ounce bottle pitted stuffed green olives, sliced		Salt and freshly ground black pepper to taste
3	to four tomatoes, peeled and sliced	2	bay leaves, crumbled
1½	teaspoons sugar	2	cups tomato juice
		½	cup butter.

1. Preheat the oven to 375 degrees.

2. Make an assembly line of the following ingredients: the bacon, pork, ham, frankfurters, mushrooms, olives, tomatoes, sugar, sauerkraut, apples, onions and cabbage. Starting with one-third of the bacon slices, make alternate layers of the ingredients in a four-quart to five-quart baking dish, leaving plenty of cabbage and tomato slices for the next-to-last layer and a few bacon slices to top everything. As galatoise is being assembled, season each layer lightly with salt and pepper and sprinkle with bits of crumbled bay leaves.

3. Pour the tomato juice over all, dot with the butter, cover the dish and bake one and three-quarter hours. Remove the cover, to brown gala-toise lightly, and bake fifteen minutes longer. Serve topped with sour cream-and-mustard sauce (recipe below).

Yield: About one dozen servings.

Sour Cream-and-Mustard Sauce
CONNECTICUT

6 cups sour cream	¼ cup chopped chives.
9 to twelve tablespoons Dijon or Düsseldorf mustard	

Stir the sour cream and mustard together and sprinkle with the chives.

Yield: About one and one-half quarts.

Stuffed Pork Chops
MASSACHUSETTS

1 cup diced dried apricots	½ cup finely chopped onion
½ cup boiling water	4 cups one-quarter-inch stale white, French or Italian bread cubes
1 tablespoon sugar	
¼ cup flour	
Salt and freshly ground black pepper to taste	1 large tart apple, peeled, cored and diced
6 one-inch-thick rib pork chops	2 tablespoons chopped parsley
3 tablespoons shortening	½ teaspoon thyme
4 tablespoons butter	¼ teaspoon marjoram.
½ cup diced celery	

1. Preheat the oven to 325 degrees.

2. Place the apricots in a bowl and add the boiling water and sugar.

3. Combine the flour, salt and pepper. Trim the excess fat from the chops and coat the chops with the flour mixture. Melt the shortening in a skillet. Add the chops, brown on both sides, remove and set aside.

4. Add the butter to the skillet. Add the celery and onion and sauté until tender but not browned.

5. Combine the bread cubes, apple, parsley, thyme and marjoram and add the cooked vegetables. Add the apricots. Season with salt and pepper.

6. Place the stuffing in the bottom of a shallow baking dish or casserole and place the chops on top of stuffing. Cover and bake one and one-half hours, or until the chops are thoroughly cooked.

Yield: Six servings.

Sweet and Sour Pork

CONNECTICUT

1 four-pound to five-pound rib end of pork	Salt and freshly ground black pepper to taste
1 clove garlic, finely minced	2 cups brown sugar
1 teaspoon finely minced rosemary	1 cup cider vinegar.

1. Preheat the oven to 450 degrees.

2. Rub the pork with the garlic, rosemary, salt and pepper. Place the roast, fat side up, in a Dutch oven. Bake, uncovered, fifteen minutes.

3. Meanwhile, put the brown sugar in a skillet. Cook over very low heat until the sugar melts and starts to caramelize, but do not let the sugar burn. Stir in the vinegar.

4. Reduce the oven temperature to 300 degrees. Pour off the fat that has accumulated from the pork. Baste the meat with the vinegar-sugar mixture. Bake, covered, basting frequently, two hours or longer, until the pork is fork-tender.

5. Serve the pork sliced. Pour off excess fat from the liquid in the Dutch oven and serve the remaining sauce separately.

Yield: Four to six servings.

Pork Chops with Spinach

CONNECTICUT

¼ cup flour	preferably Dijon or Düsseldorf
¾ teaspoon salt	
4 large pork chops, trimmed	1 pound fresh spinach, well washed and chopped, or one package frozen chopped spinach, partially defrosted
2 tablespoons olive oil	
1 clove garlic, minced	
2 tablespoons minced parsley	
1 tablespoon chopped onion	
¼ cup dry white wine	½ cup croutons, fried in oil.
½ teaspoon prepared mustard,	

1. Combine the flour and one-half teaspoon of the salt and rub mixture into pork chops. Brown chops in the oil. Cover and cook ten minutes over low heat. Transfer chops to a shallow casserole.

2. Preheat the oven to 375 degrees.

3. Add the garlic, parsley and onion to skillet and cook until onion is wilted. Add the wine, mustard, spinach and remaining salt.

4. Cook, covered, four minutes. Drain off excess liquid. Puree the spinach mixture in an electric blender or force through sieve. Pile spinach over chops.

5. Top with the crisp croutons. Cover casserole and bake twenty to twenty-five minutes.

Yield: Four servings.

Barbecued Ribs with Maple Syrup

VERMONT

3	pounds (one rack) lean spare ribs	¼	cup maple syrup
½	cup tomato puree		Salt and freshly ground black pepper to taste
¼	cup cider vinegar		Tabasco to taste.
⅓	cup finely grated onion		
2	tablespoons Worcestershire sauce		

1. Preheat the oven to 350 degrees.

2. Line a 13-by-9-inch baking dish with foil. Lay the rack of ribs on the foil.

3. Combine the remaining ingredients in a small saucepan, bring to a boil, check seasonings and adjust if necessary. Reserve one-quarter cup and pour the remaining sauce over the ribs. Close the foil over the ribs or cover with a second piece of foil. Bake one hour, or until pork is cooked.

4. Remove the ribs and cut into one-rib sections, brush on both sides with reserved sauce and broil under broiler preheated to 350 degrees, turning and basting with sauce several times until well glazed.

Yield: Four servings.

Creamed Veal
CONNECTICUT

4 tablespoons butter
1 one-pound untrimmed veal
   steak, cut as for schnitzel
   Salt and freshly ground
   black pepper to taste

3 cups heavy cream
Toast.

1. Heat two tablespoons of the butter in a skillet and add the veal steak. Sprinkle with salt and pepper and brown on both sides over high heat. Remove the skillet from the heat.

2. Trim the meat. Remove and discard the bone. Cut the meat into one-inch pieces.

3. Add the remaining butter to the skillet and cook the cubed veal once more until browned. Add the cream, partially cover and cook, stirring occasionally, thirty to forty minutes. Serve with toast.

Yield: Two servings.

Veal with Mushrooms
CONNECTICUT

1 pound boneless veal cutlet,
   cut one-third-inch to one-
   half-inch thick
   Salt and freshly ground
   black pepper to taste
¼ cup butter
3 shallots, finely chopped
¼ pound mushrooms, sliced

1 thin slice baked ham, finely
   chopped
2 tablespoons finely chopped
   parsley
1 cup dry white wine
1 teaspoon lemon juice
½ cup fine buttered soft bread
   crumbs.

1. Preheat the oven to 350 degrees.

2. Cut the veal into strips about one-half-inch wide and season with salt and pepper.

3. Melt the butter in a heavy skillet and sauté the shallots in it until tender but not browned. Add the mushrooms, ham and parsley and cook, stirring occasionally, three minutes.

4. Add the veal strips and cook, stirring constantly, two minutes longer.

5. Add the wine and lemon juice. Bring to a boil, stirring, and sim-

mer, covered, five minutes. Transfer to a shallow baking dish. Top with the bread crumbs and bake, uncovered, fifteen to twenty minutes, or until the veal is tender.

Yield: Four servings.

Hungarian-Style Veal
MASSACHUSETTS

4	slices bacon		Salt to taste
1½	pounds veal cutlet, one-half-inch thick and cut into serving pieces	1	cup sour cream
		½	cup tomato sauce, preferably homemade.
2	tablespoons chopped onion		
1	teaspoon sweet Hungarian paprika		

1. Cook the bacon until crisp. Remove from the skillet, crumble and reserve.

2. Brown the veal pieces on all sides in the bacon drippings. Add the onion and cook until lightly browned.

3. Season with the paprika and salt. Stir in the sour cream and tomato sauce. Cover and simmer, but do not boil, twenty minutes, or until the veal is tender. Serve topped with the reserved bacon bits.

Yield: Four servings.

Veal Birds
CONNECTICUT

6	veal scaloppine (about one and one-quarter pounds), lightly pounded	½	teaspoon chopped fresh thyme or one-quarter teaspoon dried thyme
	Salt and freshly ground black pepper to taste	½	teaspoon chopped fresh basil or one-quarter teaspoon dried basil
5	tablespoons butter	3	tablespoons heavy cream
¾	cup soft bread crumbs	1	tablespoon flour
1	clove garlic, finely minced	1	cup fresh or canned chicken broth
1	tablespoon freshly grated Parmesan cheese	1	tablespoon lemon juice.
¼	cup finely chopped parsley Grated rind of one lemon		

1. Preheat the oven to 350 degrees.

2. Place the scaloppine on a flat surface and sprinkle with salt and pepper.

3. Melt two tablespoons of the butter. Combine with the bread crumbs, garlic, cheese, parsley, lemon rind, thyme, basil, cream, salt and pepper. Spread equal portions of this mixture on the veal slices. Roll each slice like a jellyroll and secure with toothpicks or string.

4. Melt the remaining butter in a skillet, add the veal rolls and brown on all sides. Transfer the veal rolls to a casserole.

5. Sprinkle the flour over the fat remaining in the skillet and cook briefly. Add the broth and stir with a wooden spoon to dissolve the brown particles that cling to the bottom and sides of the skillet. Pour the mixture over the veal and sprinkle with salt and pepper. Add the lemon juice and bring to a boil. Cover and bake forty-five minutes.

Yield: Four to six servings.

Veal Scallops with Cheese
CONNECTICUT

2 eggs, lightly beaten	3 tablespoons butter
Salt and freshly ground black pepper to taste	3 tablespoons oil
	12 wafer-thin slices lemon
6 veal scaloppine (about three-quarters pound), pounded lightly until thin	6 thin slices Gruyère or Swiss cheese
½ cup strained lemon juice	1 cup half-and-half or heavy cream.
1 cup fine soft bread crumbs	

1. Preheat the oven to 400 degrees.

2. Season the eggs with salt and pepper. Dip the scaloppine into the eggs, then into the lemon juice and finally into the bread crumbs.

3. Heat the butter and oil in a heavy skillet, add the scaloppine and brown on one side only. Remove the scaloppine and place, cooked side down, in a single layer in a baking dish.

4. Cover each scallop with two lemon slices and one cheese slice. Sprinkle with salt and pepper. Pour the cream over all and bake ten to fifteen minutes, or until the cheese melts and the cream bubbles slightly. Do not overcook.

Yield: Six Servings.

Veal Shanks à la Grecque
MASSACHUSETTS

4	veal shanks	1	teaspoon oregano
	Salt and freshly ground	1	clove garlic, finely minced
	black pepper to taste	1	eggplant
	Flour	4	cups fresh or canned chick-
½	cup olive oil		en broth, approximately.
4	cups tomatoes, preferably		
	Italian plum style		

1. Preheat the oven to 450 degrees.
2. Wipe the veal shanks with a damp cloth and sprinkle them with salt and pepper. Dredge in flour.
3. Pour half the oil into a heavy casserole or Dutch oven large enough to hold the shanks. Add the shanks. Bake, basting frequently with the oil, about twenty minutes, or until meat is golden brown.
4. Pour off the fat from the casserole or Dutch oven and reduce the oven heat to 350 degrees.
5. Pour the tomatoes around the shanks and add the oregano, garlic and remaining oil. Return to the oven and continue baking and basting fifteen minutes.
6. Pare off the ends of the eggplant, but leave the skin on. Cut the eggplant into cubes and scatter these around the meat. Add one cup of the broth and continue baking and basting. Add more broth as the original broth boils away and continue baking and basting. The total cooking time for this dish is about one and one-half to two hours, depending on the size and tenderness of the veal.

Yield: Four servings.

Jelled Veal
NEW HAMPSHIRE

4	veal shanks, split	6	peppercorns, crushed
1	veal knuckle bone, cracked	1	teaspoon chervil, if avail-
1	onion, sliced		able
2	carrots, sliced	2	tablespoons chopped pars-
2	ribs celery, diced		ley
4	sprigs parsley	2	tablespoons chopped green
1	bay leaf		pepper.
1	teaspoon salt		

111

1. Place the shanks, knuckle bone, onion, carrots, celery, parsley sprigs, bay leaf, salt, peppercorns and chervil in a kettle. Add water almost to cover.

2. Bring to a boil and boil vigorously, skimming off scum, five minutes. Cover and simmer gently three hours, or until meat is very tender. Leave shanks in broth until cool enough to handle.

3. Remove and discard knuckle bone. Remove meat from shanks. Dice meat and place in a one-and-one-half-quart to two-quart bowl or ring mold. Add the chopped parsley and green pepper and toss.

4. Strain the cooking broth into a saucepan and reduce by boiling until liquid measures two cups. Pour over the meat mixture. Cool and chill until firm.

5. Unmold and serve as luncheon or buffet dish or as sandwich filling.

Yield: Six to eight servings.

Veal and Ham Picnic Loaf

CONNECTICUT

3 pounds ground veal	2 eggs, lightly beaten
2 teaspoons salt	2 tablespoons cognac
½ teaspoon freshly ground black pepper	1 pound baked ham, cut into one-quarter-inch cubes
2 teaspoons dried sage	3 hard-cooked eggs
½ teaspoon ground allspice	Cherry tomatoes.

1. Preheat the oven to 350 degrees.

2. Mix together the veal, salt, pepper, sage, allspice, beaten eggs, cognac and ham. Pack half the mixture into a greased 9-by-5-by-3-inch loaf pan. Arrange the hard-cooked eggs down the middle.

3. Pack remaining meat mixture around and over the eggs. Place on a baking sheet (to catch drips) and bake one and one-half hours. Cool and then chill in the pan.

4. To unmold loaf, set in a bowl of warm water for a moment or two; then turn out onto serving platter. Garnish the platter with tomatoes.

Yield: Ten servings

Veal-Sour Cream Meat Loaf

NEW HAMPSHIRE

1½	pounds ground veal	1½	teaspoons salt
½	pound ground pork	¼	teaspoon freshly ground
2	tablespoons grated onion		black pepper
2	carrots, finely grated or	½	teaspoon grated lemon rind
	ground	½	cup sour cream.
½	teaspoon rubbed leaf sage		
	or one teaspoon chopped		
	fresh sage		

1. Preheat the oven to 350 degrees.
2. Mix all ingredients together and pack into a 9-by-5-by-3-inch loaf pan. Bake one and one-half hours.
Yield: Six servings.

Oxtail Stew

CONNECTICUT

4	oxtails, skinned and cut into	1	pound ripe tomatoes,
	sections		peeled, seeded and
¼	cup oil		chopped, or one one-pound
¼	cup butter		can Italian plum tomatoes,
2	cups finely chopped celery		drained and chopped
¼	cup finely chopped parsley		Salt and freshly ground
2	cloves garlic, finely minced		black pepper to taste
1	bay leaf		Juice of half a lemon
2	carrots, chopped	¼	teaspoon nutmeg
2	tablespoons flour	1	cup Madeira wine
1	cup fresh or canned beef		Additional chopped parsley
	broth		(optional)
1	cup dry red wine		Boiled potatoes or noodles.
3	tablespoons cognac		

1. Preheat the oven to 350 degrees.
2. Brown the oxtails well in the oil and butter in a large skillet.
3. Line a buttered casserole with the celery, parsley, garlic and bay leaf. Transfer the oxtails to the casserole.

4. Add the carrots to the skillet and cook, stirring, until lightly browned. Sprinkle with the flour and, when it starts to brown, add a little broth. Stir to dissolve brown particles. Scrape this mixture into the casserole.

5. Add the remaining broth to the casserole. Add the red wine, cognac, tomatoes, salt and pepper. Cover and bake two and one-half to three hours. Transfer the oxtails to a hot serving dish.

6. Strain the gravy, but press as much of the cooked vegetable mixture as possible through the sieve. Bring the strained liquid to a boil and add the lemon juice, nutmeg and Madeira. Simmer five minutes and pour the sauce over the oxtails. Serve sprinkled with additional chopped parsley if desired. Serve with boiled potatoes or noodles.

Yield: Eight servings.

Meat-Filled Manicotti

MASSACHUSETTS

½	pound ground veal	1	egg, lightly beaten
½	pound ground cooked ham	2	tablespoons Marsala wine
1	tablespoon finely chopped onion	1	cup soft bread crumbs
3	tablespoons olive oil	1	cup freshly grated Parmesan cheese
½	teaspoon salt	8	four-inch pieces manicotti
¼	teaspoon freshly ground black pepper	6	quarts boiling salted water
¼	teaspoon rosemary	3	to four cups tomato sauce, preferably homemade marinara style.
⅛	teaspoon nutmeg		

1. Preheat the oven to 375 degrees.

2. Sauté the veal, ham and onion in one tablespoon of the oil until lightly browned.

3. Combine the meat mixture, salt, pepper, rosemary, nutmeg, egg, Marsala, bread crumbs and two tablespoons of the cheese in a bowl.

4. Cook the manicotti in the boiling salted water until half done, about twelve minutes. Drain and rinse in cold water. Add the remaining oil.

5. Cover the bottom of a shallow baking dish with half the sauce. Fill the manicotti with the meat mixture and arrange in a single layer on top of the sauce.

114

6. Cover with the remaining sauce, sprinkle with the remaining cheese and bake about thirty minutes, or until tender and bubbly hot.

Yield: Four servings.

Boston Tripe
MASSACHUSETTS

2	pounds honeycomb tripe	1½	tablespoons prepared mustard, preferably Dijon or Düsseldorf
1	onion, studded with two whole cloves		
2	sprigs fresh thyme or one-half teaspoon dried thyme	3	tablespoons peanut oil or vegetable oil
1	bay leaf	1	teaspoon Worcestershire sauce
1	carrot, quartered		
	Salt to taste	1	tablespoon wine vinegar
12	peppercorns	¼	teaspoon Tabasco
	Freshly ground black pepper to taste	2	cups soft bread crumbs.

1. Cut the tripe into large squares measuring about 4 by 4 inches.

2. Place the tripe in a kettle and add water to reach about one inch above the top of the tripe. Add the onion, thyme, bay leaf, carrot, salt and peppercorns. Bring to a boil and simmer until the tripe is thoroughly tender, two to three hours. Drain tripe. When cool enough to handle, pat dry with paper towels.

3. Preheat the oven to 425 degrees.

4. Sprinkle the tripe with salt and pepper.

5. Combine the mustard, oil, Worcestershire, vinegar and Tabasco. Dip the tripe, piece by piece, into the mixture; then dip each piece into the bread crumbs until thoroughly coated.

6. Generously oil a baking pan and arrange the tripe pieces in it. Bake thirty to forty-five minutes, or until crumbs are crisp and well browned. Serve with Dijon or Düsseldorf mustard on the side.

Yield: Four to six servings.

Fried Chicken with Cream Gravy
NEW HAMPSHIRE

1 two-and-one-half-pound to three-pound frying chicken, cut into serving pieces	black pepper to taste Vegetable shortening
¼ cup flour Salt and freshly ground	1½ cups milk Mashed potatoes.

1. Preheat oven to 350 degrees.
2. Coat the chicken pieces in the flour mixed with salt and pepper. Reserve the remaining flour.
3. Heat enough shortening to make a half-inch-deep layer in a heavy skillet. Fry the chicken pieces a few at a time until golden on all sides. Drain on paper towels and transfer to a baking dish. When all the chicken has been browned, bake in the oven twenty-five minutes, or until cooked through.
4. Meanwhile, drain off all but two tablespoons of the shortening from the skillet. Measure two tablespoons of the reserved flour mixture, adding more flour, salt and pepper if necessary. Sprinkle into skillet and cook, stirring to loosen browned-on particles.
5. Gradually stir in the milk and bring to a boil, stirring, until thickened. Serve over mashed potatoes with chicken pieces.
Yield: Four servings.

Oven-Baked Chicken
MAINE

1 one-pound loaf firm white bread	2 teaspoons salt Freshly ground black pepper (use a generous amount)
¾ cup freshly grated Parmesan cheese	1 four-pound chicken, cut into serving pieces
¼ cup finely chopped parsley 1 clove garlic, chopped	½ cup melted butter.

1. Preheat the oven to 350 degrees.
2. Trim the crusts from the bread and grate it by hand or cut into cubes and blend a handful at a time in an electric blender.
3. Combine the crumbs, cheese, parsley, garlic, salt and pepper.

116

4. Dip each chicken piece into the butter and then into the crumb mixture. Arrange the chicken pieces, so they do not touch each other, on a large baking pan. Pour a little of the remaining butter over the chicken and bake one hour, or until fork-tender.

Yield: Six servings.

Sautéed Chicken Livers with Madeira

CONNECTICUT

1	pound chicken livers	8	ounces noodles, cooked, drained and buttered
¼	cup butter		
	Salt and freshly ground black pepper to taste	¼	cup Madeira wine or Marsala wine.
1	teaspoon rubbed sage		
2	wafer-thin slices ham, preferably prosciutto		

1. Pick over the livers and cut each in half.
2. Melt the butter and add the livers. Sprinkle with salt, pepper and the sage. Cook, stirring gently, until the livers are cooked on all sides. Do not overcook.
3. Add the ham and toss until heated through.
4. Place the buttered noodles on a hot serving dish and pour the livers into the center.
5. Add the wine to the skillet in which the livers cooked. Simmer, stirring with a wooden spoon to scrape up brown particles that cling to the bottom and sides of the skillet. When the wine is slightly reduced, pour it over the livers and serve immediately.

Yield: Four servings.

Chicken and Noodles

NEW HAMPSHIRE

1	five-pound chicken, cut into serving pieces	2	carrots, quartered
	Water	1	onion
	Salt	2	cups flour
12	peppercorns	4	egg yolks
2	ribs celery, chopped	4	to six tablespoons hot water.

1. Place the chicken in a kettle. Add water to cover, salt to taste, the peppercorns, celery, carrots and onion. Simmer until the chicken is thoroughly tender, about one and one-quarter hours.

2. Strain the broth and pour it into a clean kettle. Simmer while preparing the remaining ingredients.

3. Remove the chicken from the bones. Discard the bones and skin. Cut the chicken into bite-size pieces.

4. Sift the flour and one-half teaspoon salt together onto a board. Make a well in the center and put the egg yolks in it. Gradually work the egg yolks into the flour until a stiff dough is formed, adding the hot water as necessary. Knead until smooth, about five minutes.

5. Cut the dough in half and roll each half until paper thin. Cut the dough into noodles about one-inch wide.

6. Add the chicken to the simmering broth and add the noodles, a few at a time. Continue boiling until the noodles are done, about five minutes.

Yield: Eight to one dozen servings.

Chicken Liver Casserole
MAINE

2	medium-size eggplants	¼	cup finely chopped parsley
	Boiling salted water	½	cup heavy cream
5	tablespoons butter	¼	teaspoon freshly grated nutmeg, or to taste
½	pound chicken livers		meg, or to taste
	Salt and freshly ground		Cayenne pepper to taste
	black pepper to taste	¾	cup soft bread crumbs
½	pound mushrooms, thinly sliced	½	cup freshly grated Parmesan cheese.
2	eggs, lightly beaten		

1. Trim off and discard the ends of the eggplants. Cut the eggplants into one-inch cubes. Barely cover with boiling salted water and simmer until tender, about ten minutes. Drain in a colander. Empty the eggplant into a mixing bowl and mash with a fork.

2. Preheat the oven to 350 degrees.

3. Heat two tablespoons of the butter in a skillet. Add the chicken livers and sprinkle with salt and pepper. Cook the livers until brown on all sides; then chop the livers in the skillet. Add them to the eggplant.

4. Heat two tablespoons of the remaining butter in the same skillet. Add the mushrooms, sprinkle with salt and pepper and cook until the mushrooms are wilted. Add them to the eggplant mixture.

5. Stir in the eggs, beating thoroughly. Add the parsley, cream, nutmeg, cayenne and all but two tablespoons of the bread crumbs. Add all but two tablespoons of the cheese. Mix well and pour the mixture into a one-quart casserole.

6. Sprinkle with the remaining bread crumbs and cheese and dot with the remaining butter. Bake twenty-five to thirty minutes.

Yield: Six to eight servings.

Elegant Chicken Pie
MASSACHUSETTS

1	three-pound chicken, trussed (reserve giblets)		Salted water
	Salt and freshly ground black pepper	½	cup diced cooked ham
		¼	pound mushrooms, sliced
¼	teaspoon nutmeg		Juice of half a lemon
¼	teaspoon cloves	3	tablespoons cognac
¼	teaspoon cinnamon	3	tablespoons port wine
6	tablespoons butter	2	cups heavy cream
1	carrot, sliced	1	tablespoon foie gras
2	small white onions		Rich pie pastry for one ten-inch crust.
1	pair sweetbreads		

1. Preheat the oven to 450 degrees.

2. Sprinkle the chicken inside and outside with salt and pepper. Add the nutmeg, cloves and cinnamon to the inside of the chicken.

3. Heat half of the butter in a large open oven-proof skillet. Add the chicken and turn to coat on all sides in the butter. Let the chicken rest on one side. Add the giblets, carrot and onions and roast fifteen minutes, basting often with a large spoon. Turn chicken to the other side and roast fifteen minutes, basting. Turn chicken on its back and continue roasting and basting about thirty minutes, or until done. Leave chicken in the skillet while completing the dish.

4. Meanwhile, soak the sweetbreads one hour and drain. Place sweetbreads in a saucepan and add salted water to cover. Bring to a boil. Simmer five minutes and drain. Rinse under cold running water. Trim or pare away the skin and tubes of the sweetbreads. Slice the sweetbreads.

5. Heat remaining butter in another skillet and add sweetbread slices. Cook, turning occasionally, about two minutes. Add the ham, mushrooms and lemon juice. Cook, stirring gently once in a while, about five minutes.

6. Cut chicken into serving pieces and place in the bottom of a deep baking dish. Add the cognac and port wine to the juices in the skillet in which chicken cooked. Bring to a boil and stir to dissolve. Add salt to taste and all but two tablespoons of cream. Strain this into a saucepan and add sweetbread mixture. Simmer three to four minutes.

7. Blend remaining cream with the foie gras and add to the saucepan. Pour this sauce over chicken and cover the dish with rolled-out pastry. Bake fifteen minutes, or until the crust is a rich golden brown.

Yield: Six servings.

Hancock Shaker Village's Sister Clymena's Chicken Pie
MASSACHUSETTS

2	three-pound chickens, quartered	4	sprigs parsley, minced
2	cups water	4	sprigs chervil, minced
3	eggs, well beaten		Salt and freshly ground
2	cups heavy cream		black pepper to taste
½	small onion, minced		Pastry for a deep two-crust ten-inch pie.

1. Place the chickens in a kettle and add the water. Cover, bring to a boil and simmer thirty minutes. Remove meat from bones, but leave in large pieces. Discard bones and skin. Reserve chicken liquid. Place chicken meat in a bowl.

2. Preheat the oven to 425 degrees.

3. Combine the eggs and cream. Add the onion, parsley, chervil, salt and pepper. Add enough hot chicken liquid to cream and egg mixture to cover chicken pieces. Combine chicken and sauce.

4. Butter a deep ten-inch pie dish well and line bottom and sides with rolled-out pastry. Fill with chicken mixture and cover with top crust, cutting small vents for steam. Bake one-half hour.

Yield: Four to six servings.

Roast Chickens with Lemon
MAINE

2 two-pound chickens
1 lemon, cut in half
Salt and freshly ground
black pepper to taste
1 cup plus one tablespoon
butter

2 cups finely chopped onions
Juice of half a lemon
2 cups chopped parsley
1 cup hot chicken broth,
approximately.

1. Rub the chickens inside and outside with the lemon halves, salt and pepper.

2. Heat one tablespoon of the butter, add the onions and cook until wilted. Sprinkle with salt, pepper and the lemon juice. Stir in the parsley and one-half cup of the remaining butter. Use this mixture to stuff the chickens.

3. Melt the remaining butter in a large pot or Dutch oven. Add the chickens and brown on all sides, turning with a wooden spoon so as not to tear the skin. Reduce the heat and add one-quarter cup of the hot broth.

4. Cover the pot with aluminum foil; then partly cover with a lid. Cook the chickens slowly until done, basting occasionally and add the remaining broth as necessary, about forty minutes.

5. Before serving, run the chickens under the broiler to crisp the surface. Strain the broth and serve separately.

Yield: Four to six servings.

Quick Chicken and Eggplant
MASSACHUSETTS

2 medium-size eggplants,
approximately
Boiling water
½ pound skinned boneless
breast of chicken
1 tablespoon cornstarch
2 tablespoons soy sauce
1 tablespoon dry sherry
2 fresh hot green peppers, or

to taste, or dried red pepper
flakes to taste
¼ cup peanut oil
1 small clove garlic, finely
minced
1 tablespoon freshly grated
ginger
½ cup fresh or canned chicken
broth.

1. Peel the eggplants and, using a sharp knife, slice them into one-quarter-inch rounds. Slice each round into very thin, matchlike strips. There should be about four cups of thin strips. Pour boiling water over the eggplant strips and let stand five minutes. Drain well in a colander.

2. Cut the chicken into thin slices; then cut each slice into thin, matchlike strips. Place the chicken strips in a mixing bowl and add the cornstarch, soy sauce and sherry.

3. Split the peppers in half and discard the seeds and stem of each. Cut the peppers into thin shreds.

4. Heat the oil, add the peppers and cook until they start to color. With a slotted spoon, remove the peppers and reserve. Add the chicken to the oil and cook, stirring briskly, until the flesh turns white. Add the egg-plant strips, garlic, ginger, chicken broth and reserved peppers. Cook just until the mixture boils and is slightly thickened.

Yield: Six servings.

Chicken with Sour Cream

CONNECTICUT

2	tablespoons shortening or butter		quantity used will depend on the strength of the spice)
2	medium-size onions, finely chopped	4	whole chicken breasts, halved
2	teaspoons salt, or more to taste	2	cups chicken broth or water
1	to two tablespoons Hungarian sweet paprika (the	2	teaspoons flour
		2	cups sour cream
			Cooked rice.

1. Heat the shortening or butter in a heavy pot and cook the onions in it until golden. Sprinkle with the salt and paprika and add the chicken. Cook briefly, turning; then add the broth or water. Cover and simmer until tender, about forty-five minutes.

2. Take the chicken from the pot and, when cool enough to handle, carefully remove and discard the skin and bones. Combine the flour and sour cream and stir the mixture into the drippings in the pot. Stir rapidly with a wire whisk. Put the sauce through a sieve. Add the chicken to the sauce. Heat thoroughly just to the boiling point, but do not boil. Serve immediately, with the rice.

Yield: Four or more servings.

Chicken Stew
VERMONT

2 tablespoons oil
1 large whole chicken breast, skinned, boned and cut into one-inch pieces
3 to four zucchini, cut into one-quarter-inch slices
1 onion, chopped
1 small clove garlic, finely minced
1 small bay leaf
1 rib celery with leaves, chopped

1 large potato, peeled and cut into six wedges
¾ cup chicken broth
½ teaspoon salt
⅛ teaspoon freshly ground black pepper
1 cup sliced mushrooms
1 tablespoon lemon juice
2 tablespoons finely chopped parsley.

1. Heat the oil in a heavy skillet. Add the chicken pieces and cook quickly on all sides until the chicken turns white.

2. Add half the zucchini, the onion, garlic, bay leaf, celery, potato, one-half cup of the broth, the salt and pepper. Stir and cook fifteen minutes, but with a slotted spoon, remove the potato wedges as soon as they are done.

3. Add the remaining broth. If the potatoes have not already been removed, remove them with a slotted spoon. Pile the potato wedges in the middle of a warm serving dish.

4. Push the chicken pieces to one side of the skillet and gently mash the vegetables in the skillet into the liquid. Add the remaining zucchini and the mushrooms. Cook, stirring, four to five minutes. The zucchini just added should remain crisp-tender and green.

5. Stir in the lemon juice and arrange the mixture around the mound of potatoes. Sprinkle the potatoes with the parsley.

Yield: Two servings.

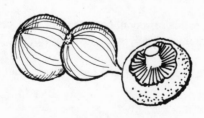

Sunday Supper Cold Chicken

NEW HAMPSHIRE

3	whole chicken breasts, halved	¼	teaspoon dry mustard
1	carrot, diced		Cayenne pepper
1	rib celery, diced	½	cup olive oil
	Salt	½	cup vegetable oil
10	peppercorns	1	envelope unflavored gelatin
1	bay leaf	¼	cup heavy cream, approximately
3	sprigs parsley		Ripe olives or truffles
1	onion, chopped		Pimentos
½	teaspoon thyme		Green leek leaves
	Freshly ground black pepper to taste	4	tomatoes, peeled and sliced
2	egg yolks	1	red onion, sliced and separated into rings
1	tablespoon tarragon vinegar	⅓	cup French dressing
1	tablespoon lemon juice		Water cress.

1. Day before, place the chicken breasts in a large skillet with the carrot, celery, one teaspoon salt, the peppercorns, bay leaf, parsley, onion and thyme. Add water to three-quarters cover the breasts.

2. Bring to a boil, cover and simmer very gently ten to fifteen minutes, or until the chicken is tender. Chill overnight, still in the broth.

3. Next day, remove the skin and bones from breasts, but keep the meat in whole pieces. Season with salt and pepper.

4. Place the egg yolks, vinegar, lemon juice, mustard and salt and cayenne to taste in an electric blender with one-quarter cup of the olive oil. Blend at high speed, gradually adding the remaining olive oil and the vegetable oil in a continuous stream.

5. Soak the gelatin in one-quarter cup water and dissolve while stirring over gentle heat. Add the gelatin to the mayonnaise in the blender and continue blending while adding enough cream to give a spreading consistency.

6. With a spatula or spoon, coat the chicken pieces with the mayonnaise and decorate immediately with olives or truffles, pimentos and leek greens. Chill.

7. Combine the tomatoes and onion rings. Pour the dressing over and chill.

8. To serve, place the tomato mixture on a platter and top with the chicken breasts. Garnish with water cress.

Yield: Six servings.

Blue Crab-Stuffed Chicken

RHODE ISLAND

Chicken:

¼	cup plus two tablespoons butter	2	two-and-one-half-pound to three-pound chickens, split
1	teaspoon salt	½	pound mushrooms, sliced
¼	teaspoon freshly ground black pepper	¼	cup dry sherry
2	teaspoons Hungarian sweet paprika	¼	cup catchup
		1	tablespoon chopped parsley.

Stuffing:

3	slices stale white bread, cut into very small cubes	⅛	teaspoon cayenne pepper
5	tablespoons heavy cream	1	teaspoon salt
12	ounces crab meat, picked over to remove bits of shell and cartilage	1	teaspoon prepared mustard
		½	teaspoon thyme
¼	cup melted butter	¼	teaspoon marjoram
		¼	teaspoon sage.

1. Preheat the oven to 350 degrees.

2. To prepare chicken, mix two tablespoons of the butter with the salt, pepper and paprika. Rub the chicken pieces with the mixture and place, skin side up, wings tucked under, in a single layer in a baking dish. Bake thirty-five minutes.

3. Heat the remaining butter and sauté the mushrooms in it. Add the sherry, catchup and parsley. Spoon one tablespoon of the butter mixture over each chicken half and bake ten minutes longer.

4. Meanwhile, to prepare stuffing, combine the ingredients in a bowl.

5. Turn the chicken pieces over and stuff with the crab stuffing. Spoon the remaining butter-mushroom mixture over all and bake thirty minutes longer, or until chicken is tender.

Yield: Four servings.

125

Roast Turkey with Oyster Stuffing
VERMONT

1	ten-pound to twelve-pound oven-ready turkey, thawed if frozen	6	slices fat bacon
			Turkey giblets
	Salt and freshly ground black pepper to taste	1	onion, sliced
		1	rib celery with leaves, diced
1	recipe oyster stuffing (see page 283)	¼	cup flour.

1. Preheat the oven to 350 degrees.

2. Wash and dry the turkey inside and out. Season the inside with salt and pepper and stuff with the oyster mixture. Truss and place on a rack in a roasting pan. Arrange the bacon slices over the breast and drumsticks.

3. Roast, uncovered, three and one-half hours, basting occasionally with the drippings in the pan. Test for doneness. When the bird is done, no pink liquid comes from the thigh joint when pricked; internal temperature of the thigh joint is 180 degrees. Cover with aluminum foil if the bird starts to brown too much.

4. Meanwhile, place the giblets, onion, celery, salt and pepper in a small saucepan. Add water to cover, bring to a boil and simmer, covered, until tender, about forty minutes, Strain the broth and reserve.

5. Remove the cooked bird to a platter and keep warm. Pour off all but three tablespoons of the drippings in the roasting pan. Sprinkle the flour over and cook, stirring, until lightly browned.

6. Gradually stir in the strained broth; bring to a boil, stirring, until the mixture thickens. Add water if the mixture is too thick. Season with salt and pepper. Add two tablespoons of the chopped gizzard if you wish. Serve with turkey.

Yield: Ten to twelve servings.

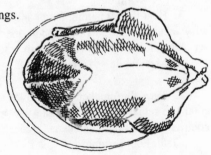

Turkey and Oysters in Patty Shells

MASSACHUSETTS

3	tablespoons butter	1	cup cooked or thawed frozen peas
1	tablespoon chopped shallots		
½	pound mushrooms, sliced	2	teaspoons lemon juice
3	tablespoons flour	2	egg yolks
½	cup dry white wine	1	cup heavy cream
1½	cups light cream	2	pimentos, diced
	Salt and freshly ground black pepper to taste	2	cups oysters with their liquor
¼	teaspoon nutmeg	6	to eight homemade or purchased patty shells, warmed.
½	teaspoon thyme		
2	to three cups diced cooked white turkey meat		

1. Melt the butter in a large skillet and sauté the shallots in it until tender. Add the mushrooms and cook two minutes.

2. Sprinkle with the flour and stir. Cook one minute.

3. Stir in the wine and light cream and bring to a boil, stirring. Season with salt, pepper, the nutmeg and thyme. Cook two minutes.

4. Add the turkey, peas and lemon juice and reheat. Beat the egg yolks with the heavy cream, add a little of the hot sauce and return all to the pan. Heat, stirring, until mixture thickens a little, but do not boil.

5. Add the pimentos and oysters and maintain low heat without boiling until the edges of the oysters just curl, about three minutes. Test the seasoning. Spoon into and over the patty shells.

Yield: Six to eight servings.

Roast Goose

VERMONT

1	seven-pound to nine-pound goose (reserve giblets)	1	bay leaf
		1	rib celery with leaves
	Salt and freshly ground black pepper to taste	3	tablespoons flour
1	recipe oyster stuffing (page 283) or fruit stuffing (page 284)		Gravy coloring and flavoring (optional)
			Crab apples or orange slices.
1	onion		

1. Preheat the oven to 450 degrees.

2. Wash and clean the goose inside and outside. Wipe dry. Burn off any hairs that remain. Season the cavity with salt and pepper.

3. Using the desired stuffing, stuff the cavity three-quarters full. Put any leftover stuffing under the neck skin. Truss the bird and place on a rack in a shallow roasting pan. Roast ten minutes.

4. Reduce the oven heat to 325 degrees and continue to roast twenty to twenty-five minutes a pound, removing fat as it accumulates.

5. Meanwhile, wash the gizzard, neck and heart (the liver goes into the stuffing or is sautéed and seasoned as a delicacy) and place in a saucepan with the onion, bay leaf, celery, salt, pepper and water to cover. Bring to a boil and simmer several hours.

6. Strain liquid. If desired, chop some of giblet meat.

7. Transfer the cooked goose to a warm platter. Pour off all but three tablespoons goose fat from the roasting pan. Sprinkle fat in pan with the flour. Cook, stirring, two minutes. Stir in three to four cups of the strained liquid and the chopped giblet meat. Cook, stirring, until gravy thickens. Season with salt and pepper and add gravy coloring and flavoring (Kitchen Bouquet) if desired.

8. Garnish the goose platter with crab apples or orange slices. Serve gravy separately.

Yield: Six servings.

Foil-Baked Venison Steak

VERMONT

2	cups flour	1 two-inch-thick cut, boned
2	eggs, beaten	top round venison, beaten
½	teaspoon salt	well with a mallet to tender-
½	cup water	ize
6	thick slices bacon	Currant jelly.

1. Combine the flour, eggs, salt and water to make a paste.

2. Preheat the oven to 425 degrees.

3. Roll out the flour mixture until thin. Cover with the bacon slices.

4. Place the venison on top of the bacon. Moisten the edges of the flour mixture, draw around the meat and pinch to seal. Wrap in heavy-duty aluminum foil, set on a baking sheet and bake fifty minutes a pound.

5. Fifteen minutes before the meat is due to be done, open up the foil, increase the oven heat to 450 degrees and bake to brown. Serve with currant jelly.

Yield: About eight servings.

Vegetables, Main Dish Accompaniments and Salads

Baked Asparagus with Cheese Sauce
RHODE ISLAND

2 pounds asparagus	½ teaspoon salt
Boiling salted water	⅛ teaspoon cayenne pepper
6 hard-cooked eggs, sliced	½ cup grated sharp Cheddar
2 tablespoons butter	cheese
2 tablespoons flour	½ cup buttered soft bread
1½ cups milk	crumbs.

1. Break the asparagus spears at the point where white or tough part starts and wash very well. Boil in the salted water in an asparagus cooker, with the stem bottoms in the water and tips steaming, or boil quickly, flat, in a covered skillet until barely tender.

2. Drain the asparagus and arrange in a greased shallow baking dish. Top with the egg slices.

3. Preheat the oven to 350 degrees.

4. Melt the butter, blend in the flour, gradually stir in the milk and bring to a boil, stirring. Cook two minutes. Add the salt, cayenne and cheese and stir just to melt the cheese. Pour over the eggs and asparagus.

5. Sprinkle with the bread crumbs. Bake twenty minutes.

Yield: Six servings.

Sister Josephine's Shaker Baked Beans
MASSACHUSETTS

4	cups dried pea beans or navy beans	½	cup butter
1	onion	1	teaspoon salt
½	cup unsulphured molasses	2	teaspoons dry mustard
		½	cup catchup.

1. Day before, pick over and wash beans. Cover beans with water and soak overnight. Next day, drain beans and add two and one-half cups hot water. Cook until tender, about forty-five minutes.

2. Preheat the oven to 325 degrees.

3. Place the onion in bottom of a well-buttered bean pot. Drain beans and save the liquid. Pour beans into bean pot.

4. Add the remaining ingredients to the reserved bean liquid and pour over beans to cover. Cover pot and cook two and one-half hours, adding more liquid whenever necessary. Remove cover and bake one-half hour longer to brown well.

Yield: Ten to one dozen servings.

Home-Baked Beans
MAINE

2	pounds dried pea beans or navy beans	⅔	cup unsulphured molasses
	Water	1	teaspoon dry mustard
¾	pound salt pork	1½	teaspoons salt
1	onion		Boiling water.

1. Day before, pick over the beans and wash well. Place in a bowl and cover with cold water so that water extends two inches above the beans. Soak overnight. Next morning, put beans and soaking water in a heavy pot.

2. Make one-half-inch deep cuts through the rind of the salt pork at one-half-inch intervals. Add to beans. Bring to a boil and simmer them until the skin cracks when a bean is held in the hand and blown on, about one hour.

3. Preheat the oven to 250 degrees.

4. Place the onion in the bottom of a bean pot or heavy three-quart casserole. Add the beans. Cube the salt pork and add.

5. Stir in the remaining ingredients, including enough boiling water to cover beans. Bake, uncovered, six to eight hours, stirring occasionally and adding more boiling water whenever necessary so that the beans are always just submerged.

Yield: Ten to one dozen servings.

Note: Beans and ham, most likely served with steamed brown bread (page 177) in Maine and Massachusetts and with johnnycakes (page 171) in Rhode Island, are a New England tradition on Saturday night. And there is never any problem with leftovers. Warmed-over beans are served for Sunday morning breakfast, and on Monday lunch-toting workers and children expect cold bean sandwiches garnished with crisp marinated onion rings for added texture and flavor.

To prepare Vermont baked beans, substitute maple syrup or honey for the molasses in the recipe above.

Baked Beans I

MASSACHUSETTS

1	pound dried pea beans or navy beans	¼	cup brown sugar
1	bay leaf	2	teaspoons dry mustard
1	celery rib, halved	2	teaspoons salt
3	sprigs parsley	¼	teaspoon freshly ground black pepper
1	sprig fresh thyme or one-half teaspoon dried thyme	1	medium-size onion, coarsely chopped
½	pound salt pork	1	cup sherry.
⅔	cup unsulphured molasses		

131

1. Soak the beans overnight in cold water to cover.

2. Next day, drain beans; then cover with fresh water. Tie the bay leaf, celery, parsley and thyme in a bundle. Add to the kettle. Bring to a boil and simmer slowly until bean skins blow off when blown upon lightly, thirty to sixty minutes.

3. Drain beans, reserving two quarts of the cooking liquid. Slice the salt pork into one-quarter-inch slices. Arrange the beans and half the sliced pork in alternate layers in a two-quart bean pot or casserole. Score the remaining pork and place in the center of the top layer of beans.

4. Preheat the oven to 300 degrees.

5. Combine the molasses, brown sugar, mustard, salt, pepper, onion and reserved cooking liquid. Pour over the beans. Bake, covered, six to eight hours. One hour before beans are to be done, pour the sherry over them. Replace the cover and bake one hour longer.

Yield: Six to eight servings.

Baked Beans II
MASSACHUSETTS

½	pound salt pork, cut into squares	½	cup unsulphured molasses
1	pound dried white Michigan or pea beans	1	teaspoon dry mustard
		1	teaspoon salt
½	cup brown sugar	1	onion, studded with two whole cloves.

1. Day before, place the salt pork and beans in a large mixing bowl and add water to cover to the depth of one inch. Let stand overnight.

2. Next day, drain beans and pork and pour into a three-quart saucepan. Add the remaining ingredients and water to barely cover, and bring to a boil. Simmer, partially covered, one hour.

3. Preheat the oven to 350 degrees.

4. Discard the onion and pour the beans into an earthenware crock or bean pot. Cover and bake two and one-half hours. Look at the beans occasionally and, if they are cooking too fast, reduce the oven heat. They should bubble nicely.

Yield: Six servings.

Bean Porridge

MAINE

½ cup dried kidney beans
1 quart meat broth (from cooking corned beef is traditional)
1 tablespoon yellow corn meal

1 tablespoon flour
  Salt to taste
2 cups milk.

1. Day before, wash beans, cover with water and let soak overnight. Next morning, place beans and soaking water in saucepan and cook thirty minutes, or until beans start to become tender.

.2. Drain off water. Add the broth to beans and cook until they are very tender. Mash slightly to thicken mixture.

3. Mix the corn meal and flour together and then make a paste with a little cold water. Stir into the bean mixture and boil until mixture thickens. Season with salt.

4. Add the milk and reheat
Yield: Six servings.

Braised Beet Greens

NEW HAMPSHIRE

Tops from two bunches of beets or two bundles (they should be young and tender)

3 to four tablespoons butter
  Salt and freshly ground black pepper to taste.

1. Remove the tough stems and wilted leaves from the beet tops. Wash very well in many changes of cold water. Place the leaves, with just water clinging to them, in a heavy kettle.

2. Cover tightly and cook over low heat until the beet greens are wilted. Drain very well. Chop and toss with the butter, salt and pepper.
Yield: Four servings.

Pease Porridge Hot
NEW HAMPSHIRE

1 pound green split peas	½ teaspoon tarragon
1 teaspoon salt	¼ teaspoon freshly ground
1 onion, studded with two	black pepper
whole cloves	3 tablespoons butter.
½ teaspoon marjoram	

1. Place the peas in a kettle and cover with water. Add the salt and onion, bring to a boil and simmer over low heat one hour, adding water as necessary.

2. Remove the cloves from the onion. Add the marjoram, tarragon and pepper and cook very slowly one hour longer, stirring occasionally to prevent sticking. The mixture should be very thick.

3. Put through a sieve, check the seasoning and dot with the butter.

Yield: Eight servings.

Bean Salad
MASSACHUSETTS

1 pound dried Great Northern beans	1 clove garlic, crushed
	1 tablespoon chopped chives
1 onion	1 green pepper, cored, seeded
2 teaspoons salt	and diced
4 ounces salt pork, sliced	1 small red onion, sliced and
⅓ cup wine vinegar	separated into rings
¾ cup olive oil	¼ cup finely chopped parsley
½ teaspoon freshly ground	4 to six slices salami, diced
black pepper	Boston lettuce cups.

1. Two days before, wash and pick over the beans. Cover with water and soak overnight. Next day, transfer to a kettle and add water, if necessary, just barely to cover the beans.

2. Bury the whole onion in the beans and add one teaspoon of the salt. Place the slices of salt pork on the top. Bring to a boil and simmer, uncovered, until just tender, about forty-five to sixty minutes. Do not overcook or beans lose their identity.

3. Meanwhile, mix together the vinegar, oil, black pepper, garlic, chives and remaining salt.

134

4. Drain the beans of excess liquid. Remove and discard the salt pork and onion. Pour the oil dressing over the hot beans, cool and chill overnight.

5. Next day, add the green pepper, red onion, parsley and salami. Check the seasoning. Serve in lettuce cups.

Yield: About ten servings.

Harvard Beets
MASSACHUSETTS

2	bunches beets	⅛	teaspoon ground allspice
	Boiling water	1½	tablespoons cornstarch
1	tablespoon cider vinegar	1	tablespoon honey
¾	cup orange juice	2	tablespoons butter.
3	tablespoons lemon juice		
2	teaspoons grated orange rind		

1. Scrub the beets and cut off the tops, leaving one inch attached. Place in a saucepan and add boiling water to cover. Add the vinegar and cook until tender, about twenty minutes.

2. Drain the beets, reserving some liquid. Skin the beets; then slice or dice them and keep warm.

3. Strain enough reserved beet liquid to yield one-quarter cup. Combine with the orange juice, lemon juice, orange rind and allspice. Add the cornstarch slowly.

4. Bring to a boil, stirring, and cook until the sauce thickens. Stir in the honey and butter and pour over the beets.

Yield: Four to six servings.

Broccoli with Mozzarella

MASSACHUSETTS

1	large bunch broccoli
	Salted water
2	tablespoons butter
1	tablespoon finely chopped shallots or scallions, including green part
1	clove garlic, finely minced
1½	tablespoons flour
1	cup fresh or canned chicken broth
4	anchovies, finely chopped
½	cup sliced ripe olives, preferably imported
	Freshly ground black pepper to taste
2	cups shredded mozzarella cheese or sharp Cheddar cheese.

1. Cook the broccoli in salted water until tender.

2. As the vegetable cooks, melt the butter in a saucepan and add the shallots and garlic. Cook, stirring, about three minutes. Do not brown.

3. Sprinkle with the flour and add the broth, stirring vigorously with a wire whisk. When the mixture is thickened, simmer five minutes.

4. Add the anchovies, olives, pepper and cheese and stir until the cheese melts.

5. Drain the broccoli. Pour the sauce over.

Yield: Four to six servings.

Broccoli Cheese Casserole

VERMONT

1	large bunch broccoli
	Salt
18	small white onions
3	tablespoons butter
3	tablespoons flour
1½	cups milk
½	cup heavy cream
1½	cups grated sharp Cheddar cheese
	Freshly ground black pepper.

1. Preheat the oven to 350 degrees.

2. Trim off the hard part of the broccoli base and stand the broccoli, stem side down, in a saucepan large enough to hold broccoli while covered. Add water to the depth of one inch and sprinkle the broccoli with a little salt. Cover and cook until vegetable is crisp-tender.

3. Meanwhile, peel the onions and put them in a saucepan with salted water barely to cover. Cook, partly covered, until the onions are nearly tender. Drain.

4. While the vegetables are cooking, melt the butter in a saucepan and, with a wire whisk, stir in the flour. When blended and smooth, add the milk, stirring rapidly with the whisk. When the sauce is thickened and smooth, stir in the cream and simmer five minutes. Remove from the heat and stir in one cup of the cheese. Season to taste with salt and pepper.

5. Drain the broccoli and cut it into bite-size pieces. Arrange layers of broccoli and onions in a buttered casserole and pour the cheese sauce over all. Sprinkle with the remaining cheese and bake one hour.

Yield: Four to six servings.

Golden Cabbage
CONNECTICUT

2 pounds white or green cabbage	2 cups milk
2 quarts water	¼ cup conrstarch
1 tablespoon sugar	¼ cup butter
1½ tablespoons plus one teaspoon salt	¼ pound Swiss cheese, grated.

1. Remove and discard the core from the cabbage. Shred or chop cabbage finely and combine it with the water, sugar and one and one-half tablespoons of the salt. Bring to a boil, cover and cook over low heat one hour. Remove cabbage and drain thoroughly in a colander.

2. Preheat the oven to 400 degrees.

3. Combine the milk, cornstarch, butter and remaining salt. Bring to a boil over moderate heat, stirring. Combine with drained cabbage. Stir in all but four tablespoons grated cheese and blend well. Pour cabbage mixture into a buttered 7½-by 12-inch baking dish. Sprinkle with the remaining cheese and bake just until throughly heated. Run the dish briefly under the broiler and serve hot.

Yield: Six servings.

Glazed Carrots

RHODE ISLAND

3	tablespoons butter	1½	teaspoons salt
4	cups sliced carrots	¼	teaspoon cinnamon
3	tablespoons orange juice	4	tablespoons honey.

Combine all the ingredients in a saucepan, cover and cook, stirring occasionally, over low heat twenty-five minutes.

Yield: Six servings

Corn Pudding I

MASSACHUSETTS

2	cups cooked whole kernel corn (one way to use left-over corn on the cob)	2	cups milk, scalded
		1½	teaspoons salt
¼	cup chopped scallions, including green part	¼	teaspoon freshly ground black pepper
3	eggs, lightly beaten	½	cup finely chopped cooked ham (optional).
2	tablespoons melted butter		

1. Preheat the oven to 325 degrees.

2. Combine all the ingredients and turn into a greased two-quart baking dish or casserole. Set in a pan with hot water extending halfway up the dish.

3. Bake one hour, replenishing the water if necessary.

Yield: Six servings.

Corn Pudding II

RHODE ISLAND

6	slices bacon	2	cups milk
2	cups freshly cut corn kernels	1	teaspoon salt
½	cup soft bread crumbs	¼	teaspoon freshly ground black pepper
½	green pepper, diced		
1	onion, finely chopped	½	cup buttered soft bread crumbs.
2	eggs, lightly beaten		

138

1. Preheat the oven to 350 degrees.

2. Cook the bacon until crisp. Remove from the skillet, crumble and combine with the corn and soft bread crumbs.

3. In the bacon drippings remaining in the skillet, sauté the green pepper and onion until tender. Add to the corn mixture.

4. Mix together the eggs, milk, salt and black pepper and pour over the vegetable mixture. Turn into a buttered casserole, top with the buttered crumbs and bake about forty-five minutes, or until set.

Yield: Six servings.

Corn Rarebit

MAINE

3 tablespoons butter	½ teaspoon salt
½ small onion, finely chopped	¼ teaspoon dry mustard
1 small green pepper, seeded and finely chopped	1 cup grated sharp Cheddar cheese
1 cup fresh corn kernels	3 egg yolks, lightly beaten
1 cup milk	Toast triangles (optional).
½ cup heavy cream	

1. Melt the butter in a saucepan and cook the onion until tender but not brown. Add the green pepper and corn and cook four minutes.

2. Add the milk and cream; bring to just below the boil. Add the salt, mustard and cheese and stir off heat to melt the cheese.

3. Add a little of the hot mixture to the egg yolks and mix well; return to the saucepan and heat, stirring, until mixture thickens, but do not boil. Serve over toast triangles if you wish.

Yield: Four to six servings.

Creamed Celery

NEW HAMPSHIRE

3 tablespoons butter	½ cup heavy cream
1 small onion, finely chopped	⅛ teaspoon nutmeg
4 cups one-half-inch-long celery pieces	1 egg yolk
½ cup boiling water	Salt and freshly ground black pepper to taste.

139

1. Heat the butter in a saucepan and cook the onion until tender but not brown. Add the celery and cook, stirring, four minutes. Add water and cook until celery is crisp-tender, about five minutes. Some of the liquid will have evaporated.

2. Beat together the cream, nutmeg and egg yolk and stir into the celery mixture. Reheat until the mixture thickens slightly, but do not boil or it will curdle. Season with salt and pepper.

Yield: Four servings.

Sautéed Dandelion Flowers
VERMONT

2	cups clean, freshly picked unsprayed dandelion flowers (see step 1)	2	eggs, lightly beaten
½	cup butter		Flour
			Salt and freshly ground black pepper to taste.

1. Do not wash the flowers or they will close, so it is important that they are clean when picked.

2. Heat the butter in a skillet. Dip each blossom into eggs, then into flour, and sauté briefly in the butter.

3. Season with salt and pepper and serve as a vegetable or special side dish.

Yield: Six servings.

Dandelion Stems
VERMONT

12	to eighteen long dandelion stems with buds	3	tablespoons lemon juice
	Boiling salted water	½	clove garlic, finely chopped
3	hard-cooked eggs, halved		Salt and freshly ground black pepper to taste.
3	tablespoons olive oil		

1. Remove the dandelion buds and discard. Tie the stems in a bundle and cook in boiling salted water to cover in an uncovered skillet until tender, about ten minutes. Drain.

2. For each serving, wind two or three dandelion stems in a basket shape and place in a small ramekin. Top with hard-cooked egg half.

140

3. Combine the remaining ingredients and drizzle over eggs and stems. Serve cold or warm. To warm, heat in 300-degree oven five minutes.

Yield: Six servings.

Leeks and Rice
CONNECTICUT

2   or three leeks
    Boiling water to cover
¼   cup butter
1   carrot, thinly sliced
1   cup uncooked rice

2   cups fresh or canned chicken broth, approximately
    Salt and freshly ground black pepper to taste.

1. Trim the leeks and split them in half lengthwise. Rinse thoroughly under cold running water to remove all sand and dirt. Cut the leeks into one-inch lengths. Place in a saucepan and add boiling water to cover. Let stand five minutes.

2. Heat the butter in a saucepan and add the carrot. Cover and cook slowly ten minutes. Add the leeks, cover and cook five minutes. Add the rice and one and one-half cups of the chicken broth. Add salt and pepper. Simmer, covered, thirty minutes, or until rice is tender, adding more broth during cooking if necessary.

Yield: Four to six servings.

Braised Lettuce with Mushrooms
RHODE ISLAND

¼   pound mushrooms, sliced
6   tablespoons butter
2   tablespoons flour
⅔   cup chicken broth
⅔   cup light cream
    Salt and freshly ground black pepper to taste
¼   teaspoon nutmeg

1   teaspoon fresh rosemary
1   tablespoon chopped parsley
2   tablespoons cognac
2   large or three small heads Boston lettuce
2   tablespoons chopped chives.

141

1. Sauté the mushrooms briefly in four tablespoons of the butter. Sprinkle with the flour. Gradually stir in the broth and cream and bring to a boil, stirring.

2. Season with salt, pepper, the nutmeg, rosemary, parsley and cognac. Hold over hot water.

3. Shred the lettuce into very wide ribbons and sauté very briefly in the remaining butter. Do not overcook.

4. Toss the lettuce with the sauce, sprinkle with the chives and serve immediately.

Yield: Six servings.

Note: Braised lettuce goes well with poached or stuffed chicken breasts.

Creamed Mushrooms with Fennel

RHODE ISLAND

5	tablespoons butter	1	cup milk
1	small onion, finely chopped	2	tablespoons chopped fennel
½	cup fennel root, diced		leaves
2	tablespoons chopped pars-		Salt and freshly ground
	ley		black pepper to taste
1½	pounds mushrooms, sliced	1	egg yolk
2	tablespoons flour	2	tablespoons sour cream.

1. Melt four tablespoons of the butter. Sauté the onion and fennel root in the butter until wilted and tender but not browned. Add the parsley and mushrooms. Cook until the mushrooms are tender and most of the liquid has evaporated, about five minutes.

2. Melt the remaining butter in a small pan and blend in the flour. Gradually stir in the milk, bring to a boil and simmer, stirring constantly, one minute. Add the fennel leaves and pour over the mushroom mixture. Stir.

3. Bring to a boil and season with salt and pepper. Blend together the egg yolk and sour cream and stir into the mushroom mixture. Reheat, but do not allow to boil.

Yield: Six servings.

Stuffed Mushrooms I
MASSACHUSETTS

24 medium-size to large mushrooms
2 cloves garlic, finely
chopped
8 tablespoons butter
1 cup soft bread crumbs
½ cup freshly grated Parmesan cheese

½ teaspoon salt
¼ teaspoon freshly ground
black pepper
2 tablespoons chopped parsley.

1. Preheat the oven to 350 degrees.

2. Remove the stems from the mushrooms, reserving the mushroom caps, and chop the stems finely. Sauté with the garlic in four tablespoons of the butter.

3. Add the bread crumbs, cheese, salt, pepper and parsley.

4. Sauté the mushrooms caps briefly in three tablespoons of the remaining butter.

5. Fill the caps with the stuffing and place in a buttered shallow casserole. Melt the remaining butter and drizzle over the mushrooms. Bake until very hot, about fifteen minutes.

Yield: Six to eight servings.

Stuffed Mushrooms II
RHODE ISLAND

24 medium-size to large mushroom caps or forty tiny caps
4 tablespoons olive oil
1 two-and-one-half-ounce
can anchovy fillets
1 clove garlic, finely chopped

1 teaspoon lemon juice
¾ cup soft bread crumbs
¼ cup chopped parsley
Freshly ground black pep-
per to taste.

1. Preheat the oven to 350 degrees.

2. Sauté the mushroom caps in three tablespoons of the oil two to three minutes.

3. Chop the anchovies with the garlic. Add the lemon juice, bread crumbs and parsley and mix. Season with pepper.

4. Fill the caps with the mixture, drizzle remaining oil over all and bake until hot, about fifteen minutes.

Yield: Six to eight servings.

Creamed Mushrooms

NEW HAMPSHIRE

¼	cup butter	1	teaspoon chopped fresh dill
½	pound medium-size mush-rooms, sliced or quartered		or one-half teaspoon dried dill
	Salt and freshly ground black pepper to taste	½	cup heavy cream.

1. Heat the butter in a skillet with a cover and, when the butter is melted, add the mushrooms. Cover and cook over medium heat, stirring or shaking the pan, about one minute.

2. Add the salt, pepper and the dill. Cover and cook five minutes. Add the cream and simmer, uncovered, until the sauce is thickened and reduced somewhat. Taste and correct the seasonings with more salt, pepper or dill if desired.

Yield: Four servings.

Fried Mushrooms

CONNECTICUT

32	mediu n-size white mush-rooms	1	teaspoon water
	Flour	1	teaspoon peanut oil or vege-table oil
	Salt and freshly ground black pepper to taste	1½	cups soft bread crumbs
			Oil for deep-frying
2	eggs		Tartar sauce.

1. Trim off the tips of the mushroom stems, but leave the stems on. Rinse the mushrooms under cold running water and drain. Do not dry.

2. Dredge the mushrooms in flour seasoned with salt and pepper.

3. Beat the eggs with the water and peanut or vegetable oil and place in a pie dish.

4. Toss or turn the mushrooms in the egg mixture until well coated.

Coat the mushrooms on all sides with the bread crumbs. Let stand until ready to cook.

5. Heat the oil in a large skillet and, when hot (375 degrees), add the mushrooms. Cook until golden brown all over. Drain on paper towels and serve hot with tartar sauce.

Yield: Four servings.

Lettuce with Bacon

NEW HAMPSHIRE

6	slices bacon, cubed	⅛	teaspoon freshly ground
¼	cup cider vinegar		black pepper
1	teaspoon brown sugar	4	cups torn-up Boston let-
½	teaspoon salt		tuce.

1. Cook the bacon until crisp, remove the bits and reserve. Remove and discard all but three tablespoons fat from the pan.

2. Add the vinegar, brown sugar, salt and pepper to pan. Bring to a boil and pour over the lettuce. Add the reserved bacon bits and toss.

Yield: Four servings.

Sour Cream and Onion Pie

MASSACHUSETTS

5	slices lean bacon	⅛	teaspoon nutmeg
3	cups thin onion rings	1	tablespoon freshly snipped
1	cup sour cream		dill weed
⅓	cup dry sherry	1	unbaked eight-inch to nine-
3	eggs, lightly beaten		inch pie shell.
½	teaspoon salt		
¼	teaspoon freshly ground		
	black pepper		

1. Cook the bacon until crisp. Remove the bacon, drain, crumble and reserve. Pour off all but four tablespoons of the bacon drippings.

2. Preheat the oven to 450 degrees.

3. Sauté the onions until golden in the bacon drippings in the skillet. Cool.

4. Combine the sour cream, sherry, eggs, salt, pepper, nutmeg and dill weed. Stir in the onions and reserved bacon.

5. Bake the pie shell ten minutes, or until set. Reduce the oven heat to 350 degrees. Pour the sour cream mixture into the pie shell and bake twenty-five to thirty minutes, or until set.

Yield: Eight servings.

Onions and Apples
MASSACHUSETTS

⅓ cup diced salt pork
4 tart apples
2 large onions, thinly sliced and separated into rings

¼ cup water, approximately.

1. Cook the salt pork in a heavy skillet until crisp. Remove the pieces and reserve.

2. Core the apples, leave the skin on and slice into one-half-inch rings. Place in the fat remaining in the skillet. Scatter the onion rings over the apples. Cook five minutes. Add one-quarter cup water, cover and cook until the apples and onions are tender, adding water during cooking if necessary. Sprinkle with reserved pork pieces.

Yield: Six servings.

Parsnip Fritters
VERMONT

5 parsnips
Boiling salted water
1 tablespoon butter
1 teaspoon flour

1 egg, lightly beaten
Salt and freshly ground black pepper to taste
Bacon drippings or butter.

1. Cook the parsnips in boiling salted water to cover.

2. Drain, peel and mash. Beat in the butter, flour, egg, salt and pepper. Form the mixture into small, flat, round or oval cakes.

3. Heat bacon drippings or butter in a large heavy skillet so that there is about one-quarter-inch depth. Fry the cakes, a few at a time until golden brown, turn and brown the other side. Drain on paper towels and keep warm until all are cooked.

Yield: Four servings.

Roasted Italian Peppers

CONNECTICUT

4	large green peppers, left whole	2	tablespoons finely chopped parsley
	Salt and freshly ground black pepper to taste	1½	tablespoons wine vinegar
1	clove garlic, finely minced	4½	tablespoons olive oil
			Lemon wedges.

1. Place the peppers on a hot griddle or over hot charcoal but not too close. Cook, turning occasionally, until skin is roasted and almost black all over. Set aside.

2. When peppers are cool enough to handle, peel away the charred skin. Remove the core and seeds from each pepper. Cut the peppers into strips and arrange symmetrically on a serving dish. Sprinkle with salt, pepper, the garlic, parsley, vinegar and oil. Chill. Serve garnished with lemon wedges.

Yield: Four to six servings.

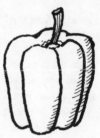

Potato Medley

MAINE

3	medium-size potatoes, peeled and sliced one-quarter-inch thick	¼	cup chopped parsley
		1	clove garlic, finely chopped
3	medium-size zucchini, sliced one-half-inch thick	¾	cup olive oil
4	tomatoes, peeled, seeded and chopped	2	medium-size onions, finely chopped
			Salt and freshly ground black pepper to taste.

1. Preheat the oven to 350 degrees.

2. Place the potatoes and zucchini in a shallow baking dish.

3. Combine the remaining ingredients and add to the dish. Toss to mix. Bake, uncovered, one and one-half hours.

Yield: Six servings.

Note: Peeled sliced eggplant can be added if desired.

Mashed Potato Casserole

MAINE

2	cups mashed potatoes	⅛	teaspoon freshly ground
1	cup sour cream		black pepper
1	cup large-curd cottage	1	tablespoon finely chopped
	cheese		green pepper
2	eggs, lightly beaten	¼	cup finely chopped scal-
2	tablespoons melted butter		lions, including green part.
¾	teaspoon salt		

1. Preheat the oven to 350 degrees.
2. Combine all the ingredients and place in a greased one-and-one-half-quart baking dish. Bake one hour.

Yield: Six servings.

Potatoes with Mustard Sauce

MAINE

3	large waxy potatoes	3	to four tablespoons Düssel-
	Boiling salted water		dorf mustard
6	tablespoons butter		Salt and freshly ground
3	tablespoons chopped onion		black pepper to taste
3	tablespoons flour	¼	cup soft bread crumbs
2	cups chicken broth	¼	cup freshly grated Parme-
1	cup heavy cream		san cheese.

1. Scrub the potatoes and cover with boiling salted water. Simmer until barely tender, about thirty minutes.
2. Meanwhile, melt three tablespoons of the butter in a saucepan. Add the onion and sauté until tender but not browned. Sprinkle with the flour and gradually stir in the broth and cream. Bring to a boil, stirring, and simmer one minute. Stir in the mustard and hold over hot water until potatoes are done.
3. Preheat the oven to 375 degrees.
4. Peel potatoes and slice into a shallow casserole, seasoning each layer with salt and pepper.
5. Pour sauce over potatoes, sprinkle with the bread crumbs and cheese and dot with remaining butter. Bake, uncovered, until bubbly hot and lightly browned.

Yield: Six servings.

Note: Potatoes in mustard sauce go particularly well with corned beef, boiled beef or roast beef.

Spinach and Onion Pie

MASSACHUSETTS

2	ten-ounce bags spinach	6	eggs, lightly beaten
	Salt		White pepper to taste
3	large bunches scallions, chopped, including green part	1½	cups water
		1½	cups flour, approximately
		2	tablespoons oil
½	pound cottage cheese	¼	cup butter.
½	pound feta cheese, crumbled		

1. Preheat the oven to 350 degrees.
2. Chop the spinach finely. Sprinkle generously with salt, add the scallions and squeeze to wilt the greens. Discard extra moisture.
3. Add the cottage cheese, feta cheese and three of the eggs to the spinach and scallions. Season with pepper.
4. Make a thin batter with the water, flour and remaining eggs (batter should be just slightly thinner than a crepe batter).
5. Put the oil in a 12-by-18-by-3-inch baking dish or roasting pan and swirl to coat the dish.
6. Pour half the batter into the dish. Top with spinach mixture. Dot with the butter. Pour the remaining batter over all and bake about one hour, or until set and browned on top.

Yield: Ten servings.

Spinach Timbale

CONNECTICUT

1	pound spinach, well washed	⅛	teaspoon nutmeg
1	tablespoon bacon drippings	1	cup milk, scalded
½	teaspoon salt	2	eggs, lightly beaten
⅛	teaspoon freshly ground black pepper	2	hard-cooked eggs, chopped.

1. Preheat the oven to 350 degrees.

2. Place the spinach in a large kettle with just the water clinging to the leaves. Cover and cook until the spinach wilts. Drain well and chop.

3. Add the bacon drippings, salt, pepper and nutmeg to the spinach. Combine the spinach mixture with the milk. Stir in the beaten eggs and hard-cooked eggs and turn into a greased shallow baking dish. Set the dish in a pan of hot water and bake thirty-five minutes, or until custard is set.

Yield: Four servings.

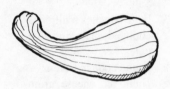

Squash and Cheese Casserole

VERMONT

2 pounds yellow squash	1 cup milk
Boiling water	¾ cup grated Gruyère or
1 cup chopped onions	Swiss cheese
3 sprigs parsley	¼ teaspoon nutmeg
½ teaspoon thyme	2 egg yolks, lightly beaten
Salt and freshly ground	¼ teaspoon cayenne pepper
black pepper to taste	¼ cup buttered soft bread
2 tablespoons butter	crumbs.
2 tablespoons flour	

1. Preheat the oven to 325 degrees.

2. Trim ends of the squash. Cut squash into rounds and place in a saucepan. Add boiling water to cover, Add the onions, parsley, thyme, salt and black pepper. Cook briefly until squash is crisp-tender. Discard parsley and drain squash mixture.

3. Heat the butter in a saucepan and add the flour. Stir until blended and add the milk, stirring rapidly with a wire whisk. When sauce is blended and smooth, remove from heat. Add half the cheese, the nutmeg, egg yolks and cayenne, beating rapidly.

4. Add squash mixture and pour into a buttered baking dish. Sprinkle with remaining cheese and bread crumbs. Bake twenty-five to thirty minutes, or until bubbling and golden brown.

Yield: Six servings.

Spiced Butternut Squash
NEW HAMPSHIRE

2	butternut squash	1	teaspoon cinnamon
8	tablespoons butter	¼	teaspoon nutmeg
¼	teaspoon ground allspice	1	tablespoon maple syrup.
½	cup light brown sugar		

1. Preheat the oven to 350 degrees.

2. Split the butternut squash in half and scoop out seeds and membranes. Dot interior and the cut surface with the butter. Place squash halves in a roasting pan or baking dish.

3. Blend the allspice, sugar, cinnamon and nutmeg and sprinkle squash cavities with mixture. Pour equal quantities of the syrup into each cavity. Bake until squash is thoroughly tender, fifty minutes to one hour.

Yield: Four servings.

Sandra's String Beans with Mint
CONNECTICUT

2	pounds tiny string beans, washed, trimmed, left whole	½	cup olive oil
		¼	clove garlic
	Boiling salted water	2	teaspoons wine vinegar
3	sprigs mint		Salt and freshly ground black pepper to taste.

1. Cook the beans in boiling salted water to cover until crisp-tender, about six minutes. Drain beans and rinse with cold water briefly to stop cooking but not to cool beans down too much.

2. Place the remaining ingredients in an electric blender and blend until smooth. Pour over hot rinsed beans.

Yield: Eight servings.

Note: These can be eaten cold, too.

String Beans with Herb Sauce

CONNECTICUT

3 tablespoons olive oil
1 tablespoon butter
1 onion, chopped
1 clove garlic, finely chopped
2 tomatoes, peeled, seeded and chopped
1 tablespoon chopped celery
1 tablespoon chopped parsley

1 teaspoon herbed vinegar
¼ teaspoon rosemary
¼ teaspoon sugar
Salt and freshly ground black pepper to taste
2 pounds string beans, cooked whole and drained.

1. Heat the oil and butter in a small skillet and sauté the onion and garlic in it until tender. Add the remaining ingredients except the beans. Bring to a boil and simmer ten minutes.

2. Pour over hot beans.

Yield: Eight servings.

Succotash

MASSACHUSETTS

2 cups fresh, or frozen, lima beans or fava beans
Boiling salted water
2 cups freshly cut corn kernels (about four large ears)
1 cup one-inch-lengths green beans

¼ cup butter
1 teaspoon sugar
1 teaspoon salt
¼ teaspoon freshly ground black pepper
1 cup heavy cream.

1. Place lima or fava beans in a saucepan. Cover with boiling salted water and cook until crisp-tender, about eight minutes.

2. Add the corn and green beans, cover and cook five minutes. Drain and run the beans and corn under cold water; drain. Pat dry with paper towels.

3. Heat the butter in a heavy skillet, add the vegetables and reheat while tossing. Add the sugar, salt, pepper and one quarter cup of the cream. Cook, uncovered, while stirring until cream has almost evaporated. Add half of the remaining cream and cook until thick. Add the remaining cream and heat until creamy.

Yield: Four to six servings.

Sweet Potatoes and Cranberries

MASSACHUSETTS

6 sweet potatoes, cooked, peeled and sliced lengthwise	¾ cup water
	½ cup brown sugar
	¾ teaspoon grated orange rind
1½ cups homemade cranberry sauce (page 265)	¾ teaspoon cinnamon
	1½ tablespoons butter.

1. Preheat the oven to 325 degrees.
2. Place the sweet potato slices in a greased two-quart casserole.
3. Combine the cranberry sauce, water, brown sugar, orange rind and cinnamon in a saucepan. Bring to a boil and simmer five minutes.
4. Add the butter and pour over the sweet potatoes. Bake twenty minutes.

Yield: Six servings.

Fried Tomato Slices

NEW HAMPSHIRE

½ cup flour	6 firm tomatoes
½ teaspoon baking powder	1 teaspoon basil
¼ teaspoon salt	Salt and freshly ground
⅓ cup milk	black pepper to taste.
1 egg, well beaten	

1. Combine the flour, baking powder and salt in a bowl. Mix the milk and egg together and stir into the dry ingredients to make a smooth batter.
2. Cut the tomatoes into one-half-inch slices. Sprinkle with the basil, salt and pepper and let drain ten minutes.
3. Dip the tomato slices into the batter and fry on a well-greased griddle until brown on one side. Turn and brown the underside.

Yield: Eight servings.

Note: Fried tomato slices are delicious with ham or bacon.

Shaker Tomato Custard

NEW HAMPSHIRE

8	to ten ripe tomatoes, chopped	4	eggs, lightly beaten
	Salt and freshly ground black pepper to taste	1	cup milk
		⅓	cup sugar
1	teaspoon basil	⅛	teaspoon nutmeg.

1. Place the tomatoes, salt, pepper and basil in a saucepan and simmer gently, uncovered, thirty minutes.

2. Pass through a sieve. Cool.

3. Preheat the oven to 350 degrees.

4. Combine the remaining ingredients. Stir in tomato mixture. Pour into ten to twelve greased custard cups. Set cups in a shallow pan with hot water coming halfway up the cups. Bake thirty minutes, or until custards are set.

Yield: Ten to one dozen servings.

Fresh Tomato Risotto

CONNECTICUT

1	cup peeled, chopped tomatoes	½	teaspoon oregano
¾	cup uncooked rice	½	teaspoon salt
½	cup finely chopped onions	1¾	cups concentrated chicken broth.
1	clove garlic, finely minced		

1. Preheat the oven to 375 degrees.

2. Combine the tomatoes, rice, onions, garlic, oregano and salt in a one-and-one-half-quart casserole.

3. Heat the broth to boiling and pour over tomato mixture. Cover and bake, stirring occasionally, about thirty-five minutes, or until rice is cooked.

Yield: Four servings.

Cheese Scalloped Rutabagas or Yellow Turnips
MAINE

3 cups thinly sliced rutabagas or yellow turnips (about one and one-half pounds)
1 cup boiling water
2 tablespoons butter
½ cup chopped onion
⅓ cup chopped celery
⅔ cup chopped green pepper
1 teaspoon salt
¼ teaspoon freshly ground black pepper
¼ teaspoon thyme
2 teaspoons cornstarch
3 tablespoons water
½ cup grated Cheddar cheese
¼ cup buttered soft bread crumbs
2 tablespoons freshly grated Parmesan cheese.

1. Place the rutabaga or turnip slices in a saucepan and add the boiling water. Bring to a boil and simmer about twenty minutes, or until the vegetable is barely tender.

2. Meanwhile, melt the butter in a heavy skillet and sauté the onion in it until tender but not browned. Add the celery and green pepper and cook three minutes longer.

3. Season with the salt, pepper and thyme. Add the undrained cooked rutabagas to the seasoned vegetables.

4. Mix the cornstarch with the water. Stir the cornstarch mixture and the Cheddar cheese into the vegetables. Heat, stirring, until vegetable mixture thickens. Cook two minutes. Pour into a heatproof serving casserole or dish. Sprinkle with the bread crumbs and Parmesan cheese and glaze under a preheated broiler.

Yield: Four servings.

Glazed Yellow Turnip
VERMONT

2 medium-size yellow turnips, peeled and sliced one-quarter-inch thick
Boiling salted water
1 cup brown sugar
½ cup orange juice
1 teaspoon grated orange rind
2 tablespoons butter.

1. Preheat the oven to 350 degrees.

2. Barely cover the yellow turnips with boiling salted water and boil five minutes. Drain turnips and place in a shallow baking dish.

3. Combine the brown sugar, orange juice, orange rind and butter in a pan and heat to melt the butter and dissolve the sugar. Pour over the vegetable and bake, basting frequently, forty-five to sixty minutes, until the turnip slices are tender.

Yield: Six servings.

Zucchini Casserole

MAINE

6	medium-size zucchini, thinly sliced	3	shallots, finely chopped
1	medium-size eggplant, thinly sliced	¼	teaspoon thyme
½	cup peanut oil	1	bay leaf
	Salt and freshly ground black pepper to taste	6	tomatoes, cored, peeled and stewed until thickened
		3	tablespoons freshly grated Parmesan cheese.

1. Preheat the oven to 350 degrees.

2. Cook the zucchini and eggplant in half the oil until wilted and browned. Sprinkle with salt and pepper. Pour into a colander to drain.

3. Cook the shallots in the remaining oil and add the drained zucchini and eggplant.

4. Add the thyme and bay leaf. Turn into a baking dish and bake twenty minutes. Remove from the oven. Increase the oven heat to 400 degrees.

5. Put half the tomatoes, then the zucchini and eggplant mixture into another baking dish. Add the remaining tomatoes and sprinkle with the cheese. Bake ten minutes, or until the cheese browns.

Yield: Four to six servings.

End-of-the-Garden Casserole
MAINE

3 onions, sliced	1 green pepper, cored, seeded and sliced
2 tablespoons oil	
2 medium-size potatoes, peeled and thinly sliced	2 tablespoons melted butter
	½ teaspoon basil
2 medium-size zucchini, thickly sliced	2 cloves garlic, finely minced
	3 large tomatoes, peeled and sliced
1 small eggplant, thinly sliced	
Salt and freshly ground black pepper to taste	

1. In a heavy casserole, sauté two of the onions in the oil until tender. Add the potatoes and cook until lightly browned.

2. Add the zucchini and eggplant in two layers. Season with salt and black pepper. Make a layer of the remaining onion slices and the green pepper and season with salt and pepper.

3. Drizzle the butter over all and sprinkle with the basil and garlic. Top with the tomatoes and season again. Cover, bring to a boil and simmer gently about twenty-five minutes, or until the vegetables are tender. Serve hot or cold, spooning down to the bottom to catch all layers.

Yield: Six servings.

Baked Zucchini
CONNECTICUT

2 tablespoons vegetable oil or olive oil	4 eggs, well beaten
	1½ cups milk
3 large or six small zucchini, peeled and diced	1 tablespoon flour
	¼ teaspoon cayenne pepper
1 teaspoon salt	½ cup grated Gruyère or Swiss cheese.
½ teaspoon freshly ground black pepper	

1. Pour the oil into a heavy saucepan and add the zucchini. Sprinkle with the salt and pepper. Cover and cook over very low heat, stirring occasionally, until zucchini is soft and mushy.

2. Preheat the oven to 400 degrees.

3. In a mixing bowl, combine the eggs, milk, flour and cayenne.

4. Drain the zucchini and add to egg mixture. Beat well with a rotary beater or wire whisk.

5. Pour the mixture into a buttered two-quart baking dish and sprinkle with the cheese. Bake at least twenty minutes, or until top is brown and the casserole is slightly puffed.

Yield: Six servings.

Asparagus Vinaigrette
CONNECTICUT

1	hard-cooked egg	1	tablespoon chopped parsley
1½	tablespoons olive oil	2	tablespoons heavy cream,
1	tablespoon cider vinegar		whipped
1	teaspoon salt	16	spears asparagus, cooked,
½	teaspoon freshly ground		drained and chilled.
	black pepper		
1	tablespoon finely grated onion		

1. Rub the yolk of the egg through a sieve. Chop the egg white. Gardually beat the oil, vinegar, salt, pepper, onion, parsley and egg white into the yolk.

2. Fold into the cream and spoon over the asparagus.

Yield: Four servings.

Canlis Salad
CONNECTICUT

2	heads romaine lettuce	¼	cup chopped scallion, including green part
1	egg		
1	pound bacon slices	½	cup freshly grated Romano
2	teaspoons vegetable oil		cheese or Parmesan cheese
1	cup one-half-inch bread cubes		Juice of two lemons
	Salt to taste	¼	teaspoon chopped fresh mint
1	clove garlic, peeled	¼	teaspoon dried oregano
⅓	cup olive oil		Freshly ground black pepper to taste.
2	tomatoes, peeled, cored and cut into eighths		

1. Trim and rinse the lettuce and cut or tear it into bite-size pieces. Pat dry, place in plastic bag and chill.

2. Place the egg in a saucepan, cover with water, bring to a simmer and simmer one minute. Drain. Set aside.

3. Cook the bacon until it is crisp. Drain on paper towels. Let bacon cool; then break or cut into small pieces.

4. Heat the vegetable oil in a skillet and add the bread cubes. Cook, shaking the skillet and stirring, until cubes are golden brown and crisp. Drain on paper towels.

5. Sprinkle the bottom of a salad bowl with salt and rub with the garlic. Remove the garlic and stir in one tablespoon of the olive oil. Add the tomato wedges and the lettuce.

6. Sprinkle with the scallion, cheese and bacon bits.

7. In a small mixing bowl, combine the remaining olive oil, the lemon juice, mint, oregano and lightly cooked egg. Stir thoroughly and pour the dressing over the salad. Add salt and pepper and toss. Add the bread cubes, toss once more and serve immediately.

Yield: Four to six servings.

Clam Mold
RHODE ISLAND

2 envelopes unflavored gelatin

¼ cup cold water

1 cup boiling water
Grated rind and juice of one lemon

1 seven-ounce can chopped clams, drained and liquor reserved

¼ teaspoon freshly ground black pepper

1½ cups clam broth or water

1 teaspoon Dijon or Düsseldorf mustard

2 scallions, finely chopped, including green part

6 large stuffed olives, sliced

1 cup cottage cheese, well beaten

¼ cup catchup

½ cup chopped parsley

1 hard-cooked egg, sliced
Salad greens.

159

1. Soften the gelatin in the cold water. Add the boiling water and stir to dissolve the gelatin. Add the lemon rind, lemon juice, reserved clam liquor, pepper and broth or water. Stir well.

2. Halve the gelatin mixture between two bowls. Stir the clams, mustard and scallions into one bowl of the gelatin mixture.

3. Pour the clam mixture into a one-and-one-half-quart mold or oblong baking dish that has been rinsed with cold water.

4. Chill until the layer just starts to set; then poke the olive slices down around the sides of the mold or dish. Chill until almost firm.

5. Reserve one-quarter cup of the gelatin mixture in the second bowl. Add the cottage cheese, catchup and six tablespoons of the parsley to the remaining mixture. Spoon the cottage cheese mixture over the setting clam mixture. Chill until firm.

6. Sprinkle the remaining parlsey over the top of the firm mixture; then arrange the egg slices in an attractive pattern over all. Spoon the reserved gelatin mixture over to coat the egg slices. Chill until firm.

7. Unmold or cut into squares. Serve on salad greens.

Yield: Six to eight servings.

Cole Slaw with Cooked Dressing

MAINE

Cooked dressing:

1 egg, lightly beaten	1 teaspoon dry mustard
¾ cup milk	⅛ teaspoon cayenne pepper
2 tablespoons flour	2 tablespoons bacon drip-
1½ tablespoons sugar	pings or butter
1 teaspoon salt	¼ cup cider vinegar.

Slaw:

4 cups shredded cabbage	½ red sweet pepper, diced
½ green pepper, seeded and diced	1 teaspoon salt.

1. To prepare cooked dressing, combine the egg and milk. In the top of a double boiler, mix together the flour, sugar, salt, mustard and cayenne. Stir in the milk mixture.

2. Cook over hot water, stirring until mixture thickens. Do not boil. Stir in the bacon drippings or butter and vinegar. Cool.

3. Combine the slaw ingredients in a bowl and toss well.
4. Stir in enough of the cooled dressing to moisten well.
Yield: Eight servings.

Marinated Bean Salad
CONNECTICUT

2	cups cooked baby lima beans	½	cup wine vinegar
2	cups cooked green beans	¼	cup olive oil
1	one-pound-fourteen-ounce can kidney beans, drained	⅓	cup water
1	cup button mushrooms or sliced large mushrooms	1	teaspoon sugar
¼	cup diced pimento	1	clove garlic, crushed
½	cup finely chopped onion	¼	teaspoon oregano
2	tablespoons chopped parsley	¼	teaspoon celery salt
		½	teaspoon salt
		¼	teaspoon freshly ground black pepper.

1. Day before, place the lima beans, green beans, kidney beans, mushrooms, pimento, onion and parsley in a bowl.
2. Place the remaining ingredients in a jar and shake well. Pour over the beans and toss. Cover and chill well overnight.
Yield: One dozen servings.

Cucumber Salad
NEW HAMPSHIRE

1	large cucumber	3	tablespoons cider vinegar
1	cup sour cream	¼	teaspoon salt
1	tablespoon chopped onion	⅛	teaspoon white pepper.

1. Peel the cucumber. Run the tines of a fork lengthwise over cucumber and cut crosswise into thin slices.
2. Combine the remaining ingredients and pour over the sliced cucumber. Marinate thirty minutes at room temperature.
Yield: Four servings.

161

Wilted Dandelion Greens

VERMONT

4	slices bacon, diced	¼	cup cider vinegar
½	cup sugar	1	cup light cream
½	teaspoon salt	4	cups dandelion greens
1	tablespoon cornstarch	1	hard-cooked egg, chopped.
1	egg, lightly beaten		

1. Cook the bacon until crisp. Reserve drippings and bacon.

2. Combine the sugar, salt and cornstarch. Mix well. Gradually stir in the egg, vinegar and cream.

3. Pour into the bacon mixture and cook, stirring, until the mixture thickens. Pour over the greens and garnish with the egg.

Yield: Six servings.

Escarole Salad

MASSACHUSETTS

2	red onions, thinly sliced	1	cucumber
3	tablespoons cider or wine vinegar	1	green pepper, cored, seeded and diced
	Salt	1	bunch radishes, sliced
1	head escarole, chopped	1	cup Greek olives
3	tomatoes, peeled and chopped	½	pound feta cheese, cut into slivers.

Dressing:

¼	cup wine vinegar	1	cup olive oil
1	teaspoon dry mustard		Salt and freshly ground
1	teaspoon sugar		black pepper to taste.

1. To prepare salad, place the onions and vinegar in a bowl. Sprinkle generously with salt. Squeeze vigorously with the hand. Let mixture set twenty to thirty minutes.

2. Place the escarole, onion mixture and tomatoes in a salad bowl.

3. Cut the top off the cucumber. Salt and rub surfaces together several minutes. This removes the bitterness.

4. Peel the cucumber and score the outside before chopping. Add to the salad bowl. Add the green pepper, radishes, olives and feta cheese.

5. To prepare dressing, shake together the vinegar, mustard and sugar in a jar. Add the oil, salt and pepper. Shake again. Toss the salad with the dressing just before serving.

Yield: Ten servings.

Creamed Horseradish
MASSACHUSETTS

3 roots of fresh horseradish	¼ cup flour
3 cups milk	1 tablespoon sugar
¼ cup butter	1½ teaspoons salt.

1. Peel the roots and grate the horseradish on a very fine grater. There should be about two cups. Alternately, the horseradish can be grated in an electric blender in small quantities, using one cup of the milk to give the necessary liquid.

2. Melt the butter in a heavy skillet. Stir in the flour and cook, stirring, until lightly browned. Add the horseradish and cook three minutes longer, stirring constantly.

3. Stir in the sugar, salt and (remaining) milk and bring to a boil, stirring. Cover and simmer very slowly, stirring occasionally, or cook in a double boiler over boiling water, forty-five to sixty minutes, or until the horseradish is tender.

Yield: About three cups.

Note: During long cooking, the horseradish loses much of its pungency.

Serve with roast beef, ham or corned beef.

Mushroom Salad
CONNECTICUT

1½ tablespoons lemon juice	¼ cup olive oil
3 tablespoons Dijon mustard	½ pound mushrooms, sliced.
¼ teaspoon salt	
⅛ teaspoon freshly ground black pepper	

1. Place the lemon juice, mustard, salt and pepper in a bowl. With a wire whisk, gradually whisk in the oil. Mixture will become the consistency of mayonnaise.

2. Add the mushrooms, toss and chill.

Yield: Three servings.

Picnic Potato Salad

VERMONT

⅓ cup French dressing
4 cups hot diced, cooked potatoes
4 hard-cooked eggs
1 cup sour cream
¼ cup sliced scallions, including green part
2 tablespoons snipped parsley
2 tablespoons chopped dill pickle

2 tablespoons diced pimento
2 tablespoons cider vinegar
1 tablespoon prepared mustard, preferably Dijon or Düsseldorf
1 teaspoon salt
⅛ teaspoon freshly ground black pepper
1 cup chopped celery
Parsley sprigs.

1. Pour the dressing over the potatoes and toss to coat. Refrigerate until potatoes are throughly chilled.

2. Chop three of the hard-cooked eggs.

3. Combine the sour cream, scallions, snipped parsley, pickle, pimento, vinegar, mustard, salt and pepper. Add to potatoes along with the celery and chopped eggs. Toss gently and chill.

4. Cut the remaining egg in wedges. Garnish potato salad with egg wedges and the parsley sprigs.

Yield: Six servings.

Jane's Potato Salad

MAINE

6 medium-size baking potatoes
1 cup chopped celery
1 cup thinly sliced red onion rings
Salt and freshly ground black pepper to taste

1½ teaspoons celery seeds
½ cup wine vinegar
½ cup peanut oil
2 tablespoons olive oil
⅛ teaspoon cayenne pepper
1½ cups chopped parsley
Lettuce leaves.

164

1. Cook the potatoes in jackets until tender. Peel and slice thinly while still hot.

2. Combine the potato slices, celery, onion rings, salt, black pepper, celery seeds, vinegar, peanut oil, olive oil, cayenne and one cup of the parsley. Mix well.

3. Cover with the remaining parsley. Serve at room temperature, on lettuce leaves.

Yield: Six servings.

New England Potato Salad

MASSACHUSETTS

1	pound waxy potatoes	2	tablespoons cider vinegar
2	tender ribs celery, approximately		Juice of half a lemon
¾	cup heavy cream		Salt and freshly ground black pepper to taste
¼	cup sour cream	¼	cup cooked ham.

1. Cook the potatoes in jackets, taking care not to overcook. Let cool; then chill.

2. Peel the potatoes. Cut them first into thin slices; then cut each slice into thin, matchlike strips. Place the strips in a mixing bowl.

3. Cut the celery ribs into two-inch lengths. Cut each length of celery into very thin strips. There should be about half as much celery as potatoes. Add the celery to the potatoes.

4. Whip the heavy cream until it is the consistency of thin mayonnaise. Do not whip until stiff. Stir in the sour cream, vinegar, lemon juice, salt and pepper. Pour over the potatoes and celery. Mix gently without breaking potatoes.

5. Cut the ham into very thin strips and scatter over the salad. Serve as soon as possible.

Yield: Four servings.

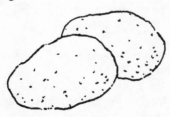

Hot Apple and Potato Salad
MASSACHUSETTS

½ cup golden raisins
1 cup boiling water
3 cups sliced cooked potatoes
1 cup diced celery
2 tablespoons chopped parsley
2 teaspoons salt
¼ teaspoon freshly ground black pepper

4 slices bacon
2 tablespoons cider vinegar
2 tablespoons tarragon vinegar
¼ cup sugar
1 teaspoon grated lemon rind
3 unpeeled Red Delicious apples, cored and diced.

1. Place the raisins in a bowl, pour the boiling water over raisins and let stand three minutes. Drain.
2. Combine the potatoes, celery, parsley, salt and pepper in a skillet.
3. In another skillet, cook the bacon until crisp. Add the cider vinegar, tarragon vinegar, sugar and lemon rind and bring to a boil.
4. Pour over the potato mixture. Heat gently. Add the apples and raisins and heat mixture to serving temperature.
Yield: Eight servings.

Crisp Rutabaga Salad
MAINE

½ cup grated raw rutabaga
½ cup thinly sliced celery
2 scallions, including green part, chopped
2 radishes, sliced paper-thin
3 cups shredded romaine lettuce
3 tablespoons olive oil

1 tablespoon wine vinegar
½ teaspoon salt
¼ teaspoon freshly ground black pepper
⅛ teaspoon dry mustard
¼ teaspoon sugar
¼ teaspoon basil.

1. Combine the rutabaga, celery, scallions, radishes and romaine in a bowl and chill well.
2. Combine the remaining ingredients in a jar and shake. Chill. Toss the salad with the dressing just before serving.
Yield: Four servings.

Maine Sardine Salad

1	clove garlic, crushed or quartered	½	teaspoon salt
¾	cup oil	¼	teaspoon freshly ground black pepper
1½	cups small bread cubes	2	tablespoons lemon juice
1	egg	⅓	cup freshly grated Parmesan cheese
1	small onion, sliced and separated into rings	3	three-and-three-quarter-ounce to four-ounce cans sardines
8	cups bite-size pieces romaine lettuce	6	cherry tomatoes, peeled.

1. Let the garlic stand in the oil one hour or longer. Remove garlic and discard.

2. Heat one-half cup of the oil in a skillet, add the bread cubes and cook until golden and crisp. Drain on paper towels. Set aside.

3. Place the egg in a saucepan, cover with water, bring to a simmer and simmer one minute. Drain. Set aside.

4. Place the onion, romaine, salt and pepper in a salad bowl. Pour remaining oil over all and toss lightly. Break the egg into the salad.

5. Add the lemon juice and toss thoroughly. Add the cheese, bread cubes and sardines. Toss. Garnish with the tomatoes.

Yield: Six servings.

Spinach Salad with Marinated Mushrooms
CONNECTICUT

1	pound button mushrooms Boiling water	¼	teaspoon freshly ground black pepper
3	large cloves garlic, crushed	2	tablespoons lemon juice
1	bay leaf	½	cup olive oil
½	teaspoon thyme	¾	cup malt vinegar or wine vinegar
½	teaspoon rosemary, crushed with mortar and pestle	2	quarts spinach leaves, washed.
¼	teaspoon basil		
¼	teaspoon salt		

1. Trim the mushroom stems, rinse the mushrooms and place in a saucepan. Cover with boiling water. Cover and boil five minutes. Drain.

2. Meanwhile, combine the remaining ingredients except the spinach. Shake or beat well. Pour over the hot drained mushrooms and chill.

3. Place the spinach leaves in a salad bowl and add the mushrooms and enough of the marinade to dress the greens. Toss.

Yield: Eight servings.

Spinach Salad with Mustard Dressing
VERMONT

1	pound spinach	7	tablespoons olive oil
	Salt		Freshly ground black pepper to taste
1	clove garlic		
¼	teaspoon dry mustard	2	hard-cooked eggs, finely chopped.
	Tabasco		
3	tablespoons wine vinegar		

1. Wash the spinach well, dry it and cut into bite-size pieces. Discard any tough stems.

2. Sprinkle the bottom of a salad bowl with salt, rub with the garlic and add the mustard. Add a few drops Tabasco, the vinegar, oil and pepper. Stir with a fork until the mixture is well blended. Add the spinach and toss until the leaves are coated with dressing. Lift onto individual salad plates and sprinkle with the eggs.

Yield: Four to six servings.

Tossed Salad with Honey Dressing
CONNECTICUT

Salad:

1	medium-size head leaf lettuce or romaine lettuce, washed, drained and crisped	¼	cup finely diced celery
		⅓	cup finely diced carrot
¼	head red cabbage, finely shredded	½	clove garlic, finely chopped
		1	teaspoon oregano
1	cucumber, peeled and thinly sliced	1	tablespoon finely grated onion
1	bunch scallions, including some green part, chopped		Salt and freshly ground black pepper to taste.

Honey dressing:
½ cup oil
¼ cup cider vinegar
¼ cup honey.

1. To prepare salad, break the lettuce into a salad bowl. Add the cabbage, cucumber, scallions, celery and carrot. Toss.
2. Sprinkle with the garlic, oregano, grated onion, salt and pepper.
3. To prepare honey dressing, combine the oil, vinegar and honey. Mix well. Pour over salad and toss.
Yield: Eight servings.

Vegetable Salad
CONNECTICUT

¼ cup chicken broth
1 tablespoon curry powder, or to taste
½ cup chopped scallions, including green part
⅓ cup mayonnaise
1¼ cups sour cream
2 teaspoons lemon juice
1 cup cooked peas
⅓ cup chopped celery

½ cup diced cooked carrot
½ cup cooked corn kernels
¼ cup diced green pepper
Salt and freshly ground black pepper to taste
1 teaspoon chopped fresh mint
Lettuce leaves (optional)
Mint sprigs.

1. Combine the broth and curry powder. Bring to a boil, stirring, and simmer gently until reduced by at least half.
2. Combine the curry mixture with the scallions, mayonnaise, sour cream and lemon juice. Mix well.
3. Add the vegetables, salt, pepper and the chopped mint. Chill.
4. Serve on lettuce leaves if desired. Garnish with mint sprigs.
Yield: Four servings.

Poppy Seed Dressing
CONNECTICUT

½ cup sugar
1 teaspoon dry mustard
1 teaspoon paprika
¼ teaspoon salt
5 tablespoons tarragon vinegar
⅓ cup honey

1 tablespoon lemon juice
2 tablespoons onion juice or finely grated onion
1 cup vegetable oil (not olive oil)
1 tablespoon poppy seeds.

1. Mix together the sugar, mustard, paprika, salt and vinegar until sugar dissolves completely.
2. Add the honey, lemon juice and onion juice or onion. Gradually beat in the oil. Chill.
3. Add the poppy seeds just before serving.
Yield: About one and one-half cups.

Mayonnaise
CONNECTICUT

½ teaspoon dry mustard
1 teaspoon cold water
2 egg yolks
Salt to taste
Pinch of cayenne pepper

3 tablespoons wine vinegar or lemon juice
1¼ cups peanut oil or vegetable oil.

1. Place the mustard in a mixing bowl. Add the water to make a paste. Let stand ten minutes.
2. Add the egg yolks, salt, cayenne and half the vinegar or lemon juice. Start beating with a wire whisk, rotary beater or electric mixer, gradually adding the oil. Continue beating, adding the oil and remaining vinegar alternately until all the ingredients are used. Taste for seasoning and add more salt, cayenne or vinegar if desired.
Yield: About one and one-half cups.

Breads

Rhode Island johnnycakes or Massachusetts johnnycakes were originally called journey cakes because the circuit riders carried the bread with them on their travels to preach the gospel. Massachusetts johnnycakes usually have wheat flour and corn meal in them.

Johnnycakes
RHODE ISLAND

1 cup waterground white corn meal	1 teaspoon sugar (optional)
1 teaspoon salt	½ cup milk, approximately
1 cup boiling water	Butter and maple syrup.

1. Place the corn meal and salt in a bowl. Gradually stir in the boiling water. Add the sugar if desired and enough milk to make a batter that is a little thicker than a regular pancake batter.

2. Spoon onto a greased griddle and cook eight to ten minutes on one side before turning to cook and brown the other side. Split cakes and serve with butter and syrup.

Yield: Fourteen.

Corn Bread

MASSACHUSETTS

1 cup yellow corn meal
1 cup flour
1 teaspoon sugar
½ teaspoon salt
4 teaspoons baking powder

1 egg
1 cup milk
¼ cup melted lard or shortening.

1. Preheat the oven to 425 degrees.
2. Sift the corn meal, flour, sugar, salt and baking powder into a mixing bowl. Add the egg, milk and lard or shortening and stir with a wooden spoon until blended. Do not overbeat.
3. Grease an eight-inch square pan or iron skillet. Heat on top of the stove and pour in the batter. Place in the oven and bake twenty to twenty-five minutes.

Yield: Eight to ten servings.

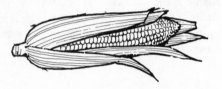

Caraway Corn Bread

RHODE ISLAND

1½ cups flour
1 teaspoon baking soda
4 teaspoons baking powder
3 tablespoons sugar
1½ teaspoons salt
1½ cups waterground yellow corn meal

3 teaspoons caraway seeds
½ teaspoon nutmeg
3 eggs, lightly beaten
1½ cups buttermilk
5 tablespoons melted shortening or bacon drippings.

1. Preheat the oven to 425 degrees.
2. Sift together the flour, baking soda, baking powder, sugar and salt. Add the corn meal, caraway seeds and nutmeg.
3. Stir in the eggs, buttermilk and shortening or bacon drippings. Turn into a greased nine-inch square baking tin and bake twenty-five to thirty minutes.

Yield: Six to eight servings.

Spider Corncake

CONNECTICUT

1⅓	cups yellow corn meal	2	teaspoons sugar
⅓	cup flour	½	teaspoon salt
1	teaspoon baking soda	2	tablespoons bacon drip-
1	cup buttermilk		pings or butter.
2	cups regular milk		

1. Preheat the oven to 350 degrees.
2. Combine the corn meal, flour and baking soda in a mixing bowl. Add the buttermilk, one cup of the regular milk, sugar and salt. Stir to blend well.
3. Meanwhile, put the bacon drippings or butter in a nine-inch cast-iron skillet or other baking dish and place it in the oven.
4. When skillet is thoroughly hot, withdraw it and pour in the batter. Carefully pour the remaining milk over the top. Bake fifty minutes.
Yield: Six servings.

Biscuits

MASSACHUSETTS

1½	cups flour	6	tablespoons melted shorten-
2	teaspoons baking powder		ing
¼	teaspoon salt		Milk.

1. Preheat the oven to 450 degrees.
2. Combine the flour, baking powder and salt.
3. Stir in the shortening and enough milk to make a soft, mangeable dough.
4. Knead the dough ten strokes. Pat to a thickness of one-half inch and cut with a biscuit cutter. Bake on a greased baking sheet about twelve minutes.
Yield: Two dozen.

Potato Biscuits

MAINE

⅓	cup shortening, melted	4	teaspoons baking powder
1	cup mashed potatoes	2	tablespoons sugar
1½	cups flour	½	cup milk.
½	teaspoon salt		

1. Preheat the oven to 400 degrees.
2. Stir the shortening into the potatoes. Sift together the flour, salt, baking powder and sugar and add to the potato mixture. Mix well.
3. Add the milk all at once and mix just enough to moisten.
4. Turn out onto a lightly floured board and knead twenty times.
5. Flatten dough into one-inch-thick rectangle. Cut into rounds. Bake on a greased baking sheet about twenty minutes, or until done.
Yield: Ten to twelve.

Clam Biscuits

MASSACHUSETTS

2	cups flour	1	cup clams, drained and
½	teaspoon baking soda		chopped
1	teaspoon cream of tartar	2	tablespoons butter
½	teaspoon salt		Salt and freshly ground
¼	cup lard		black pepper to taste.
1	cup milk, approximately		

1. Preheat the oven to 425 degrees.
2. Sift the flour, baking soda, cream of tartar and salt into a bowl. With the finger tips or a pastry blender, work in the lard.
3. Add enough milk to make a soft dough. Turn out onto a floured board and knead thirty seconds. Flatten with the hands to one-half-inch thickness and cut into two-inch rounds.
4. Place two teaspoons of the clams on half of biscuits. Top with dot of the butter, salt and pepper. Moisten edges of biscuits and top with second biscuit. Press to seal. Place on a greased baking sheet and bake fifteen to twenty minutes, or until done and golden.
Yield: Eight.

Quahog Popovers

MASSACHUSETTS

6	medium-size quahogs	2	eggs
¼	cup water	1	tablespoon oil
1	cup flour	½	cup milk.
⅛	teaspoon freshly ground black pepper		

1. Preheat the oven to 425 degrees.

2. Place the quahogs and water in a pan and steam until quahogs open, about five minutes. Remove meat and chop. Reserve quahog liquid.

3. Place the flour and pepper in a bowl. Add the eggs, oil, milk and one-half cup of the reserved quahog liquid. Beat until smooth.

4. Grease six deep muffin tins very well and heat in oven three minutes.

5. Stir chopped quahogs into batter and pour into muffin tins. Bake thirty-five to forty minutes.

Yield: Six.

Cranberry Corn Meal Muffins

MASSACHUSETTS

1½	cups flour	⅓	cup oil
1½	cups yellow corn meal	½	cup finely chopped cooked smoked ham
3	tablespoons sugar		
2	tablespoons baking powder	1	tablespoon chopped chives
1	teaspoon salt	1½	cups cranberries, rinsed and drained.
3	eggs, lightly beaten		
1½	cups milk		

1. Preheat the oven to 425 degrees.

2. Combine the flour, corn meal, sugar, baking powder and salt in a bowl.

3. Beat the eggs into the milk and oil and add to dry ingredients. Stir to moisten. Add the ham, chives and cranberries and mix.

4. Spoon into well-greased muffin tins. Bake fifteen to twenty minutes, or until done. Serve warm.

Yield: Two dozen.

Blueberry Muffins

MAINE

3	cups flour	2	eggs, lightly beaten
1	cup sugar	½	cup oil
4	teaspoons baking powder	1	cup milk
1	teaspoon salt	1½	cups blueberries.

1. Preheat the oven to 400 degrees.

2. Mix together the flour, sugar, baking powder and salt in a bowl. Combine the eggs, oil and milk and stir into the dry ingredients until just moistened.

3. Stir the berries into the batter and spoon into medium-size muffin tins lined with cupcake liners until about half full. Bake twenty minutes.

Yield: Two dozen.

Anadama Bread

CONNECTICUT

½	cup yellow corn meal, preferably waterground	1	tablespoon salt
2	cups boiling water	2	packages active dry yeast
2	tablespoons shortening	½	cup warm water
½	cup dark molasses	7	to eight cups sifted flour
			Melted butter.

1. Add the corn meal to the boiling water, stirring constantly. Add the shortening, molasses and salt and let cool to lukewarm.

2. Soften the yeast in the warm water and stir into the corn meal mixture. Add the flour gradually, stirring in just enough to make a stiff dough. Knead well and place in a bowl rubbed with shortening. Cover with a cloth and let stand in a warm place until doubled in bulk.

3. Slash through dough with a knife or punch dough with the fingers. Cover and let rise in a warm place forty-five.minutes longer. Pull out onto a lightly floured board and knead well, adding more flour if necessary.

4. Shape the dough into two loaves and place in two 9-by-5-by-3-inch loaf pans rubbed with shortening. Cover and let stand in a warm place until nearly doubled in bulk.

5. Preheat the oven to 400 degrees.

6. Bake the two loaves fifteen minutes and reduce the oven heat to 350 degrees. Bake about forty-five minutes longer. Brush the tops of the loaves with the melted butter and remove the bread from the oven to a rack.

Yield: Two loaves.

Brown Bread I
MASSACHUSETTS

¾ cup graham flour
¾ cup yellow corn meal
¾ cup flour
¾ cup dry bread crumbs
¾ cup molasses

2 cups sour milk or buttermilk
2 teaspoons baking soda
1 teaspoon salt
¾ cup ground raisins (optional).

1. Grease two coffee tins, each with a one-quart capacity. Or use other one-quart utensils suitable for steaming.

2. Combine all the ingredients in a mixing bowl and pour the batter into the prepared tins. The tins should be about two-thirds full. Cover with aluminum foil.

3. Steam in a closed steamer two hours.

Yield: Two loaves.

Brown Bread II
MAINE

1 cup yellow corn meal
1 cup rye flour
1 cup graham flour
2 teaspoons baking soda

1 teaspoon salt
2 cups buttermilk
¾ cup unsulphured molasses
1 cup raisins.

1. Combine the corn meal, rye flour, graham flour, baking soda and salt in a mixing bowl.

2. Mix together the buttermilk, molasses and raisins. Add to dry ingredients. Mix well. Fill well-greased pudding molds or cans two-thirds full with the batter. It will fill about three No. 2 cans or two No. 2½ cans.

3. Cover with greased mold covers or can lids and cover over with aluminum foil.

4. Place the molds or cans on a rack in a large kettle, with water ex-

tending at least halfway up the sides of the molds or cans. Cover and cook three hours, replenishing water as necessary.

Yield: Two or three loaves.

Blueberry Nut Bread

CONNECTICUT

2 cups flour	½ cup chopped nuts
¼ teaspoon salt	2 eggs, well beaten
3 teaspoons baking powder	1 cup milk
1 cup sugar	3 tablespoons oil.
1 cup blueberries, preferably wild	

1. Sift together the flour, salt, baking powder and sugar. Add the berries and nuts.

2. Combine the eggs, milk and oil and stir in just to moisten. Pour into a wax-paper-lined 9-by-5-by-3-inch loaf pan. Let stand twenty minutes.

3. Preheat the oven to 350 degrees.

4. Bake loaf one hour, or until done.

Yield: One loaf.

High Fiber Bread

NEW HAMPSHIRE

2 cups flour	1 cup whole bran cereal
⅓ cup sugar	½ cup raisins
1 tablespoon salt	2 eggs, lightly beaten
1 teaspoon baking soda	1⅓ cups buttermilk
1½ cups rolled oats	½ cup light molasses.

1. Preheat the oven to 350 degrees.

2. Sift together the flour, sugar, salt and baking soda. Stir in the oats, bran and raisins.

3. Combine the eggs, buttermilk and molasses. Add to dry ingredients and stir until just moistened. Pour into a greased 9-by-5-by-3-inch loaf pan. Bake one hour, or until done.

Yield: One loaf.

Banana Bread

CONNECTICUT

½	cup shortening	1	teaspoon lemon juice
1	cup sugar	2	cups flour
2	eggs, lightly beaten	3	teaspoons baking powder
1	cup mashed sieved ripe ba- nanas	½	teaspoon salt
		1	cup chopped walnuts.

1. Preheat the oven to 375 degrees.
2. Cream the shortening and sugar together until light and fluffy. Beat in the eggs. Mix the bananas with the lemon juice and mix into batter.
3. Sift together the flour, baking powder and salt. Stir into the batter. Fold in the walnuts.
4. Turn into a greased loaf pan and bake one and one-quarter hours, or until done.

Yield: One loaf.

Parker House Rolls

MASSACHUSETTS

1	cup milk, scalded	½	package active dry yeast
¼	cup sugar	¼	cup warm water
¼	cup plus three tablespoons butter	2	eggs, lightly beaten
¼	cup shortening	4	to five cups flour
1	teaspoon salt	2	tablespoons melted butter.

1. Combine the milk with the sugar, one-quarter cup of the butter, the shortening and salt. Stir to melt the shortening and dissolve the sugar. Cool to lukewarm.
2. Soften the yeast in the water. Stir until dissolved.
3. Add the eggs to the lukewarm milk mixture. Stir in the softened yeast. Add three cups of the flour and beat until smooth. Add enough remaining flour to make a soft ball of dough.
4. Knead the dough on a lightly floured board or in the bowl until dough is smooth and elastic, about eight minutes. Place the dough in a clean bowl, grease the top surface, cover with a damp towel and let dough rise in a warm place until doubled in bulk, about one hour.

5. Knock down the dough. Let rest, covered, about ten minutes. Knead three minutes on a lightly floured board.

6. Soften the remaining butter. Divide the dough in half. Roll out each half to one-quarter-inch thickness and spread each with one and one-half tablespoons softened butter. With a biscuit cutter, cut into two-inch rounds.

7. With the back of a knife, make a light cut, slightly off center, in each round and fold the smaller half over the larger, pressing edges together to secure. Place rolls close together on a greased baking sheet. Cover with a damp cloth and let rise in a warm place until doubled in bulk, about fifteen to twenty minutes.

8. Preheat the oven to 425 degrees.

9. Bake the rolls about fifteen minutes, or until golden brown. Brush with the melted butter and serve hot or, if desired, let rolls cool on a rack.

Yield: Three dozen.

Crescent Rolls
CONNECTICUT

2½ teaspoons active dry yeast granules or one three-quarter-ounce cake compressed yeast	¾ cup scalded milk, cooled to lukewarm, for dry yeast or one cup scalded milk, cooled to lukewarm, for compressed yeast
¼ cup warm water for dry yeast or one tablespoon warm water for compressed yeast	1 cup plus one tablespoon butter
2½ cups flour	1 egg yolk
1 teaspoon salt	2 tablespoons heavy cream.

1. Dissolve or soften yeast in warm water.

2. Put the flour and salt in a bowl and make a well in the center. Into this pour the cooled milk, the dissolved or softened yeast and one tablespoon of the butter.

3. Blend well and knead until the dough is smooth and elastic.

4. Refrigerate the dough on the bottom shelf of the refrigerator fifteen minutes. Roll out on a board to a 12-by-18-inch rectangle.

5. Soften the remaining butter. Score the dough rectangle into thirds

and spread half the softened butter over the center third. Fold one end of the dough over the butter. On this spread the remaining butter. Fold the other end over this and press the edges to seal.

6. With a rolling pin, roll out the dough to a 12-by-18-inch rectangle. Fold in thirds as before. Wrap dough in wax paper and chill one hour.

7. Roll dough into 12-by-18-inch rectangle, fold in thirds, wrap in wax paper and refrigerate two hours.

8. Roll out dough to one-eighth-inch thickness in a 12-by-18-inch rectangle. Cut into six-inch squares and then cut each square into four triangles. Starting with the wide end, roll the triangles; then bend into crescents. Place on a buttered baking sheet.

9. Cover with wax paper and refrigerate thirty minutes or longer.

10. Preheat the oven to 475 degrees.

11. Blend the egg yolk with the cream and brush over the crescents. Bake five minutes and reduce oven heat to 400 degrees. Bake until crescents are golden, about ten minutes longer.

Yield: Two dozen.

Pumpkin Rolls
NEW HAMPSHIRE

1	cup canned or homemade pumpkin puree	¼	cup warm water
½	cup sugar	½	cup melted shortening
1½	teaspoons salt	2	teaspoons grated lemon rind
1	cup milk, scalded	5	cups flour
1	package active dry yeast		Melted butter.

1. Day before, combine the pumpkin, sugar, salt and milk in a large bowl and beat until smooth and lukewarm.

2. Dissolve the yeast in the water and add to the lukewarm mixture. Add the shortening and lemon rind and mix well.

3. Add about half the flour and beat until batter is smooth. Add remaining flour to make a soft dough. Mix well with the hands or a wooden spoon. Cover and let rise in a warm place until doubled in bulk. Cover dough with wax paper and a towel and chill overnight in the refrigerator.

4. Next day, shape the dough by dividing into thirty-two equal portions. For cloverleaf rolls, make three balls out of each portion and drop

into greased medium-size muffin tins. The dough may be made into other shapes if desired.

5. Brush the top of the rolls lightly with melted butter. Cover and let rise in a warm place until doubled in bulk, about one and one-quarter hours.

6. Preheat the oven to 375 degrees.

7. Bake rolls twenty-five to thirty-minutes, or until done. Brush with melted butter and cool on a rack.

Yield: Thirty-two.

Round Rye Loaves

RHODE ISLAND

3	packages active dry yeast	2¾	cups rye flour
1½	cups warm water	2	tablespoons shortening
¼	cup molasses	3½	cups to four cups flour
⅓	cup sugar	1	egg white
4	teaspoons salt	2	tablespoons water.
3	tablespoons caraway seeds		

1. Dissolve the yeast in the warm water. Stir in the molasses, sugar, salt and caraway seeds.

2. Stir in the rye flour until smooth.

3. Work in the shortening. With the hands, work in enough of the regular flour to make a dough that can be handled. Turn onto a floured board and knead until smooth, about ten minutes.

4. Place in a clean greased bowl, cover and let rise in a warm place until doubled in bulk.

5. Shape into two round, slightly flattened loaves. Place far apart on a greased large baking sheet. Cover with a damp cloth and let rise in a warm place until doubled in bulk.

6. Preheat the oven to 375 degrees.

7. Mix the egg white with the water and use to brush the loaves. Bake thirty to forty minutes, or until done.

Yield: Two loaves.

Pumpkin Bread
NEW HAMPSHIRE

1	cup warm water	2	teaspoons salt
¾	cup sugar	1	cup pumpkin puree
1	package active dry yeast	½	cup non-fat dry milk solids
3	tablespoons oil	5	cups flour, approximately.

1. Place the water, sugar and yeast in mixing bowl. Let stand five minutes.

2. Add the oil, salt, pumpkin and milk solids and beat well.

3. Gradually beat in enough flour to give a manageable dough. Knead on a lightly floured board until smooth. Place in a clean greased bowl, cover and let rise until doubled in bulk.

4. Knead briefly, cover and let rise again until doubled in bulk.

5. Punch dough down and shape into two rolls to fit two greased 8½-by-4½-by-2½-inch loaf pans. Put dough into pans, cover and let rise until doubled in bulk.

6. Preheat the oven to 400 degrees.

7. Bake twenty-five to thirty minutes.

Yield: Two loaves.

Potato Bread
MAINE

1	package active dry yeast	1	teaspoon salt
½	cup lukewarm water	2	eggs, lightly beaten
1	cup milk, scalded	½	cup mashed potatoes
⅔	cup sugar	6	cups flour, approximately.

1. Dissolve the yeast in the water. Combine the milk, sugar and salt and let stand until lukewarm.

2. Beat the eggs into the mashed potatoes and gradually beat in the cooled milk mixture. Add the dissolved yeast.

3. Stir in enough flour to make a manageable dough. Turn onto a lightly floured board and knead until smooth, about ten minutes. Place in a clean greased bowl, cover and let rise until doubled in bulk, about one hour.

4. Knock dough down and shape into two loaves. Place in two

greased 9-by-5-by-3-inch loaf pans. Cover with a damp cloth and let rise in a warm place until doubled in bulk.

5. Preheat the oven to 375 degrees.

6. Bake forty minutes, or until done.

Yield: Two loaves.

Zucchini Bread
NEW HAMPSHIRE

3	eggs	¼	teaspoon baking powder
1	cup vegetable oil	2	teaspoons baking soda
1½	cups sugar	2	teaspoons ground cinnamon
3	medium-size zucchini, grated and well drained	1	teaspoon salt
		1	cup raisins
2	teaspoons vanilla	1	cup chopped walnuts.
2	cups flour		

1. Preheat the oven to 375 degrees.

2. Beat the eggs lightly in a large bowl. Stir in the oil, sugar, zucchini and vanilla.

3. Sift together the flour, baking powder, baking soda, cinnamon and salt and stir into the egg mixture. Stir in the raisins and walnuts and spoon the batter into two well-greased 8-by-4½-by-2½-inch loaf pans.

4. Bake one hour, or until the centers spring back when lightly pressed with finger tips. Cool in pans on rack ten minutes. Remove from pans and cool on rack.

Yield: Two loaves.

Apple Bread
MASSACHUSETTS

1	package active dry yeast	¼	cup sugar
¼	cup lukewarm water	6	cups to six and one-half
2	cups lukewarm applesauce		cups flour
2	tablespoons butter		Melted butter.
1	teaspoon salt		

184

1. Soften the yeast in the water.

2. Combine the applesauce, two tablespoons butter, salt and sugar. Stir to dissolve sugar. Add the softened yeast and half the flour. Mix well.

3. Continue adding flour until a soft manageable dough is formed.

4. Knead on a lightly floured board until smooth.

5. Place in a clean greased bowl, cover and let rise until doubled in bulk, about one hour.

6. Knock dough down and divide into two. Let rest, covered, ten minutes. Shape into two oblong loaves and place on a greased baking sheet. Cover and let rise until doubled in bulk, about forty-five minutes.

7. Preheat the oven to 400 degrees.

8. Bake thirty to thirty-five minutes, or until done. Brush with melted butter.

Yield: Two loaves.

Rich Tea Loaf
CONNECTICUT

1	package active dry yeast	2	egg yolks
¼	cup lukewarm water	½	teaspoon salt
⅓	cup milk, scalded	1½	teaspoons grated lemon
¼	cup sugar		peel
¼	cup butter	¼	teaspoon lemon extract
1	egg, lightly beaten	3	cups flour, approximately.

1. Dissolve the yeast in the water.

2. Place the milk in a large bowl and add the sugar and butter. Stir to melt butter and dissolve sugar and let cool to lukewarm.

3. Beat the egg and egg yolks together and add to the yeast. Stir into the milk mixture. Add the salt, lemon peel and lemon extract.

4. Gradually stir in the flour to make a soft dough. Beat in the bowl with dough hook of electric mixer or with a wooden spoon until smooth.

5. Place the dough in a clean greased bowl, cover and let rise in a warm place until doubled in bulk, about one and one-quarter hours.

6. Knock dough down and knead lightly on a floured board. Roll into a 10-by-14-inch rectangle and roll up from the short end. Tuck the ends under and place in a greased 9-by-5-by-3-inch loaf pan.

7. Cover and let rise until doubled in bulk, about one hour.

8. Preheat the oven to 375 degrees.

9. Bake ten minutes, reduce the oven heat to 350 degrees and bake thirty minutes longer, or until done. Cool on a rack.

Yield: One loaf.

Jennie's Coffeecake Ring

VERMONT

Coffeecake ring:

2	packages active dry yeast	1	teaspoon salt
⅓	cup lukewarm water	2	eggs, lightly beaten
1	cup milk, scalded	1	teaspoon grated lemon rind
¼	cup butter	5	cups flour, approximately.
½	cup granulated sugar		

Filling:

¼	cup melted butter	½	cup raisins
⅓	cup light brown sugar	1	teaspoon cinnamon.
½	cup granulated sugar		

Frosting:

2	cups confectioners' sugar	¼	cup chopped walnuts or pecans.

1. To prepare coffeecake ring, dissolve the yeast in the water.

2. Combine the milk, butter, granulated sugar and salt in a bowl and cool to lukewarm.

3. Add the dissolved yeast, the eggs, lemon rind and enough flour to make a stiff batter. Beat well. Add more flour to make a soft dough. Turn out onto a lightly floured board and let rest, covered with a towel, ten minutes. Knead gently until smooth and satiny, about ten minutes.

4. Place in a clean greased bowl, cover and let rise in a warm place until doubled in bulk, about one hour.

5. Punch dough down and roll out into a large rectangle about one-quarter-inch thick.

6. For filling, brush the dough rectangle with the butter and sprinkle with the brown sugar, granulated sugar, raisins and cinnamon. Roll up from the long side like a jellyroll.

7. Arrange roll in a ring shape on a lightly greased baking sheet, pinching dough ends together. With scissors, cut slashes at an angle, about

two inches apart, three-quarters of the way through the dough from the outer edge. Turn the sections over on their side so that they are flat on the tin or slightly twisted.

8. Cover with a towel and let rise about twenty-five minutes, until almost doubled in bulk.

9. Preheat the oven to 375 degrees.

10. Bake twenty-five minutes, or until well browned and done. Cool on a rack.

11. To prepare frosting, combine the confectioners' sugar with enough water to give a smooth coating consistency. Spoon over the hot coffecake. Springle with the nuts.

Yield: One dozen servings.

Doughnuts
MASSACHUSETTS

3 eggs	1½ teaspoons baking powder
1 cup granulated sugar	½ teaspoon nutmeg
1 cup sour cream	½ teaspoon cinnamon
4 cups flour	Fat or oil for deep-frying
½ teaspoon salt	Confectioners' sugar.
½ teaspoon baking soda	

1. Beat the eggs until thick. Gradually beat in the granulated sugar. Stir in the sour cream.

2. Sift together the flour, salt, baking soda, baking powder, nutmeg and cinnamon and stir to make a soft dough.

3. Roll out the dough to one-half-inch thickness on a lightly floured pastry cloth or board and cut with a doughnut cutter.

4. Fry until golden, a few at a time, in the fat or oil heated to 375 degrees, turning once. Drain on paper towels. Dust with confectioners' sugar while hot.

Yield: About three dozen.

Orange Quick Bread
NEW HAMPSHIRE

3	oranges	3	teaspoons baking powder
	Lightly salted boiling water	1	cup milk
2	cups sugar	2	eggs, lightly beaten
2	tablespoons water	¼	teaspoon salt
4	cups flour	¾	cup chopped walnuts.

1. Preheat the oven to 350 degrees.

2. With a swivel-edge potato peeler, cut the orange part of the rind from the oranges. With scissors, cut the rind into slivers. Add the rind to a saucepan of lightly salted boiling water and simmer until tender, about ten minutes. Drain the rind.

3. Add one cup of the sugar and the two tablespoons water to the rind in a small saucepan. Boil until clear, about one minute. Cool. Sift the flour with the baking powder.

4. Add the remaining sugar, milk, eggs, salt and flour mixture to the cooled rind. Mix. Fold in the walnuts. Turn into two greased 9-by-5-by-3-inch loaf pans that have the bottoms lined with oiled paper. Bake about fifty minutes, or until the loaves test done.

Yield: Two loaves.

Pies, Cakes, Desserts and Cookies

Squash-Apple Pie
MASSACHUSETTS

1 cup cooked, mashed and sieved squash	½ teaspoon mace
	⅛ teaspoon ground cloves
1 cup thick tart applesauce	4 eggs, lightly beaten
½ teaspoon salt	1½ cups heavy cream
1 cup light brown sugar	1 unbaked ten-inch pie shell with stand-up edge.
1 teaspoon cinnamon	
1 teaspoon ginger	

1. Preheat the oven to 425 degrees.

2. Place the squash and applesauce in a bowl. Stir in the salt, brown sugar, cinnamon, ginger, mace and cloves.

3. Combine the eggs and cream and add to the squash mixture. Pour into the pie shell. Bake twenty minutes. Reduce oven heat to 350 degrees

and bake twenty to twenty-five minutes longer (a knife inserted into filling should come out clean). Cool and chill.

Yield: Eight servings.

Note: This pie can be made with egg yolks and beaten egg whites folded in or used for a meringue topping.

Apple Pie with Sour Cream
MASSACHUSETTS

⅓	cup plus two tablespoons flour	½	teaspoon vanilla
		1	cup sour cream
⅓	cup plus three-quarters cup sugar	6	medium-size apples, peeled, cored and sliced
1¼	teaspoons cinnamon	1	unbaked nine-inch pie shell, chilled
⅛	teaspoon salt		
1	egg	¼	cup butter.

1. Preheat the oven to 400 degrees.

2. Sift together two tablespoons of the flour, three-quarters cup of the sugar, three-quarters teaspoon of the cinnamon and the salt. Stir in the egg, vanilla and sour cream. Fold in the apples and spoon into the pie shell. Bake fifteen minutes.

3. Reduce the oven temperature to 350 degrees and bake thirty minutes longer. Meanwhile, combine the remaining flour, sugar and cinnamon. With a pastry blender or the finger tips, blend in the butter until the mixture is crumbly.

4. Increase the oven temperature to 400 degrees. Sprinkle crumb mixture over the pie. Bake ten minutes longer.

Yield: Six servings.

Brandied Apple Pie
MASSACHUSETTS

3	pounds tart green apples	¾	cup light brown sugar
	Juice of half a lemon	¼	cup granulated sugar
¼	cup brandy	¾	cup flour.
½	cup sweet butter		

1. Preheat the oven to 350 degrees.

2. Take two of the apples and reserve for another use. Peel the remaining apples and core them. Cut into thick slices and immediately arrange them in a buttered baking dish. Sprinkle with the lemon juice. Pour the brandy over the apples.

3. With the fingers, cream together the remaining ingredients. Spread this mixture over the apples and bake one hour. Serve hot.

Yield: Six servings.

Martha's Apple Pie
MASSACHUSETTS

	Pastry for a two-crust ten-inch pie	¾	cup light brown sugar
1	tablespoon butter	½	cup granulated sugar
¼	cup dry vermouth	1	teaspoon cinnamon
1	cup golden raisins	¼	teaspoon allspice
6	cups peeled, sliced tart apples	¼	teaspoon nutmeg
1	tablespoon lemon juice		Sweetened whipped cream (optional).

1. Preheat the oven to 375 degrees.

2. Roll out half the pastry and use it to line a ten-inch pie dish. Reserve the remaining pastry for the top.

3. Heat the butter and vermouth in a saucepan and add the raisins. Simmer until the raisins are soft. Drain and set aside.

4. Combine the apples, lemon juice, brown sugar, granulated sugar, cinnamon, allspice and nutmeg. Add the raisins and toss lightly. Pour the mixture into the pie dish. Roll out the remaining pastry and make a latticework top for pie. Bake about forty minutes, or until the crust is golden brown. If desired, serve with sweetened whipped cream on the side.

Yield: Six to ten servings.

Dutch Apple Sack Pie

MAINE

5 to six apples, peeled and sliced	1½ tablespoons butter, cut up very finely
½ cup light brown sugar	1 unbaked nine-inch pie shell
⅓ cup granulated sugar	3 tablespoons heavy cream
⅛ teaspoon salt	1 tablespoon milk
⅛ teaspoon allspice	½ teaspoon cinnamon.
2 tablespoons flour	

1. Preheat the oven to 425 degrees.

2. Mix together the apples, brown sugar, granulated sugar, salt, allspice, flour and butter. Turn into the pie shell.

3. Mix the cream and milk together and pour over the pie filling. Sprinkle with the cinnamon.

4. Slide the pie into a heavy, unglazed brown paper sack and fold over the open end. Place on shelf in middle of oven and bake about thirty minutes, or until apples are almost tender.

5. Remove pie carefully from the sack and allow to brown lightly, about fifteen minutes.

6. Cool the pie to lukewarm on a rack before serving.

Yield: Six servings.

Apple Turnovers

MASSACHUSETTS

Pastry:

2 cups flour	¼ cup sugar
½ teaspoon salt	½ cup sour cream.
¾ cup butter	

Filling:

2 tablespoons flour	4 tart green apples, peeled, cored and thinly sliced
½ cup sugar	
¼ teaspoon cinnamon	¼ cup butter.

1. To prepare pastry, sift the flour and salt into a bowl. With a pastry blender or two knives, cut in the butter until the mixture resembles coarse oatmeal. Mix in the sugar and sour cream.

2. Roll out the dough on a lightly floured pastry cloth or board into an approximate 18-by-9-inch rectangle. Fold lengthwise into three. Wrap in aluminum foil and chill two hours.

3. Preheat the oven to 375 degrees.

4. To prepare filling, combine the flour, sugar and cinnamon and toss with the apples.

5. Roll out the chilled pastry to one-eighth-inch thickness on a lightly floured pastry cloth or board. Cut into four-and-one-half-inch rounds.

6. Place a tablespoon or two of apple mixture in the middle of each round. Dot with the butter. Moisten the edges of each round, fold over and pinch with a fork to seal.

7. Place on an ungreased baking sheet and bake twenty minutes, or until golden and done.

Yield: One dozen to fourteen.

Blueberry Pie
MAINE

Pastry:

2	cups flour	⅔	cup shortening
½	teaspoon salt		Ice water.

Filling:

4	cups wild blueberries	¼	teaspoon salt
¾	cup to one cup sugar, depending on tartness of berries	¼	teaspoon lemon juice
		2	tablespoons butter, cut into three parts.
¼	scant cup flour		

1. Preheat the oven to 400 degrees.

2. To prepare pastry, combine the flour and salt in a bowl. With a pastry blender or the finger tips, blend the shortening in until mixture resembles coarse oatmeal. With a fork, mix to a dough with ice water. Chill twenty minutes if desired.

3. Roll out two-thirds of the pastry and use to line a nine-inch pie plate.

4. To prepare filling, combine the blueberries, sugar, flour, salt and lemon juice. Pour into the pie plate. Dot with the butter. Cover with the remaining pastry, rolled out.

5. Slit the crust in several places. Bake the pie fifty minutes, or until the crust is well browned.

Yield: Six servings.

Deep-Dish Blueberry Pie

MAINE

4 cups blueberries, picked over, rinsed and drained	Grated rind of half a lemon
¾ cup sugar	1 tablespoon lemon juice
1½ teaspoons tapioca	1 tablespoon butter
⅛ teaspoon salt	Pastry for one-crust pie
	Whipped cream.

1. Preheat the oven to 400 degrees.

2. Combine the blueberries, sugar, tapioca, salt, lemon rind and lemon juice. Turn the mixture into a 10-by-6-by-2-inch baking dish. Dot with the butter.

3. Roll the pastry into a rectangle one-eighth-inch thick and about one and one-half inches larger than the baking dish. Arrange the pastry lightly over the berries and trim the edges, leaving one-half inch overhanging. Moisten the rim of the dish, turn the overhanging edges of the pastry under and press it onto the rim. Flute or crimp the edge with the tines of a fork. Cut slits in the pastry for steam to escape. Bake the pie thirty to forty-five minutes, or until the crust is browned. Serve with whipped cream.

Yield: Six to eight servings.

Blueberry Sour Cream Pie

MAINE

1¼ cups graham cracker crumbs	¼ pound cream cheese
⅓ cup melted butter	2 cups sour cream
½ cup plus one teaspoon sugar	1 cup blueberries.

1. Preheat the oven to 350 degrees.

2. Combine the cracker crumbs, butter and one-quarter cup of the sugar. Line a nine-inch pie plate with the mixture and press down firmly. Bake eight to ten minutes, or until lightly browned.

3. Mix together the cream cheese, sour cream, and one-quarter cup of the remaining sugar. Pour into pie shell. Top with the blueberries and sprinkle with the remaining sugar. Bake five minutes. Cool and chill.

Yield: Six servings.

Custard Pie with Blueberries
MAINE

4 eggs	1 unbaked nine-inch pie shell
⅔ cup granulated sugar	1 cup blueberries, picked
½ teaspoon salt	over, rinsed and drained
½ teaspoon nutmeg	2 tablespoons orange juice
2⅔ cups milk	3 tablespoons confectioners'
1 teaspoon vanilla	sugar.

1. Preheat the oven to 425 degrees.
2. Beat the eggs with a rotary beater until throughly blended. Add the granulated sugar, salt, nutmeg, milk and vanilla and stir until smooth.
3. Pour the mixture into the pie shell. Bake fifteen minutes; then reduce oven temperature to 350 degrees and bake thirty minutes longer, or until a knife inserted in the filling about one inch from the pastry edge comes out clean. Cool.
4. Blend the blueberries, orange juice and confectioners' sugar and spoon over the custard before serving pie.

Yield: Six to eight servings.

Cape Cod Cranberry Pie
MASSACHUSETTS

2 cups cranberries	1 cup flour
1½ cups sugar	½ cup melted butter
½ cup chopped nuts	¼ cup melted shortening.
2 eggs, well beaten	

1. Preheat the oven to 325 degrees.
2. Spread the cranberries in the bottom of a well-greased ten-inch pie plate.
3. Sprinkle with one-half cup of the sugar and the nuts.

195

4. Add the remaining sugar to the eggs, beating well. Beat in the flour, butter and shortening. Pour over the cranberries.

5. Bake about one hour, or until crust is golden brown.

Yield: Six to eight servings.

Cranberry-Pumpkin Chiffon Pie
MASSACHUSETTS

1	tablespoon unflavored gelatin	1	baked nine-inch pie shell
¼	cup cold water	2	eggs, separated
1	cup cranberries	¼	teaspoon salt
1	cup plus two tablespoons sugar	½	teaspoon ginger
¼	cup chopped citron	½	teaspoon nutmeg
¼	cup chopped nuts	½	teaspoon cinnamon
½	cup chopped raisins	¾	cup mashed pumpkin
		⅓	cup milk
		½	cup heavy cream, whipped.

1. Soften one teaspoon of the gelatin in two tablespoons of the water and place over hot water to melt gelatin.

2. Put the cranberries through a food chopper, using medium blade. Add six tablespoons of the sugar, the citron, nuts and raisins. Add the melted gelatin and let mixture stand until thickened.

3. Spread over the bottom of the baked pie shell and chill until firm.

4. In the top part of a double boiler, beat the egg yolks with one-half cup of the sugar, the salt and spices. Stir in the pumpkin and milk. Cook over hot water, stirring constantly, until thick, ten to fifteen minutes. Remove from the heat.

5. Soften the remaining gelatin in the remaining cold water and add to the pumpkin mixture. Chill over ice water, stirring frequently, until thick.

6. Beat the egg whites until they stand in soft peaks, then gradually beat in the remaining sugar. Fold into the pumpkin mixture. Pour over the cranberry layer in the pie shell. Chill until firm. Top with whipped cream.

Yield: Six servings.

Vermont Pumpkin Pie

2 cups pumpkin puree
1 cup cottage cheese, sieved
½ teaspoon ginger
½ teaspoon cinnamon
1 teaspoon salt
¼ cup sour cream

2 eggs, lightly beaten
½ cup milk
¼ cup dry sherry
1 unbaked nine-inch pie shell
  Whipped cream.

1. Preheat the oven to 450 degrees.
2. Mix the pumpkin with the cottage cheese, ginger, cinnamon, salt and sour cream.
3. Beat the eggs with the milk and sherry and gradually stir into the pumpkin mixture. Pour into the pie shell.
4. Bake ten minutes. Reduce the oven temperature to 350 degrees and bake thirty minutes longer, or until set. Cool and chill. Serve cold, garnished with whipped cream.
   Yield: Six to eight servings.

Green Tomato Pie

VERMONT

6 to 8 medium-size green tomatoes, peeled and sliced
2 tablespoons lemon juice
2 tablespoons grated lemon rind
½ teaspoon salt

½ teaspoon cinnamon
2½ tablespoons cornstarch
¾ cup sugar
1 tablespoon butter
  Pastry for a two-crust nine-inch pie.

1. Place the tomato slices in a skillet. Add the lemon juice, lemon rind, salt and cinnamon. Bring to a simmer and cook, uncovered, about fifteen minutes, or until tomatoes are barely tender. Stir frequently.
2. Combine the cornstarch and sugar and stir into the hot mixture. Cook, stirring, until it thickens. Add the butter. Cool mixture to room temperature.
3. Preheat the oven to 425 degrees.
4. Line a nine-inch pie plate with half the pastry and turn the cooled tomato mixture into it. Top with the remaining pastry. Seal and decorate the edges and make a steam hole.

5. Bake about thirty-five minutes, or until the pastry is golden and cooked. Serve warm or cool.

Yield: Six servings.

Mince Pies

NEW HAMPSHIRE

Mincement:

1	pound beef suet, ground	1½	pounds currants
1½	pounds golden raisins, ground	1	pound dark brown sugar
½	pound prunes, pitted and ground	6	ounces chopped blanched almonds
½	pound dates, ground		Grated rind and juice of two lemons
½	pound mixed candied fruits, ground	1	teaspoon nutmeg
¼	pound citron peel, ground	1	teaspoon cinnamon
3	tart green apples, peeled, cored and grated or finely chopped	½	teaspoon ground ginger
		½	teaspoon ground allspice
		1	teaspoon salt
		½	cup dark rum or cognac.

Pastry:

Short crust pastry for two-crust pie

1   egg, lightly beaten.

1. Combine all the mincemeat ingredients very well, using the hands. Turn into clean jars and store, covered, in a cool, dark, dry place. The mincemeat will keep for months.

2. Preheat the oven to 425 degrees.

3. Roll out half the pastry to one-eighth-inch thickness and cut into two-inch rounds. Fit into small muffin tins. Fill with mincemeat. Roll out the remaining pastry and cut the tops to fit the pies.

4. Moisten the edges and pinch to seal. Make a steam hole in each pie, brush with the egg and bake about twenty-five minutes, or until golden brown. The pies are best eaten warm.

Yield: About six pounds mincemeat; pastry makes one dozen little pies.

Pioneer Lemon Pie

MASSACHUSETTS

3	slices stale firm white bread	2	teaspoons grated lemon rind
3	tablespoons butter	⅓	cup lemon juice
1	cup sugar		Pastry for a two-crust nine-
1	cup boiling water		inch pie.
2	eggs, separated		

1. Spread the bread with the butter and place in a bowl. Add the sugar and boiling water and let stand until cool
2. Preheat the oven to 425 degrees.
3. Beat the bread mixture until smooth. Stir in the egg yolks, lemon rind and lemon juice.
4. Roll out half the pastry and use to line a nine-inch pie plate.
5. Beat the egg whites until stiff but not dry and fold into the bread mixture. Pour into the pie plate. Cover with remaining pastry, rolled out. Seal the edges.
6. Bake pie thirty-five minutes, or until golden and done. Let cool to room temperature.
Yield: Six servings.

Yankee Pine Nut Pie

MASSACHUSETTS

½	cup sugar	1	teaspoon vanilla
	Salt to taste	2	tablespoons melted butter
1	tablespoon flour	1	cup pignoli (pine nuts)
1	cup dark corn syrup	1	unbaked nine-inch pie
2	eggs, lightly beaten		shell.

1. Preheat the oven to 300 degrees.
2. Sift the sugar, salt and flour into a mixing bowl. Stir in the syrup and eggs. Add the vanilla, butter and pignoli
3. Pour mixture into the pie shell and bake one hour. Let cool
Yield: Eight servings.

Pecan-Maple Pie
VERMONT

4	eggs	1	cup maple syrup
⅔	cup sugar	1	cup pecan halves
½	teaspoon salt	1	unbaked nine-inch pie
⅓	cup melted butter		shell, chilled.

1. Preheat the oven to 375 degrees.
2. With a rotary beater, beat together the eggs, sugar, salt, butter and syrup. Mix in the pecans and pour into the pie shell.
3. Bake fifteen minutes. Reduce the oven heat to 350 degrees and bake twenty-five minutes longer, or until the filling is set and the pastry is browned. Serve cold or slightly warm.

Yield: Six servings.

Peach Pie
CONNECTICUT

5	cups peeled, sliced ripe peaches	¼	teaspoon nutmeg
½	cup light brown sugar	⅛	teaspoon salt
1	tablespoon cornstarch		Pastry for a two-crust nine-inch or ten-inch pie
½	teaspoon cinnamon	1½	cups sour cream.

1. Preheat the oven to 425 degrees.
2. Combine the peaches, brown sugar, cornstarch, cinnamon, nutmeg and salt. Line the bottom of a nine-inch or ten-inch pie plate with the rolled-out pastry.
3. Turn the fruit into the pie plate. Pour the sour cream over all. Top with the remaining pastry, rolled out. Seal and decorate the edges and make a steam hole. Bake twenty-five to thirty-five minutes, or until the pastry is golden.

Yield: Six servings.

Raisin Sour Cream Pie

CONNECTICUT

Crust:

1	cup flour	3	tablespoons water, approximately.
¼	teaspoon salt		
3	tablespoons butter		
2	tablespoons lard or shortening		

Filling:

3	eggs, lightly beaten	1	cup cooked, pitted, chopped prunes
¾	cup honey	1	cup raisins
1	cup sour cream	½	cup chopped walnuts.
1	tablespoon lemon juice		

1. Preheat the oven to 350 degrees.

2. To prepare crust, sift the flour and salt into a bowl. With a pastry blender or the finger tips, blend in the butter and lard or shortening.

3. Using a fork, mix to a dough with the water.

4. Roll out the dough on a lightly floured board and use to line a nine-inch pie plate. Decorate the edge.

5. To prepare filling, blend the eggs with the honey, sour cream and lemon juice. Fold in the prunes and raisins. Pour into the pie shell and sprinkle the walnuts over the top.

6. Bake fifty to sixty minutes, or until a knife inserted in the middle comes out clean.

Yield: Six servings.

Sour Cream, Raisin and Walnut Pie

VERMONT

2	eggs, lightly beaten	½	teaspoon vanilla
1	cup instant superfine sugar	⅛	teaspoon salt
1	cup sour cream	2	teaspoons lemon juice
1	cup chopped raisins		Pastry for a two-crust nine-inch pie.
¼	cup coarsely chopped walnuts		

1. Preheat the oven to 450 degrees.

2. Combine the eggs and sugar and beat with a wire whisk until light and fluffy. Add the sour cream, raisins, walnuts, vanilla, salt and lemon juice. Blend well.

3. Line the bottom of a nine-inch pie dish with the rolled-out pastry and pour in the filling. Top with the remaining pastry, rolled out, and seal. Slit the top to permit steam to escape. Bake fifteen minutes and reduce the oven heat to 350 degrees. Bake one-half hour longer.

Yield: Six to eight servings.

Rutabaga Pie

MAINE

1½ cups cooked, mashed and sieved rutabaga or yellow turnip	1 teaspoon cinnamon
	½ teaspoon nutmeg
	¼ teaspoon cloves
1 cup light brown sugar	½ teaspoon salt
2 tablespoons unsulphured molasses	1 teaspoon vanilla
	1 unbaked deep nine-inch pie shell
2 eggs, lightly beaten	
1¼ cups light cream	½ cup heavy cream, whipped
½ teaspoon ginger	Sliced filberts.

1. Preheat the oven to 450 degrees.

2. Beat together the rutabaga, brown sugar, molasses, eggs, light cream, ginger, cinnamon, nutmeg, cloves, salt and vanilla. Pour into the pie shell and bake fifteen minutes. Reduce the oven heat to 350 degrees and bake about forty minutes longer, or until set. Do not overbake.

3. Cool. Serve topped with the whipped cream and sliced filberts.

Yield: Six servings.

Angel Food Cake

MASSACHUSETTS

1½ cups egg whites (nine large eggs)	1 cup granulated sugar
	1 teaspoon vanilla
1 teaspoon cream of tartar	1 cup confectioners' sugar
½ teaspoon salt	1 cup cake flour.

1. Preheat the oven to 375 degrees. Heat a nine-inch angel food pan in the oven five to ten minutes before using.

2. Beat the egg whites with the cream of tartar and salt until very stiff. Gradually beat in three-quarters cup of the granulated sugar until the mixture is very smooth and glossy.

3. Beat in the vanilla.

4. Sift together the confectioners' sugar and flour three times. Fold with the remaining granulated sugar into the egg white mixture.

5. Turn the batter into the prepared pan. Bake thirty-five minutes. Cool in the pan turned upside down.

Yield: Ten servings.

Apple Upside-Down Cake

CONNECTICUT

¼	cup butter	1¾	teaspoons baking powder
½	cup light brown sugar	¼	teaspoon salt
¼	teaspoon nutmeg	3	tablespoons shortening, at
2	large apples, peeled, cored		room temperature
	and thinly sliced	½	cup milk
1	teaspoon lemon juice	1	teaspoon vanilla
1⅓	cups cake flour	1	egg.
¾	cup sugar		

1. Preheat the oven to 375 degrees.

2. Melt the butter in an eight-inch square pan. Add the brown sugar and nutmeg and blend well. Remove from heat.

3. Arrange the apple slices, slightly overlapping them, on the brown sugar mixture. Sprinkle apples with the lemon juice and set aside.

4. Sift the flour with the sugar, baking powder and salt. Stir the shortening just to soften and stir in the flour mixture, milk and vanilla. Mix until the flour is dampened.

5. Beat two minutes with electric mixer at medium speed or beat 300 strokes by hand. Add the egg and beat one minute longer with the mixer or 150 strokes by hand. Pour the batter over the apples.

6. Bake thirty-five-minutes, or until done. Cool cake in the pan five minutes and then invert onto serving plate. Let stand one minute; then remove pan. Serve warm.

Yield: Six to eight servings.

Apple Coffeecake
CONNECTICUT

6 apples, peeled, cored and sliced (three cups)
5 tablespoons plus two cups sugar
5 teaspoons cinnamon
3 cups flour
3 teaspoons baking powder
1 teaspoon salt
1 cup oil
4 eggs
¼ cup orange juice
1 tablespoon vanilla
Whipped cream.

1. Preheat the oven to 375 degrees.

2. Combine the apples, five tablespoons of the sugar and the cinnamon and set aside.

3. Sift the flour, baking powder, salt and remaining sugar into a bowl. Make a well in the center and pour in the oil, eggs, orange juice and vanilla. Beat with a wooden spoon until well blended.

4. Drain the reserved apple mixture of excess moisture.

5. Spoon one-third of the batter into a greased nine-inch or ten-inch angel food pan. Make a ring of half the drained apple mixture on top of batter, taking care not to have any apple touching sides of pan.

6. Spoon another third of the batter over, make a ring of remaining apples and top with remaining batter. Bake one and one-quarter hours, or until done. Cover top with aluminum foil if top begins to overbrown.

7. Allow to cool to lukewarm in pan before turning out onto a serving plate. Serve immediately, with whipped cream.

Yield: Ten servings.

Note: This cake can also be made with peeled, pitted and sliced peaches.

204

Cottage Cheese Cheesecake

VERMONT

Crust:

2	cups zwieback crumbs	1½	teaspoons cinnamon
½	cup sugar	½	cup butter, melted.

Filling:

4	eggs	3	cups creamed cottage cheese
1	cup sugar		
1½	tablespoons lemon juice	¼	cup flour
⅛	teaspoon salt	2	teaspoons grated lemon rind
1	cup light cream	¼	cup chopped walnuts.

1. Preheat the oven to 350 degrees.
2. To prepare crust, combine all ingredients. Reserve three-quarters cup of the crumb mixture. With a spoon, press the remaining mixture into the bottom and sides of an eight-inch springform pan.
3. To prepare filling, beat the eggs with an electric mixer on low speed until light. Add the sugar gradually; then add the lemon juice, salt, cream, cottage cheese, flour and lemon rind. Pour into the prepared pan and sprinkle the top with the reserved crumb mixture and the walnuts.
4. Bake one hour. Turn off the oven heat, leave the door ajar and let the cake cool in the oven one hour. Chill on a rack in the refrigerator. Remove the sides of the pan before serving the cake.

Yield: Ten to one dozen servings.

Cheesecake

MASSACHUSETTS

1½	cups graham cracker crumbs	4	eggs
		2	egg yolks
¼	cup butter, melted	¼	cup heavy cream
4	eight-ounce packages cream cheese	¼	cup beer
		½	cup pineapple preserves, if desired, or three to four cups Strawberry Glaze (see below).
½	cup freshly grated Cheddar cheese		
1½	cups sugar		
1	teaspoon vanilla		

205

1. Preheat the oven to 300 degrees.

2. Mix the cracker crumbs with the butter. Press the mixture over the bottom and around the sides of a buttered nine-inch springform pan.

3. Beat the cream cheese until soft and creamy. Add the Cheddar cheese and gradually beat in the sugar.

4. Add the vanilla. Beat in the eggs and egg yolks, one at a time. Continue to beat until the mixture is smooth and satiny. Fold in the cream and beer.

5. Spoon the pineapple preserves, if used, over the bottom of the prepared pan. Pour in the cheese mixture. Bake about one and one-half hours, or until set.

6. Turn off the oven heat and allow the cheesecake to remain thirty minutes in the oven with the door ajar.

7. Cool cake on a rack. Chill thoroughly before serving. If the pineapple preserves were not used, the cake may be topped with Strawberry Glaze.

Yield: Eight servings.

Strawberry Glaze
MASSACHUSETTS

2	one-pound cartons frozen whole strawberries, thawed Cherry juice or water	2	tablespoons cornstarch or arrowroot.

1. Drain the strawberries very well, reserving the juice. Add the cherry juice or water to it until the liquid measures two cups. Set the berries aside.

2. Slowly mix the cornstarch with the liquid in a small pan. Gradually bring the mixture to a boil, stirring, and cook two to three minutes, or until thick and translucent. Cool and chill. Fold in the strawberries.

Yield: Three cups.

Rich Cheesecake
MASSACHUSETTS

Crust:

1	cup flour	½	cup butter
¼	teaspoon sugar	1	egg yolk, lightly beaten
1	teaspoon grated lemon rind	¼	teaspoon vanilla.

Filling:

5	eight-ounce packages cream cheese	3	tablespoons flour
¼	teaspoon vanilla	¼	teaspoon salt
1	teaspoon grated lemon rind	5	eggs
1¾	cups sugar	2	egg yolks
		¼	cup heavy cream.

1. Preheat the oven to 400 degrees.

2. To prepare crust, combine the flour, sugar and lemon rind. Cut in the butter until the mixture is crumbly. Add the egg yolk and vanilla. Mix.

3. Pat one-third of the dough over the bottom of a nine-inch spring-form pan with the sides removed. Bake about six minutes, or until golden. Cool.

4. Butter the sides of the pan and attach to the bottom. Pat the remaining dough around the sides to a height of two inches.

5. Increase the oven heat to 475 degrees.

6. To prepare filling, beat the cream cheese until fluffy. Add the vanilla and lemon rind.

7. Combine the sugar, flour and salt. Gradually blend into the cheese mixture. Beat in the eggs and egg yolks, one at a time, and the cream. Beat until smooth and creamy.

8. Pour the mixture into the prepared pan. Bake eight to ten minutes, or until the top edge is golden.

9. Reduce the oven heat to 200 degrees. Bake one hour longer, or until set. Turn off the oven heat and allow the cake to remain thirty minutes in the oven with the door ajar.

10. Cool the cake on a rack. Chill before serving. Top with strawberry glaze (recipe above) if desired.

Yield: Eight servings.

Aunt Maude's Cheesecake

NEW HAMPSHIRE

16	zwieback, crushed into crumbs	1½	pounds small-curd cottage cheese, forced through a sieve
¼	cup butter, melted		
1¼	cups sugar	1	teaspoon grated lemon rind
3	eggs, separated	¼	cup lemon juice
¼	cup flour	1	cup heavy cream, whipped.
⅛	teaspoon salt		

207

1. Preheat the oven to 300 degrees.

2. Combine the zwieback crumbs, butter and one-quarter cup of the sugar. Press half the mixture into the bottom of a buttered nine-inch spring-form pan.

3. Beat the egg yolks until thick. Add the flour, salt, cottage cheese, lemon rind, lemon juice and three-quarters cup of the remaining sugar. Mix well.

4. Beat the egg whites until foamy. Gradually add the remaining sugar. Beat until stiff. Fold with the whipped cream into the cheese mixture. Pour into the prepared pan. Sprinkle with the remaining crumbs. Bake one and one-half hours, or until set.

5. Turn off the oven heat and allow the cake to remain forty-five minutes in the oven with the door ajar. Cool on a rack. Chill.

Yield: Eight servings.

Maggie Murphy's Aunt's Coffeecake
MASSACHUSETTS

½	cup butter	1	cup milk
1¼	cups sugar	½	cup chopped dates
1	egg	½	cup chopped nuts
2¼	cups flour	1	teaspoon grated orange rind
4	teaspoons baking powder	2	teaspoons cinnamon.
¼	teaspoon salt		

1. Preheat the oven to 350 degrees.

2. Cream the butter and three-quarters cup of the sugar together until light and fluffy. Beat in the egg.

3. Sift the flour with the baking powder and salt. Add alternately with the milk to the batter.

4. Fold in the dates, nuts and orange rind. Spoon into a greased 9-by-9-by-2-inch pan. Mix remaining sugar with the cinnamon and sprinkle over cake. Bake forty-five minutes, or until done. Serve warm.

Yield: One dozen servings.

Sour Cream Coffeecake

MASSACHUSETTS

Cake:

1½ cups sour cream	3 eggs
1½ teaspoons baking soda	3 cups flour
¾ cup butter	1½ teaspoons baking powder
1½ cups sugar	1¾ teaspoons vanilla.

Topping:

¼ cup chopped pecans	1½ teaspoons cinnamon.
½ cup sugar	

1. Preheat the oven to 350 degrees.

2. To prepare cake, combine the sour cream and baking soda and set aside.

3. Beat the butter with the sugar until light and fluffy. Beat in the eggs, one at a time. Sift the flour and baking powder together and add to the batter alternately with the sour cream mixture. Stir in the vanilla.

4. Pour into a greased and floured nine-inch tube pan.

5. Combine the topping ingredients and sprinkle over the top of the cake. Bake one hour and ten minutes, or until cake tests done.

Yield: Ten to one dozen servings.

One-Bowl Coffeecake

CONNECTICUT

2 cups flour	Milk
3 teaspoons baking powder	2 nectarines, peeled, pitted
½ teaspoon salt	and sliced
¼ cup granulated sugar	3 tablespoons light brown
⅓ cup shortening	sugar.
1 egg	

1. Preheat the oven to 375 degrees.

2. Sift together the flour, baking powder, salt and granulated sugar. With a pastry blender or the finger tips, blend in the shortening.

3. Break the egg into a measuring cup and beat lightly. Add milk to

209

make two-thirds cup. Stir into the dry ingredients. Turn onto a floured board and knead thirty seconds.

4. Press into a greased nine-inch square pan. Cover with the nectarine slices and sprinkle with the brown sugar. Bake twenty-five minutes.

Yield: Nine servings.

Boston Cream Pie
MASSACHUSETTS

4	eggs	¼	teaspoon salt
⅛	teaspoon cream of tartar	2	cups milk
1¼	cups sugar	2	teaspoons vanilla
½	cup plus three tablespoons flour		Sweetened whipped cream (optional).

1. Preheat the oven to 350 degrees.

2. Separate three of the eggs. Beat the yolks until they are light and lemon-colored.

3. In a separate bowl, beat the egg whites until they are foamy. Add the cream of tartar and continue beating until stiff but not dry. Beat in one-half cup of the sugar.

4. Fold the yolks into the whites; then fold in one-half cup of the flour and half the salt.

5. Butter and lightly flour the bottom of a nine-inch cake pan. Pour the batter into the pan and bake thirty-five to forty minutes. Let cool.

6. Meanwhile, heat the milk in a saucepan. Beat the remaining egg lightly with the vanilla and remaining sugar, flour and salt. Stir into milk and cook, stirring, until thickened. Cool and chill.

7. Split the cake in half and fill with the custard. Chill. Serve with sweetened whipped cream if desired.

Yield: Six to ten servings.

Chocolate Cake

CONNECTICUT

Cake:

½	cup shortening	2¼	cups flour
½	cup sugar	1	teaspoon baking soda
3	eggs	1	teaspoon salt
1	teaspoon vanilla	⅔	cup cocoa powder
1	cup honey	¾	cup sour cream
1	teaspoon grated orange rind	¼	cup orange juice.

Frosting:

1¼	cups sugar	1	tablespoon lemon juice
¼	cup honey	2	egg whites
¼	teaspoon cream of tartar	¼	teaspoon salt.
½	cup minus one tablespoon orange juice		

Honey crumb topping:

1	cup flour	1	tablespoon honey
3	tablespoons light brown sugar	½	cup butter
		½	cup chopped walnuts.

1. Preheat the oven to 350 degrees.

2. To prepare cake, beat the shortening and sugar together until light and fluffy. Beat in the eggs, one at a time, very well. Stir in the vanilla, honey and orange rind.

3. Sift together the flour, baking soda, salt and cocoa powder. Stir the dry ingredients into the batter alternately with the sour cream and orange juice.

4. Divide the batter between two greased and floured nine-inch layer pans. Bake twenty-five to thirty minutes, or until done.

5. Let cool on a rack.

6. To prepare frosting, place all ingredients in the top of a double boiler over rapidly boiling water.

7. Beat constantly for about seven minutes, remove from the heat and continue to beat until the frosting is the correct consistency for filling and frosting the layers.

8. Meanwhile, increase the oven heat to 400 degrees. Combine the ingredients for the crumb topping and spread on a baking sheet. Bake twelve to fifteen minutes, stirring every three minutes.

9. The crumb topping may be stirred into the frosting before using to fill and frost the layers or may be sprinkled over the filling and the frosted cake.

Yield: Ten servings.

Rich Chocolate Cake
NEW HAMPSHIRE

½	cup butter	1	cup buttermilk
½	cup shortening	¾	cup cocoa powder
2	cups sugar	⅔	cup boiling water
4	eggs	1	teaspoon vanilla
2½	cups cake flour		Chocolate frosting (recipe
¼	teaspoon salt		below).
3	teaspoons baking soda		

1. Preheat the oven to 350 degrees.

2. Beat the butter, shortening and sugar together very well until light and fluffy. Beat in the eggs, one at a time.

3. Sift the flour with the salt and baking soda and fold into the batter alternately with the buttermilk.

4. Stir the cocoa powder into the boiling water until smooth. Stir with the vanilla into the batter.

5. Pour into three greased and floured eight-inch layer pans and bake about thirty-five minutes, or until done. Cool. Fill and frost with chocolate frosting.

Yield: Ten to one dozen servings.

Chocolate Frosting
NEW HAMPSHIRE

6	ounces (squares) unsweetened chocolate	⅛	teaspoon salt
		¾	cup milk
6	tablespoons butter	1½	teaspoons vanilla.
1½	pounds confectioners' sugar		

1. Melt the chocolate and butter in the top of a double boiler over hot water. Combine the remaining ingredients in a bowl and blend.

2. Beat in the chocolate mixture and let stand, stirring occasionally, until the frosting is of spreading consistency.

Yield: About three and one-half cups.

Coffeecake
CONNECTICUT

½ cup soft butter	1 teaspoon baking powder
1½ cups sugar	1 teaspoon baking soda
2 eggs	¼ teaspoon salt
1 cup sour cream	⅓ cup chopped pecans
2 teaspoons vanilla	1 teaspoon cinnamon.
2 cups flour	

1. Preheat the oven to 325 degrees.

2. Beat the butter and one cup of the sugar together until fluffy. Beat in the eggs, one at a time. Stir in the sour cream and the vanilla.

3. Sift together the flour, baking powder, baking soda and salt and stir into the batter until it is smooth.

4. Spoon half the batter into a greased nine-inch square baking pan. Combine the pecans, cinnamon and remaining sugar and sprinkle two-thirds of the mixture over the batter. Top with remaining batter and sprinkle with remaining nut mixture.

5. Bake fifty minutes, or until done. Serve warm.

Yield: Nine servings.

Old-Fashioned Cream Cake
MASSACHUSETTS

1½ cups sugar	1 cup heavy cream
4 eggs	1 teaspoon vanilla.
1¾ cups self-rising flour	

1. Preheat the oven to 400 degrees.

2. Beat the sugar and eggs together until very thick and pale. Fold in the flour alternately with the cream.

3. Stir in the vanilla.

4. Pour into a greased and floured nine-inch tube pan and bake fifteen

minutes. Reduce the oven heat to 300 degrees and bake thirty minutes longer, or until done.

Yield: Eight to ten servings.

Italian Custard Dessert
RHODE ISLAND

Spongecake:

6	eggs, separated	1	cup cake flour
1	cup sugar	1½	teaspoons baking powder
1	tablespoon lemon juice	¼	teaspoon salt.
1	tablespoon grated orange rind		

Custard filling:

½	cup sugar	½	teaspoon vanilla
¼	cup cornstarch	2	tablespoons crème de cacao
⅛	teaspoon salt	¼	cup Marsala wine
2	cups milk	1	cup heavy cream, whipped
3	egg yolks, lightly beaten	2	tablespoons chopped mixed candied fruits.
½	cup dark rum		

1. Preheat the oven to 350 degrees. Grease and flour a nine-inch springform pan.

2. To prepare spongecake, beat the egg yolks until they are very thick and pale; then gradually beat in the sugar until the mixture spins a rope when dropped from the beaters.

3. Beat in the lemon juice and orange rind. Sift together, twice, the flour, baking powder and salt and gently fold into the yolk mixture.

4. Beat the egg whites until stiff but not dry and fold into the batter. Pour into the prepared pan and bake about forty-five minutes, or until the cake tests done. Cool in the pan on a rack.

5. To prepare custard filling, combine the sugar, cornstarch and salt in a saucepan. Stir in the milk. Bring to a boil, stirring, and cook one minute.

6. Pour a little of the hot mixture into the egg yolks, mix and return all to the pan. Heat one to two minutes to cook the yolks.

7. Divide the custard into three bowls. Add two tablespoons of the

rum to the first bowl and chill. Add the vanilla to the second bowl and the crème de cacao to the third bowl and chill.

8. Combine the remaining rum with the Marsala. Split the cooled spongecake into three layers and sprinkle all layers with the rum mixture. Place the bottom layer in a shallow dish or deep plate. Spread with one of the cooled custards. Repeat with the other layers and the two other custards.

9. Frost with whipped cream and garnish with candied fruit. Serve immediately or refrigerate until serving time.

Yield: One dozen servings.

Old-Fashioned Fruitcake
NEW HAMPSHIRE

1½	cups shelled Brazil nuts, left whole	½	cup green maraschino cherries, drained
1½	cups walnut halves	½	cup raisins
1	eight-ounce package pitted dates, left whole	¾	cup flour
⅔	cup chopped candied orange peel	¾	cup sugar
		½	teaspoon baking powder
½	cup red maraschino cherries, drained	½	teaspoon salt
		3	eggs
		1	teaspoon vanilla.

1. Preheat the oven to 300 degrees.

2. Mix together the Brazil nuts, walnut halves, dates, orange peel, red cherries, green cherries and raisins. Sift together the flour, sugar, baking powder and salt and sprinkle over the fruit mixture.

3. Beat the eggs until light and fluffy, add the vanilla and combine with the fruit mixture. The resulting mixture will be stiff.

4. The baking utensil(s) to be used should be greased, lined with unglazed brown paper, parchment paper or wax paper and greased again. Spoon the fruitcake mixture into a prepared 9-by-5-by-3-inch loaf pan or one-and-one-half-quart mold or into two prepared one-pound coffee cans.

5. Bake the loaf one and three-quarter hours and the other tins two hours. Cool cake in baking utensil(s) ten minutes; then loosen and finish cooling on a rack.

Yield: About fourteen servings.

Christmas Cake
CONNECTICUT

½ cup shortening	½ teaspoon salt
½ cup butter	1 cup milk
1 cup granulated sugar	1 cup golden raisins
1 cup light brown sugar	½ cup green glacé cherries,
3 eggs	chopped
1 teaspoon vanilla	¾ cup drained maraschino
1 teaspoon lemon extract	cherries, chopped
1 teaspoon almond extract	1 cup chopped mixed glacé
3 cups flour	fruits
1½ teaspoons baking powder	½ cup chopped walnuts.

1. Preheat the oven to 250 degrees.

2. Beat the shortening, butter, granulated sugar and brown sugar together until light and fluffy. Beat in the eggs, one at a time. Beat in the vanilla, lemon and almond extracts.

3. Sift together the flour, baking powder and salt. Reserve one-half cup of the flour mixture and stir remainder into batter alternately with the milk.

4. Mix together the raisins, glacé cherries, maraschino cherries, mixed fruits and nuts. Toss with reserved flour mixture and stir into batter.

6. Grease a nine-inch tube pan with removable bottom, line with unglazed brown paper or parchment paper and grease again. Spoon batter into pan.

7. Bake three hours, or until the cake tests done. Cool thirty minutes in the pan, remove and finish cooling on a rack.

Yield: About fourteen servings.

Edna's Blueberry Gingerbread
MAINE

½ cup sugar	1 teaspoon ground ginger
½ cup shortening	2 teaspoons baking soda
2 eggs	1 cup boiling water
1 cup unsulphured molasses	1 cup blueberries, lightly
2 cups flour	floured
½ teaspoon salt	Whipped cream or vanilla
¼ teaspoon ground cloves	ice cream.
¼ teaspoon nutmeg	

1. Preheat the oven to 350 degrees.

2. Beat the sugar and shortening together until light and fluffy. Beat in the eggs, one at a time, very well. Beat in the molasses.

3. Sift together the flour, salt, cloves, nutmeg and ginger and stir into the batter.

4. Stir the baking soda quickly into the boiling water and stir into the batter. The mixture will be thin. Pour into a well-greased 10-by-14-inch pan or 11-by-16-inch pan.

5. Sprinkle the top with the blueberries and bake thirty to thirty-five minutes, or until done. The blueberries sink to the bottom. Serve warm straight from the pan, with whipped cream or vanilla ice cream.

Yield: About twenty servings.

Note: A delicious unfruited gingerbread can be made from this recipe by omitting the blueberries and adding two teaspoons ground ginger, instead of one, to the flour mixture.

Old-Fashioned Jellyroll
VERMONT

4	eggs, broken into a bowl and warmed to lukewarm without drying out	⅔	cup sugar
		1	teaspoon vanilla
		⅔	cup cake flour
1	teaspoon baking powder		Confectioners' sugar
¼	teaspoon salt	1	cup preserves.

1. Preheat the oven to 400 degrees.

2. Beat the eggs with the baking powder and salt until thick and very pale. Gradually beat in the sugar and continue to beat until thick. Beat in the vanilla.

3. Sift the flour twice and fold into the egg mixture. Spread the mixture over a 10-by-15-inch jellyroll pan that has been greased, lined with wax paper and greased again.

4. Bake twelve to fifteen minutes, or until golden. Turn out onto a cloth towel sprinkled with confectioners' sugar. Peel off the paper. Roll up from the long side, enclosing the towel.

5. Cool on a rack. When cake is cool, unroll, spread with the preserves and reroll without the towel. Serve in slices.

Yield: Ten servings.

Maple Sugar Cake

VERMONT

1	cup soft maple sugar	2	teaspoons baking powder
¼	cup shortening	1	cup milk
2	egg yolks	1	cup chopped nuts
1½	cups flour		Maple frosting (recipe be-
1	teaspoon salt		low).

1. Preheat the oven to 350 degrees.

2. Cream together the maple sugar and shortening until light and fluffy. Beat in the egg yolks.

3. Sift together the flour, salt and baking powder. Add to the batter alternately with the milk. Fold in the nuts.

4. Spoon into two greased eight-inch layer pans and bake about twenty-five minutes, or until done. Cool on a rack before filling and frosting with maple frosting.

Yield: Six to eight servings.

Maple Frosting

VERMONT

¾	cup maple syrup	1	egg white, stiffly beaten.
¼	cup sugar		

1. Place the syrup and sugar in a small pan and heat until the mixture spins a thread or registers 220 degrees on a candy thermometer.

2. Immediately pour the syrup slowly into the stiffly beaten egg white, continuing to beat until the mixture is cold.

Yield: About two cups.

Julia's Glazed Orange Cake

MASSACHUSETTS

Cake:

1 cup butter	3 cups cake flour
2 cups sugar	3 teaspoons baking powder
5 eggs	¼ teaspoon salt
½ teaspoon vanilla	¾ cup milk.
2 tablespoons grated orange rind	

Glaze:

¼ cup butter	⅓ cup orange juice.
⅔ cup sugar	

1. Preheat the oven to 350 degrees.

2. To prepare cake, cream the butter and sugar together until light and fluffy. Beat in the eggs, one at a time, very well. Beat in the vanilla and orange rind.

3. Sift together the flour, baking powder and salt and add to the batter alternately with the milk, ending with the flour mixture.

4. Spoon into a greased and floured ten-inch tube pan. Bake one hour, or until done. Cool in the pan on a rack two minutes.

5. Heat the glaze ingredients in a small pan until the sugar just dissolves.

6. Pour the hot glaze over the hot cake. Allow the cake to cool thoroughly in the pan before removing.

Yield: Ten to one dozen servings.

Greek Orange Cake

MASSACHUSETTS

Filling:

1 cup sugar	Grated rind of half a large orange
4 cups milk, boiling	
½ cup farina	2 eggs, lightly beaten.
¼ cup butter	

Syrup:

2 cups sugar	1 stick cinnamon.
2 cups water	

Pastry:

1 pound phyllo pastry or stru- del dough	½ cup melted butter, approxi- mately.

1. To prepare filling, add the sugar to the boiling milk and bring to a boil, stirring. Gradually stir in the farina and cook until thickened. Stir in the butter and orange rind.

2. Add a little of the hot mixture to the eggs. Return all to the pan and cook one minute longer. Allow to cool to room temperature.

3. Preheat the oven to 350 degrees.

4. To prepare syrup, combine the sugar, water and cinnamon stick and bring to a boil. Boil five minutes. Set aside to cool.

5. Remove one leaf of the phyllo pastry at a time, keeping the remaining leaves covered. Dot the edges with melted butter, fold in half, dot the edges with melted butter again and fold in half again.

6. Place two tablespoons of the cooled filling mixture at one end of the pastry. Dot the edges of the pastry with melted butter. Turn in the sides and roll up like a jellyroll. Continue shaping the rolls until all the filling is used.

7. Place the rolls with space between in a well-oiled baking pan.

8. Bake about twenty-five minutes, or until golden brown. Spoon the cooled syrup over the hot pastries.

Yield: Three dozen to four dozen.

Pound Cake
CONNECTICUT

1 cup butter	1 teaspoon almond extract
1 cup granulated sugar	3 cups cake flour
1 cup confectioners' sugar	2 teaspoons baking powder
4 eggs, separated	⅛ teaspoon salt
1 teaspoon vanilla	1 cup milk.

1. Preheat the oven to 350 degrees.

2. Cream the butter and gradually beat in the granulated sugar and confectioners' sugar until the mixture is light and fluffy.

3. Beat in the egg yolks, one at a time, well.

4. Beat in the vanilla and almond extract.

5. Sift together the flour, baking powder and salt and add to the batter alternately with the milk.

6. Beat the egg whites until stiff but not dry and fold into the batter. Turn into a well-greased heavy cast aluminum bundt pan and bake one and one-quarter hours. Cool in the pan thirty minutes before turning onto a rack to finish cooling.

Yield: Two dozen servings.

Note: Bundt pans are sold in specialty kitchen stores and large department stores.

Pumpkin Cake

VERMONT

2	cups sugar	2	teaspoons cinnamon
1¼	cups oil	1	teaspoon salt
1½	cups canned pumpkin	½	cup dark raisins
4	eggs	½	cup golden raisins
3	cups flour	1	cup chopped walnuts or pecans.
2	teaspoons baking powder		
2	teaspoons baking soda		

1. Preheat the oven to 350 degrees.

2. Place the sugar, oil and pumpkin in a large mixer bowl and beat well with the mixer at a medium speed.

3. Add the eggs, one at a time, beating well after each addition.

4. Sift together the flour, baking powder, baking soda, cinnamon and salt and fold into the batter. Stir in the raisins and nuts.

5. Pour into a greased ten-inch tube pan. Bake one and one-quarter hours, or until done. Do not open the oven door under one hour. Let cool slightly in the pan before turning out onto a rack.

Yield: One dozen servings.

Celebration Shortcake

MAINE

1¼ cups flour
¼ teaspoon salt
1 teaspoon baking powder
¾ cup 100 percent bran
1 three-ounce package cream cheese
⅔ cup soft butter
  Sugar
1 teaspoon grated lemon rind

1 tablespoon lemon juice
1 egg, lightly beaten
¼ cup apricot preserves
1 pint strawberries
1½ cups blueberries
1 cup ricotta cheese
¼ cup milk
½ teaspoon vanilla.

1. Preheat the oven to 375 degrees. Grease an 11-by-7-by-1½-inch baking dish or a ten-inch springform pan. Line the dish or pan with wax paper, allowing the paper to extend one inch above the top.

2. Sift together the flour, salt and baking powder. Stir in the bran.

3. Cream together the cream cheese and butter. Add one-half cup of the sugar and beat until fluffy. Beat in the lemon rind, lemon juice and egg. Stir in the dry ingredients.

4. Spread the dough in a very thin layer over the bottom of the prepared pan and up the sides in a thin layer to form a shell. Press a piece of greased wax paper down into the shell. Fit close to the dough at all points and let extend an inch above the pan. Fill with dried beans or rice.

5. Bake twenty minutes, or until the dough is set. Remove the top wax paper with the beans or rice. Reduce the oven heat to 350 degrees and bake fifteen minutes longer, or until done.

6. Set the pan on a rack and let cool thirty minutes. Lift out the shell and let cool. Spread the bottom of the shell with the apricot preserves.

7. Slice the strawberries and sprinkle with sugar to taste. Sprinkle the blueberries with sugar to taste. Alternating the berries, arrange them in four segments on top of the preserves.

8. Beat the ricotta with the milk until smooth. Blend in two tablespoons sugar, or to taste, and the vanilla. Serve on each piece of shortcake.

Yield: Six servings.

222

Maine Shortcake

Shortcake:

2	cups flour	½	cup shortening
3	teaspoons baking powder	⅔	cup milk
1	teaspoon salt	2	tablespoons butter.
3	tablespoons sugar		

Sauce:

½	cup sugar	2	pints blueberries
2	teaspoons cornstarch	1	tablespoon lemon juice
⅛	teaspoon salt	1	teaspoon grated lemon rind
½	cup water	1	cup heavy cream, whipped.

1. Preheat the oven to 450 degrees.

2. To prepare shortcake, sift the flour, baking powder, salt and sugar into a bowl. Cut in the shortening until the mixture resembles oatmeal.

3. With a fork, blend in the milk until the mixture is just moistened. Knead lightly twenty seconds and turn onto a lightly floured board. Pat or roll into a large round one-half-inch thick roll.

4. Place the dough on a greased sheet and bake twenty minutes, or until done. Split and spread with the butter.

5. While the shortcake bakes, prepare sauce by mixing the sugar, cornstarch and salt together in a small pan. Stir in the water and one pint of the blueberries. Bring to a boil and simmer until clear and thickened, about four minutes. Remove from the heat and add the lemon juice and lemon rind. Cool.

6. Spoon the sauce and remaining pint of the blueberries between and on top of the shortcake layers. Decorate with the whipped cream.

Yield: Six servings.

Spice Cake

MAINE

Cake:

1	cup raisins	½	teaspoon ground allspice
2⅔	cups cake flour	¾	cup butter
1	teaspoon baking soda	1½	cups light brown sugar
1	teaspoon salt	¾	cup buttermilk
1	teaspoon cinnamon	3	eggs
½	teaspoon nutmeg	1	cup finely chopped nuts.

Frosting:

2	egg whites	1	tablespoon light corn syrup
1½	cups light brown sugar	1¼	teaspoons vanilla
⅛	teaspoon salt		Toasted flaked coconut (see
½	cup water		note).

1. Preheat the oven to 350 degrees.

2. To prepare cake, rinse the raisins in hot water, drain and chop. Sift the flour with the baking soda, salt and spices.

3. Beat the butter to soften and cream it. Add the flour mixture, brown sugar and buttermilk and mix to moisten. Beat two minutes with electric mixer on medium speed. Add the eggs and beat one minute longer.

4. Stir in the raisins and nuts. Pour batter into three eight-inch layer pans lined on the bottom with paper. Bake twenty-five minutes, or until done. Cool.

5. To prepare frosting, combine the egg whites, brown sugar, salt, water and syrup in the top of a double boiler. Beat about one minute, or until mixed. Place over boiling water and beat constantly with a rotary beater or electric mixer seven minutes, or until frosting stands in stiff peaks.

6. Pour the frosting into a bowl, add the vanilla and beat until thick enough to spread. Use to fill and frost the cooled layers. Sprinkle with toasted coconut.

Yield: Ten to one dozen servings.

Note: To toast flaked coconut, spread in shallow pan and toast in 350-degree oven seven minutes.

Spongecake
CONNECTICUT

9 large egg yolks	2½ cups cake flour
1½ cups sugar	¾ teaspoon salt
¾ cup boiling water	3 teaspoons baking powder.
1 teaspoon lemon extract	

1. Preheat the oven to 350 degrees.
2. Beat the egg yolks until light. Gradually beat in the sugar until the mixture is light and creamy.
3. Beat in the boiling water and the lemon extract.
4. Sift the flour with the salt and baking powder and fold into the batter. Turn into a greased 15-by-10-by-2-inch baking or roasting pan and bake forty-five minutes, or until done. Cool in the pan on a rack.
Yield: Ten to one dozen servings.

Velvet Lunch Cake
MAINE

1 cup sugar	½ teaspoon nutmeg
½ cup butter	½ teaspoon ground cloves
1 egg	½ teaspoon cinnamon
1 tablespoon unsulphured molasses	1 cup sour milk or buttermilk
2 cups flour	½ cup raisins
½ teaspoon salt	½ cup chopped walnuts or pecans.
1 teaspoon baking soda	

1. Preheat the oven to 350 degrees.
2. Cream the sugar and butter together until very light and fluffy. Beat in the egg and molasses.
3. Sift together the flour, salt, baking soda, nutmeg, cloves and cinnamon and stir into the batter alternately with the milk.
4. Stir in the raisins and nuts and spoon into two greased and lightly floured eight-inch layer pans. Bake twenty-five minutes. Cool on a rack.
Yield: One dozen servings.

Yellow Cake

MASSACHUSETTS

Cake:

4 eggs, separated	1 cup cake flour
1 cup sugar	1½ tablespoons cornstarch
3 tablespoons water	¼ teaspoon salt
1 teaspoon vanilla	1 teaspoon baking powder.

Frosting:

1 envelope unflavored gelatin	1 cup sugar
1 cup cold milk	1 cup heavy cream, whipped
2 egg yolks, lightly beaten	½ cup buttered and lightly
1 teaspoon vanilla	salted pecans.

1. Preheat the oven to 350 degrees.

2. To make cake, beat the egg yolks with the sugar and water until very stiff and pale. Beat in the vanilla.

3. Sift together the flour, cornstarch, salt and baking powder and fold into the batter.

4. Beat the egg whites until stiff but not dry and fold in. Pour the batter into a lightly greased and floured nine-inch angel food pan. Bake forty minutes, or until done. Turn the cake upside down in the pan to cool.

5. To make frosting, sprinkle the gelatin over the milk to soften. Gradually bring to a boil and pour over the egg yolks, stirring vigorously. Stir in the vanilla and sugar until dissolved.

6. Let the mixture cool and, when almost stiff, fold in the whipped cream.

7. Remove the cake from the pan after loosening with a spatula. Pour the frosting over. Sprinkle with the pecans. If desired, the cake layer may be sliced crosswise through the middle to make two layers and filled with some of the pecan mixture.

Yield: Eight to ten servings.

Apple Cobbler

NEW HAMPSHIRE

2	cups thinly sliced, peeled and cored apples	3	teaspoons baking powder
½	cup light brown sugar	3	tablespoons sugar
¼	teaspoon almond extract	½	teaspoon salt
½	teaspoon cinnamon	⅓	cup shortening
½	teaspoon nutmeg	½	cup milk
1½	cups flour	1	egg, well beaten.

1. Preheat the oven to 400 degrees.
2. Arrange the apples in the bottom of a greased eight-inch square baking pan. Combine the brown sugar, almond extract, cinnamon and nutmeg and sprinkle over the apples. Place the pan in the oven.
3. Sift together the flour, baking powder, one tablespoon of the sugar and the salt.
4. With the fingers or a pastry blender, blend the shortening into the flour mixture until it resembles coarse oatmeal.
5. Add the milk and egg and mix just enough to moisten.
6. Spread the dough over the hot apples. Sprinkle with the remaining sugar and bake thirty-five to forty minutes.
Yield: Six to eight servings.

Apples in Cider

MASSACHUSETTS

4	cups cider	6	apples, peeled, cored and cut into three-quarter-inch slices
6	whole cloves		
1	two-inch piece cinnamon stick		
		¼	cup grenadine syrup
2	slices fresh gingerroot		Arrowroot.

1. Combine the cider, cloves, cinnamon stick and gingerroot in a saucepan, bring to a boil and simmer fifteen minutes. (If you prefer sweet desserts, one-half cup sugar, or more to taste, may be added to the cider mixture.)
2. Add the apple slices and poach until barely tender. Remove the apple slices to a serving dish and keep warm.

3. Add the grenadine to the cider syrup and boil to reduce the quantity by half. Strain the syrup, measure it and then thicken with one and one-half teaspoons arrowroot mixed with a little cold water for each cup of the syrup. Pour over the apples.

Yield: Six servings.

Maple Apples
VERMONT

6 tart firm apples, such as Cortland or McIntosh	2 cups water
2 cups maple syrup	Sweetened whipped cream (optional).

1. Remove the core from each apple, but otherwise leave them whole. Remove the peel from the upper half of each apple.

2. Combine the syrup and water, add the apples and simmer until tender, about one hour. Serve cold, with sweetened whipped cream if desired.

Yield: Six servings.

Apple Crisp
MASSACHUSETTS

Apple rolls:

2 cups flour	¼ cup melted butter
2 teaspoons baking powder	½ cup light brown sugar
1 teaspoon salt	2 cups peeled and diced tart apples
2 tablespoons lard	
1 tablespoon butter	½ teaspoon cinnamon.
¾ cup milk, approximately	

Sauce:

1 cup granulated sugar	1 teaspoon cinnamon
1 tablespoon flour	Whipped cream or ice cream.
½ teaspoon salt	
1 cup hot water	

1. Preheat the oven to 350 degrees.

2. To prepare apple rolls, sift together the flour, baking powder and

salt. With the finger tips, work in the lard and one tablespoon butter as though making pastry.

3. Mix to a soft dough with the milk. Knead one-half minute on a lightly floured board. Roll out to a rectangle one-quarter-inch thick.

4. Brush with the melted butter and sprinkle with the brown sugar, apples and cinnamon. Starting with the long side, roll like a jellyroll. Cut into one-inch slices and, with cut sides up, fit into a greased nine-inch square pan.

5. To prepare sauce, combine the granulated sugar, flour and salt in a small saucepan. Gradually stir in the water. Bring to a boil, stirring, and boil three minutes. Add the cinnamon and pour sauce while hot over rolls.

6. Bake forty-five to fifty-five minutes. Serve warm with whipped cream or ice cream.

Yield: Eight or nine servings.

Apple Pan Dowdy

NEW HAMPSHIRE

1½	cups sugar	2	teaspoons baking powder
⅓	cup molasses	⅔	cup shortening
½	teaspoon cinnamon	¾	cup milk, approximately
¼	teaspoon nutmeg	4	cups sliced, peeled and
¼	teaspoon salt		cored apples
2	cups hot water	2	tablespoons butter
2	cups flour		Heavy cream (optional).
½	teaspoon salt		

1. Preheat the oven to 350 degrees.

2. Combine the sugar, molasses, cinnamon, nutmeg, salt and hot water in a 13-by-9-by-2-inch baking pan. Set aside.

3. Sift the flour, salt and baking powder into a bowl. With a pastry blender or the fingers, blend the shortening into the flour until the texture resembles coarse oatmeal. Using a fork, mix in enough milk to give a soft biscuit consistency.

4. Roll out on a lightly floured board to one-quarter-inch thickness. Spread the apples over the dough. Roll up like a jellyroll and cut into five to six pieces.

5. Stand the pieces on end in the prepared baking pan, dot with the butter, cover with a dome of heavy foil and bake one and one-half hours, or until done. Serve with heavy cream if you wish.

Yield: Six servings.

Apple Pudding

MASSACHUSETTS

5 cups soft bread crumbs,
   made from three-day-old
   firm white bread with crusts
   removed
2 cups buttermilk
2 cups regular milk
3 pounds firm tart apples,
   such as greenings, peeled,
   cored and thickly sliced
¼ cup water

½ cup unsulphured molasses
⅓ cup sugar
4 eggs, lightly beaten
¾ teaspoon ginger
1 teaspoon cinnamon
¾ teaspoon nutmeg
⅛ teaspoon ground cloves
¼ teaspoon salt
⅛ teaspoon freshly ground
   black pepper.

1. Place the bread crumbs in a bowl and pour the buttermilk and regular milk over the crumbs. Set aside.

2. Preheat the oven to 350 degrees.

3. Place the apples and water in a skillet. Cover and cook gently until the apples start to soften but still retain their shape. Cool slightly.

4. Beat the remaining ingredients into the soaked bread mixture. Fold in the apples. Pour into a greased three-quart casserole or baking dish. Bake fifty to sixty minutes, or until set. Serve warm.

Yield: Ten servings.

Apple Snow with Custard Sauce

VERMONT

2 cups applesauce
¾ cup confectioners' sugar
1 teaspoon lemon juice
½ teaspoon grated lemon rind
½ teaspoon salt
½ teaspoon almond extract

2 eggs, separated
2 tablespoons granulated sugar
¾ cup milk
½ teaspoon vanilla.

1. Place the applesauce, confectioners' sugar, lemon juice, lemon rind, salt, almond extract and egg whites in the large bowl of an electric mixer. Beat at high speed until mixture holds peaks when beaters are lifted from the bowl.

2. Spoon into dessert glasses. Chill.

3. Meanwhile, combine the egg yolks, granulated sugar, milk, and

230

vanilla in a small saucepan and heat slowly, stirring constantly until mixture coats spoon. Do not allow mixture to boil.

4. Pour custard sauce into a small bowl, cover and cool. Spoon over chilled apple snow.

Yield: Four servings.

Blueberry Pinwheels
MAINE

1 cup blueberries	2½ teaspoons baking powder
2 tablespoons lemon juice	½ teaspoon salt
¼ cup plus two tablespoons sugar	¼ cup butter
	2 eggs
2 cups flour	½ cup milk, approximately.

1. Place the blueberries in a bowl and sprinkle with the lemon juice and two tablespoons of the sugar.

2. Preheat the oven to 375 degrees.

3. Sift together the flour, baking powder, salt and remaining sugar. With a pastry blender or the finger tips, work in the butter.

4. Beat the eggs lightly in a measuring cup and add the milk as necessary to make three-quarters cup. Stir the liquid into the flour mixture to make a dough.

5. Roll out the dough on a floured board into a one-half-inch-thick oblong measuring about 10-by-15 inches. Sprinkle the berries over the dough and press them gently into the dough. Roll up the dough from the long end and place on a greased jellyroll pan. Bake forty-five minutes.

Yield: Eight servings.

Fresh Blueberry Buckle
MAINE

½ cup butter, at room temperature	⅓ cup milk
	2 cups blueberries, picked over, rinsed and drained
1 cup sugar	
1 egg	½ teaspoon ground cardamon or allspice
½ teaspoon vanilla	
1⅓ cups flour	¼ teaspoon nutmeg
1 teaspoon baking powder	Sweetened whipped cream.
¼ teaspoon salt	

231

1. Preheat the oven to 375 degrees.

2. Using an electric mixer, cream together half the butter and half the sugar. Beat in the egg and vanilla.

3. Sift together one cup of the flour with the baking powder and salt. Starting and ending with the flour mixture, add alternately with the milk to the creamed mixture. Pour into a greased nine-inch square baking dish. Pour the blueberries over the batter.

4. Combine the remaining sugar, remaining flour, the cardamon and nutmeg. Using a pastry blender, cut in the remaining butter until the texture resembles that of coarse corn meal. Sprinkle over the blueberries and bake forty to forty-five minutes. Cool slightly before serving with sweetened whipped cream.

Yield: Six to eight servings.

Down-East Blueberry Cobbler
MASSACHUSETTS

2	tablespoons cornstarch	1	teaspoon cinnamon
⅔	cup sugar	1	cup flour
¾	cup water	1½	teaspoons baking powder
3	cups blueberries	½	teaspoon salt
1	teaspoon plus three table-spoons oil	⅓	cup milk
			Whipped cream.

1. Mix the cornstarch and sugar together in a saucepan. Stir in the water. Bring to a boil, stirring, and cook one minute.

2. Preheat the oven to 425 degrees.

3. Add the blueberries to the syrup and pour into a one-and-one-half-quart baking dish or a nine-inch pie pan. Sprinkle with one teaspoon of the oil and the cinnamon.

4. Sift together the flour, baking powder and salt. Combine the milk and remaining oil and add all at once to the flour mixture.

5. Stir with fork until mixture forms a ball. Drop spoonfuls onto fruit. Bake twenty-five to thirty minutes, or until lightly browned. Serve hot or warm, with whipped cream.

Yield: Six servings.

Cheese Delights
CONNECTICUT

1 one-pound-six-ounce loaf
extra-fresh soft white bread
1 seven-and-one-half-ounce
package farmer cheese
⅓ cup granulated sugar
½ teaspoon vanilla

1 egg
½ pound butter, melted and
clear yellow liquid poured
off for cooking (discard
milky solids)
¼ cup confectioners' sugar.

1. Remove the crusts from the bread slices. With a rolling pin, roll each slice until very thin.

2. Beat together the cheese, granulated sugar, vanilla and egg and spread one tablespoon of the mixture on each slice of rolled bread.

3. Roll up each slice and pinch the sides to hold together.

4. Heat the butter in a very heavy skillet and sauté the rolls, a few at a time, over medium heat until golden. Roll in the confectioners' sugar while hot.

Yield: Twenty-six pieces; about eight servings.

Steamed Chocolate Pudding
CONNECTICUT

6 tablespoons soft butter
¾ cup sugar
6 eggs, separated
5 ounces (five squares) semi-
sweet chocolate
1 cup milk
8 small slices firm white
bread, crusts removed and

bread cut into small cubes
(about two cups cubes)
⅓ cup ground almonds
Grated rind of half a lemon
2 tablespoons cracker crumbs
Whipped cream
Chocolate sauce (recipe below).

1. Cream the butter and sugar together and beat in the egg yolks, one at a time.

2. Melt the chocolate over low heat and beat into the creamed mixture.

3. Add the milk to the bread cubes. Soak five minutes; then squeeze dry, discarding any excess milk. Crumble the bread cubes and add with the almonds and lemon rind to the chocolate mixture. Mix well.

4. Beat the egg whites until stiff but not dry and fold into the pudding.

5. Butter a two-quart mold for steaming and sprinkle with the cracker crumbs. Pour the pudding mixture into mold and seal with a tight-fitting cover or aluminum foil and string.

6. Pour water to the depth of two to four inches in a kettle and bring to a boil. Place the sealed mold on a rack in the kettle and steam one hour.

7. To serve, unmold the pudding while hot and decorate with a border of whipped cream and a little of the chocolate sauce. Serve the remaining chocolate sauce separately.

Yield: Six or more servings.

Chocolate Sauce
CONNECTICUT

2	cups plus two tablespoons water	4	ounces (four squares) semisweet chocolate
1	cup sugar	1	teaspoon cornstarch
1	teaspoon vanilla	2	tablespoons butter.

1. Combine two cups of the water and the sugar in a saucepan and bring to a boil. Stir until the sugar is dissolved. Add the vanilla and chocolate and stir until the chocolate is dissolved.

2. Blend the cornstarch with the remaining water. Add to the chocolate mixture and bring to a boil. Stir in the butter and serve.

Yield: About two and one-half cups.

Chocolate-Walnut Mousse
CONNECTICUT

1	six-ounce package semi-sweet chocolate bits	¼	cup cognac
½	cup milk	1½	cups heavy cream, whipped
2	teaspoons unflavored gelatin	½	cup chopped toasted walnuts
2	tablespoons cold water	1	ounce (one square) semisweet chocolate, melted and cooled
2	eggs, separated		
⅛	teaspoon salt	½	teaspoon instant coffee powder
⅛	teaspoon cream of tartar		Walnut halves.
3	tablespoons sugar		

1. Day before, combine the chocolate bits and milk in a heavy saucepan and heat over very low heat, stirring occasionally, until chocolate melts.

2. Soften the gelatin in the water.

3. Beat the egg yolks lightly and add a little of the hot chocolate mixture. Return all to the pan and cook, stirring, until mixture thickens slightly. Do not allow to boil. Stir softened gelatin into hot chocolate mixture until dissolved. Cool to room temperature.

4. Beat the egg whites with the salt and cream of tartar until stiff. Gradually beat in the sugar.

5. Stir the cognac into the cooled chocolate mixture. Fold in the egg whites, one cup of the whipped cream and the walnuts. Turn into a six-cup dish or serving bowl and chill overnight.

6. Next day, fold the melted chocolate and coffee powder into the remaining cream. Using a pastry bag fitted with a star tube, pipe rosettes around the top of the mousse. Decorate with the walnut halves.

Yield: Six to eight servings.

Christmas Pudding
CONNECTICUT

1 cup dark brown sugar	2 cups flour
2 cups finely grated or ground beef kidney suet	½ teaspoon salt
	½ teaspoon ground cloves
1 cup soft bread crumbs	½ teaspoon cinnamon
1 cup currants	½ teaspoon nutmeg
1 cup raisins	2 eggs, lightly beaten
1 cup mixed candied fruit peels	1 cup unsulphured molasses
	1 tablespoon baking soda,
1 cup finely chopped, peeled tart apple	dissolved in one cup boiling water.

1. Mix together the brown sugar, suet, crumbs, currants, raisins, peels, apple, flour, salt and spices.

2. Beat the eggs and molasses together and add to sweet mixture. Stir in the dissolved baking soda. Spoon into greased one-pound pudding basins or coffee cans. Cover with wax paper and then a cloth or alumimum foil. Set in a steamer or on a rack in a pan with boiling water extending two-thirds the way up basins or cans.

3. Steam three hours. Cool. Store in freezer or refrigerator. Steam to reheat, about forty-five minutes. Serve with hard sauce (recipe below) or foamy sauce (recipe below).

Yield: Three one-pound puddings.

Hard Sauce
CONNECTICUT

1 cup sweet butter	⅛ teaspoon salt.
1 cup confectioners' sugar	
¼ cup dark rum, cognac or dry sherry	

Cream the butter and confectioners' sugar together very well. Beat in remaining ingredients and chill thoroughly.

Yield: About two cups.

Foamy Sauce
CONNECTICUT

½ cup butter	1 teaspoon vanilla or two tablespoons cognac
1 cup confectioners' sugar	
1 egg, beaten	⅛ teaspoon salt.
2 tablespoons hot water	

1. Cream the butter. Add the confectioners' sugar, egg and hot water.

2. Place bowl over hot water and beat until sauce thickens. Stir in the vanilla or cognac and salt and serve warm.

Yield: About two cups.

Coffee-Walnut Soufflés
CONNECTICUT

2 envelopes unflavored gelatin	4 eggs, separated
	2½ cups milk
1 cup sugar	1 teaspoon vanilla
4 tablespoons instant coffee powder	2 cups heavy cream
¼ teaspoon salt	½ cup finely chopped walnuts.

1. Combine the gelatin, one-half cup of the sugar, the coffee powder and salt in a two-and-one-half-quart saucepan.

2. Beat the egg yolks with the milk. Add to gelatin mixture. Stir over low heat until gelatin dissolves and mixture thickens slightly, about ten to twelve minutes.

3. Remove from heat and add the vanilla. Chill, stirring occasionally, until mixture mounds slightly when dropped from spoon.

4. Meanwhile, prepare collars on dessert glasses or demitasse cups by binding a double strip of alumimum foil firmly around top of each glass extending one inch above top rim of glass.

5. Beat the egg whites until stiff but not dry. Add remaining sugar gradually. Beat until very stiff.

6. Fold in gelatin mixture. Whip the cream and fold in with the walnuts. Spoon into prepared dessert glasses. Chill until firm.

7. To serve, remove collars. Garnish soufflés with additional chopped walnuts if desired.

Yield: Eight to one dozen servings.

Steamed Cranberry Pudding
MASSACHUSETTS

6	tablespoons butter	¼	teaspoon salt
¾	cup sugar	½	cup milk
2	eggs	2	cups cranberries
2¼	cups flour	½	cup chopped pecans
2½	teaspoons baking powder		Eggnog sauce (page 243).

1. Cream the butter and sugar together until smooth and creamy. Beat in the eggs, one at a time.

2. Sift the flour with the baking powder and salt and stir alternately with the milk into the batter. Stir in the cranberries and pecans.

3. Turn mixture into a greased six-cup mold or pudding basin. If the mold has its own cover, grease and place over pudding. If the mold has no cover, cover with aluminum foil and secure tightly.

4. Place mold on a rack in a kettle with boiling water extending halfway up the mold. Cover and steam one and one-half to two hours, or until done.

5. Let stand ten minutes. Unmold and serve with eggnog sauce.

Yield: Ten to one dozen servings.

Note: The pudding can be made several days ahead and kept refrigerated. To heat, wrap the pudding in aluminum foil and bake forty-five minutes in a 325-degree oven.

Cranberry Sherbet
MASSACHUSETTS

1	envelope unflavored gelatin	2	cups buttermilk
¼	cup lemon juice	1½	cups sugar
3	cups cranberry juice cocktail	1	teaspoon nutmeg.

1. Sprinkle the gelatin over the lemon juice and let stand five minutes. Heat gently, stirring until the gelatin dissolves.

2. Add the remaining ingredients, stirring until the sugar dissolves. Pour into an ice cube tray or metal pan and freeze until mushy.

3. Scoop mixture into a bowl and beat until smooth and fluffy. Return to the freezer and freeze until firm.

Yield: Five cups.

Hancock Village Steamed Ginger Sponge
MASSACHUSETTS

1	cup butter		ger, drained and cut into small pieces
2	teaspoons granulated sugar		
2	eggs, well beaten	7	teaspoons syrup from preserved ginger
2½	cups flour		
3	teaspoons baking powder	1	cup heavy cream
¼	teaspoon salt	4	tablespoons confectioners' sugar.
1	cup milk		
½	cup Canton preserved gin-		

1. Cream the butter and gradually add the granulated sugar. Stir in the eggs.

2. Sift the flour with the baking powder and salt and add alternately with the milk to the batter. Add the ginger and one teaspoon ginger syrup. Pour into a buttered one-quart mold and steam one and three-quarters hours.

3. Beat the cream until stiff, sweeten with the confectioners' sugar and flavor with the remaining ginger syrup. Unmold the ginger sponge and serve hot, with the ginger cream.

Yield: Six servings.

Homemade Ice Cream
NEW HAMPSHIRE

2 cups sugar	4 cups milk, scalded
2 eggs	2 cups heavy cream
⅛ teaspoon salt	2 teaspoons vanilla.
2 tablespoons flour	

1. Beat the sugar with the eggs, salt and flour until light, fluffy and pale.

2. Add two cups of the milk, beating well. Cool the remaining milk. Pour the egg mixture into a saucepan and heat, stirring, until the mixture thickens. Cool.

3. Add the cream and vanilla and pour into the can of an ice cream freezer. Add enough of the remaining cooled milk to fill the can within one inch of capacity level. Freeze according to manufacturer's instructions.

Yield: About one gallon.

Lemon Ice
CONNECTICUT

3 cups water	2 cups strained fresh lemon
2 cups sugar	juice
2 tablespoons grated lemon rind	Mint sprigs (optional).

1. Combine the water and sugar in a saucepan and bring to a boil. Simmer five minutes and cool.

2. Add the lemon rind and lemon juice.

3. Pour the mixture into a freezer tray and freeze.

4. When preparing to serve, shave the mixture by scraping the surface with a heavy spoon. Spoon into sherbet glasses and return to the freezer until ready to serve. Garnish with mint sprigs if desired.

Yield: Eight to one dozen servings.

Indian Pudding
MASSACHUSETTS

4	cups milk	½	teaspoon cinnamon
1	cup yellow corn meal	¼	teaspoon ground cloves
2	eggs, lightly beaten	¼	teaspoon ground ginger
⅓	cup finely minced suet	⅛	teaspoon allspice
½	cup sugar	⅛	teaspoon nutmeg
⅔	cup light molasses		Vanilla ice cream.
¾	teaspoon salt		

1. Bring the milk to a boil and add the corn meal gradually, beating vigorously with a wire whisk. When mixture starts to thicken, set it aside to cool.

2. Preheat the oven to 325 degrees.

3. When the mixture is nearly cool, stir in the remaining ingredients except the ice cream and mix well.

4. Pour into a buttered baking dish. Bake two hours. Serve piping hot, with vanilla ice cream on top.

Yield: Ten to one dozen servings.

Charles Street Indian Pudding
MASSACHUSETTS

4	cups milk	½	teaspoon salt
⅓	cup yellow corn meal	½	cup unsulphured molasses
¼	cup water		Butter
½	teaspoon ground ginger		Ice cream, heavy cream or
½	teaspoon cinnamon		hard sauce (page 236).
¼	cup sugar		

1. Pour three cups of the milk into a saucepan and bring just to a boil.

2. Moisten the corn meal with the water and stir mixture rapidly into the hot milk, using a wire whisk to prevent lumps. Simmer twenty minutes, stirring frequently.

3. Preheat the oven to 325 degrees.

4. Combine the ginger, cinnamon, sugar and salt and add to the mush. Stir in the molasses.

5. Butter a one-and-one-half-quart casserole and add the corn meal mixture. Gently pour the remaining cup of cold milk over the top, but do

not stir milk in. Dot the casserole with butter. Bake two hours. Serve hot, with cream, heavy cream or hard sauce.

Yield: Six servings.

Lemon Mousse
CONNECTICUT

3 eggs, separated	1 cup heavy cream, whipped
1 cup plus one tablespoon sugar	½ cup vanilla cookie crumbs.
Grated rind and juice of one lemon	

1. Combine the egg yolks, one cup of the sugar, the lemon rind and juice in the top of a double boiler. Heat over hot water, stirring until the mixture thickens. Do not boil. Cool.

2. Beat the egg whites until frothy, add the remaining sugar and beat until stiff. Fold into the cooled custard. Fold in the cream.

3. Pour into a buttered freezer tray. Sprinkle with the crumbs and freeze.

Yield: Four servings.

Orange Mousse
CONNECTICUT

3 eggs, separated	1 teaspoon grated orange rind
¾ cup sugar	2 cups heavy cream, whipped.
¾ cup orange juice	
1 envelope unflavored gelatin	

1. Beat the egg yolks until light and lemon-colored. Gradually add the sugar and continue beating until thick and creamy.

2. Add one-half cup of the orange juice and beat well.

3. Soften the gelatin in the remaining orange juice and melt over hot water. Add the gelatin mixture and the orange rind to the egg yolk mixture and blend well.

4. Beat the egg whites stiffly. Fold the whites and the whipped cream into the orange mixture. Pour into a deep serving bowl and refrigerate at least two hours before serving.

Yield: Six servings.

241

Grandma's Plum Pudding

MASSACHUSETTS

¾ pound ground beef suet
1¼ cups flour
1 teaspoon nutmeg
2 slices fresh firm white bread, crusts removed and bread made into fine crumbs
½ teaspoon salt
1 fifteen-ounce box seeded muscat raisins
1 fifteen-ounce box seedless raisins
2 eleven-ounce boxes currants
1½ pounds mixed candied fruit, finely chopped

½ pound pitted dates, chopped
6 ounces whole candied cherries, halved
4 ounces candied pineapple, chopped
Grated rind of one lemon
1⅛ cups firmly packed dark brown sugar
5 eggs, lightly beaten
1 cup cold strong black coffee
Cognac or dark rum (optional)
Eggnog sauce (recipe below).

1. Place the suet in a large bowl and add the flour, nutmeg, bread crumbs and salt.

2. Pull the seeded muscat raisins apart, removing any tiny stems or seeds. Add the muscat raisins to the flour mixture and toss to coat.

3. Pick over the seedless raisins and currants and add. Stir in the remaining fruits and lemon rind. Add the brown sugar, eggs and coffee and mix well.

4. Pack firmly into pudding molds or basins. Cover with aluminum foil. Set in a steamer or on a rack in a pan with hot water halfway up the molds.

5. When the water boils, reduce the heat and steam four hours, replenishing water as needed. Let the molds cool until they can be handled. Remove the foil and wash the outside of the molds. Cognac or rum can be poured over the puddings and they can be covered with fresh foil or plastic wrap. Reheat for serving by steaming one hour longer. Flame with cognac or dark rum. Serve with eggnog sauce.

Yield: Three three-and-one-half-cup puddings, each serving eight.

Eggnog Sauce
MASSACHUSETTS

1 cup butter	1 cup eggnog
1½ cups sugar	¼ cup dark rum.

Combine the butter, sugar and eggnog in a saucepan. Heat over low heat, stirring occasionally, until the mixture reaches serving temperature. Stir in the rum and serve.

Yield: Three cups.

Raspberry Cooler
CONNECTICUT

4 cups raspberries	4 teaspoons unflavored gelatin
2 eight-ounce containers plain yogurt	½ cup cold water.
6 tablespoons sugar	

1. Place three cups of the raspberries in an electric blender. Add the yogurt and sugar and blend until smooth.

2. Soften the gelatin in the water and then heat over hot water to dissolve. Stir into raspberry mixture.

3. Chill until mixture starts to thicken. Beat until creamy and then pile into serving dishes. Top with remaining raspberries, whole or pureed.

Yield: Six servings.

Honey Soufflé
VERMONT

4 eggs, separated	½ cup unsalted margarine, melted
2 tablespoons flour	1 teaspoon grated lemon rind
¼ teaspoon nutmeg	2 tablespoons finely ground almonds.
¾ cup confectioners' sugar	
2 tablespoons cream sherry	
½ cup honey	

243

1. Preheat the oven to 350 degrees.

2. Beat the egg yolks until light and creamy. Sift the flour, nutmeg and confectioners' sugar together and stir into the yolks.

3. Add the sherry. Mix the honey and margarine together and add slowly to the egg mixture. Add the lemon rind and beat until smooth.

4. Beat the egg whites until stiff but not dry and fold into honey mixture. Pour into an ungreased one-and-one-half-quart soufflé dish. Sprinkle with the almonds.

5. Place the dish in a shallow pan of hot water and bake thirty to forty minutes.

Yield: Four servings.

Sweet Potato Pudding
NEW HAMPSHIRE

⅓	cup peanut butter	½	teaspoon ground ginger
1¼	cups light corn syrup	¼	teaspoon nutmeg
2	cups mashed sweet potatoes	1	cup undiluted evaporated
½	teaspoon salt		milk
1	teaspoon cinnamon	3	eggs.

1. Preheat the oven to 350 degrees.

2. Mix the peanut butter and syrup together. Add the sweet potatoes, salt, cinnamon, ginger and nutmeg. Mix well.

3. Add the milk and eggs and stir until well blended. Pour into a greased baking dish and bake thirty-five to forty-minutes, or until set.

Yield: Four to six servings.

Almond Sheet Cookies
CONNECTICUT

1	cup butter	½	teaspoon cinnamon
1	cup sugar	1	tablespoon water
1	egg, separated	½	cup chopped blanched al-
2	cups flour		monds.

1. Preheat the oven to 350 degrees.

2. Cream together the butter and sugar until very light and fluffy. Beat in the egg yolk very well.

3. Sift together the flour and cinnamon and stir into the creamed mixture. Spread in a greased 10-by-15-inch jellyroll pan.

4. Beat the water and egg white together lightly. Brush over the top of the cake and sprinkle with the almonds. Bake twenty to twenty-five minutes, or until golden brown. Cut into squares or bars while hot.

Yield: Three dozen to four dozen.

Filled Applesauce Squares
MASSACHUSETTS

½	cup butter	¼	teaspoon nutmeg
1	cup light brown sugar	⅛	teaspoon ground cloves
1	egg	1⅓	cups quick-cooking rolled oats
½	teaspoon vanilla		
1⅓	cups flour	½	cup applesauce, preferably homemade
¾	teaspoon baking soda		
¼	teaspoon salt	½	cup chopped pecans
½	teaspoon cinnamon	1	cup raisins.

1. Preheat the oven to 350 degrees.

2. Cream the butter and brown sugar together until light and fluffy. Beat in the egg and vanilla.

3. Sift the four with the baking soda, salt, cinnamon, nutmeg and cloves and stir into the batter. Stir in the oats.

4. Pat two-thirds of the dough into a greased nine-inch square pan. Combine the applesauce, pecans and raisins and spread over the dough.

5. Flour a piece of wax paper generously and then, with flour-dipped finger tips, spread the remaining dough on the paper to form a nine-inch square. Invert dough square over the filling, releasing dough with the the help of a spatula. (Don't be upset if there are holes in the layer; this does not spoil the end result.) Bake about thirty minutes, or until lightly browned. Cool in the pan and cut into bars or squares.

Yield: Sixteen to twenty servings.

245

Apricot Bars

NEW HAMPSHIRE

6	cups flour	6	egg yolks
1	pound butter	2	tablespoons sour cream
½	teaspoon salt	1	cup to one and one-half
1½	cups sugar		cups apricot preserves.
2	teaspoons baking powder		
	Grated rind and juice of half		
	a lemon		

1. Preheat the oven to 350 degrees.

2. Place the flour in a large bowl and cut in the butter with a pastry blender or the finger tips as though starting pastry dough. The mixture should resemble coarse oatmeal.

3. Add all remaining ingredients except the preserves and work with the hands into a dough.

4. Cut off one-eighth of the dough and set aside. Using the fingers, spread the bulk of the dough evenly in a lightly greased 10-by-15-inch jelly-roll tin. Spread with the preserves.

5. Roll out the reserved dough to one-eighth-inch thickness on a lightly floured pastry cloth or board. Cut into pencil-thin strips and arrange over the cake in a crisscross lattice design. Bake twenty-five minutes, or until lightly browned.

6. Cool in the tin on a rack and cut into squares, triangles or bars. This is very rich.

Yield: About forty.

Carrot Cookies

MAINE

Cookies:

1	cup shortening	1	teaspoon vanilla
¾	cup granulated sugar	2	cups flour
1	egg	2	teaspoons baking powder
1	cup mashed cooked carrots,	½	teaspoon salt.
	cooled		

Frosting:

¼	cup orange juice		Confectioners' sugar.
1	tablespoon grated orange		
	rind		

1. Preheat the oven to 350 degrees.

2. To prepare cookies, cream the shortening and granulated sugar together until light and fluffy. Beat in the egg.

3. Beat in the carrots and the vanilla. Sift together the flour, baking powder and salt and stir into the batter.

4. Drop by teaspoonfuls, two inches apart, onto a greased baking sheet. Bake twenty minutes, or until done. Cool on a rack.

5. To prepare frosting, combine the orange juice, orange rind and enough confectioners' sugar to make a spreading consistency. Spread over the cooled cookies.

Yield: About thirty.

Coconut-Almond Bars

MASSACHUSETTS

1½ cups light brown sugar	1 cup shredded coconut
½ cup butter	2 tablespoons regular flour
1 cup cake flour	½ teaspoon baking powder
2 eggs, lightly beaten	⅛ teaspoon salt
1 cup slivered blanched almonds	¼ teaspoon vanilla.

1. Preheat the oven to 350 degrees.

2. Cream one-half cup of the brown sugar with the butter and stir in the cake flour.

3. Spread the mixture in a greased nine-inch square baking pan. Bake fifteen minutes.

4. Combine the remaining ingredients and spread over the partially baked mixture. Return to the oven and bake about twenty minutes longer, or until well browned. Cool in the pan; then cut into squares.

Yield: Three dozen one-and-one-half-inch squares.

Sour Cream Cookies

NEW HAMPSHIRE

½ cup shortening	½ teaspoon baking soda
1½ cups sugar	2 teaspoons baking powder
2 eggs	1 cup sour cream
2½ cups flour	1 teaspoon lemon extract
½ teaspoon salt	Grated rind of two lemons.

1. Preheat the oven to 350 degrees.

2. Cream the shortening and sugar together until light and fluffy. Beat in the eggs, one at a time.

3. Sift together the flour, salt, baking soda and baking powder and add alternately with the sour cream to the batter. Stir in the lemon extract and lemon rind.

4. Drop by teaspoonfuls, two inches apart, onto greased baking sheets. Bake fifteen minutes, or until lightly browned at the edges. Tops will be pale.

Yield: About four dozen.

Currant Cookies

MAINE

1	cup butter	3½	cups flour
1½	cups sugar	1½	teaspoons nutmeg
2	eggs	½	cup currants.
2	tablespoons cognac		

1. Beat together the butter and sugar until very light and creamy. Beat in the eggs, one at a time. Beat in the cognac.

2. Sift together the flour and nutmeg and add the currants. Toss.

3. Stir the flour mixture into the batter. Wrap in wax paper and chill several hours or overnight.

4. Preheat the oven to 350 degrees.

5. Roll out the dough to one-quarter-inch thickness and cut with a three-inch round cookie cutter. Transfer to a lightly greased baking sheet and bake fifteen to twenty minutes, or until lightly browned at the edges. The center remains pale. Cool on a rack.

Yield: Two dozen.

Isabella's Cookies

MASSACHUSETTS

1	cup shortening	1	teaspoon cinnamon
2	cups light brown sugar	1	teaspoon nutmeg
2	eggs	½	cup cold regular-strength
3	cups flour		black coffee
2½	teaspoons baking powder	2	cups raisins
½	teaspoon salt	1	cup chopped nuts.

248

1. Cream the shortening and brown sugar together until light. Beat in the eggs, one at a time.

2. Sift the flour with the baking powder, salt, cinnamon and nutmeg and add to batter alternately with the coffee. Stir in the raisins and nuts. Chill one hour or longer.

3. Preheat the oven to 375 degrees.

4. Drop batter by teaspoonfuls onto a greased baking sheet. Bake ten to twelve minutes. Remove at once from baking sheet and cool on a rack. Store tightly covered.

Yield: Six dozen.

Brownie Drops
NEW HAMPSHIRE

2 four-ounce packages German sweet chocolate	¼ teaspoon baking powder
1 tablespoon butter	⅛ teaspoon salt
2 eggs	¼ teaspoon cinnamon
¾ cup sugar	¾ cup finely chopped pecans
¼ cup flour	½ teaspoon vanilla.

1. Preheat the oven to 350 degrees.

2. Melt the chocolate and butter together in top of a double boiler over hot water, stirring constantly. Remove from heat and allow to cool.

3. Beat the eggs until foamy. Add the sugar, two tablespoons at a time, beating constantly until the mixture is very thick. (This takes at least five minutes with an electric mixer at high speed. It is egg, not flour, that thickens this mixture.)

4. Blend cooled chocolate mixture into egg mixture. Add the flour, baking powder, salt, cinnamon, pecans and vanilla.

5. Drop from a teaspoon onto greased baking sheets. Bake ten to twelve minutes, or until the cookies feel set when touched lightly. Cool on a rack. Store in tightly covered container.

Yield: About three dozen.

German Sweet Chocolate Brownies

NEW HAMPSHIRE

1 four-ounce bar German sweet chocolate	½ teaspoon lemon juice
5 tablespoons butter, at room temperature	1½ teaspoons vanilla
4 ounces cream cheese, at room temperature	½ teaspoon baking powder
1 cup sugar	¼ teaspoon salt
3 eggs	½ cup chopped walnuts or pecans
½ cup plus one tablespoon flour	½ teaspoon almond extract.

1. Preheat the oven to 350 degrees.

2. Melt the chocolate with three tablespoons of the butter over boiling water. Remove from the heat and let cool.

3. Cream together the cream cheese, one-quarter cup of the sugar and the remaining butter until light and fluffy. Beat in one of the eggs. Stir in one tablespoon of the flour, the lemon juice and one-half teaspoon of the vanilla. Set aside.

4. In another bowl, beat the remaining eggs until they are thick, gradually beat in the remaining sugar and continue beating until the mixture is thick.

5. Mix together the baking powder, salt and remaining flour and fold into the beaten egg mixture. Stir in the chocolate mixture, nuts, almond extract and remaining vanilla.

6. Spread all but one cup of the chocolate batter in a greased 9-by-9-by-2-inch baking pan. Top with the reserved cream cheese mixture and then spoon the remaining chocolate batter over the cheese mixture. Swirl through the batter with a spatula or knife to marble.

7. Bake twenty-five to thirty minutes. Cool. Cut into bars or squares and store in the refrigerator.

Yield: About twenty.

Gingerbread Men

RHODE ISLAND

¾	cup unsulphured molasses	2	teaspoons cinnamon
¾	cup butter	1	egg, lightly beaten
¾	cup dark brown sugar		Royal icing (recipe below)
4½	cups flour		Cinnamon candies
1	teaspoon baking powder		Candied cherries
1	teaspoon salt		Currants
½	teaspoon baking soda		Raisins.
2	teaspoons ground ginger		

1. Heat the molasses to the simmering point, remove from the heat and stir in the butter until it melts. Stir in the brown sugar. Cool.

2. Sift together the flour, baking powder, salt, baking soda, ginger and cinnamon. Stir along with the egg into the cooled molasses mixture. Mix well. Wrap in wax paper and chill one to two hours, or until firm enough to roll.

3. Preheat the oven to 350 degrees.

4. Roll out the dough to one-quarter-inch thickness on a lightly floured board or pastry cloth. Cut with a gingerbread man cutter.

5. Transfer to a lightly greased baking sheet and bake twelve to fifteen minutes. Cool on a rack. The gingerbread men may be decorated as desired with royal icing (recipe below), cinnamon candies, candied cherries, currants and raisins.

Yield: About eighteen.

Royal Icing

RHODE ISLAND

2	to three cups confectioners' sugar	⅛	teaspoon cream of tartar
		1	egg white.

Combine two cups of the confectioners' sugar with the cream of tartar and egg white and mix well. Add enough confectioners' sugar to make the icing a suitable consistency for forcing through a decorating bag or tube or for spreading with a spatula.

Yield: About three-quarters cup.

Miniature Holiday Cookies

MASSACHUSETTS

1	cup butter	5½	cups flour
1	cup shortening	1	teaspoon salt
1¼	cups sugar	1	teaspoon baking powder
1	egg		Chopped candied cherries
1	tablespoon vanilla		or citron peel.
¼	teaspoon lemon extract		

1. Preheat the oven to 375 degrees.

2. Cream the butter, shortening and sugar together until fluffy. Beat in the egg, vanilla and lemon extract.

3. Sift together the flour, salt and baking powder and add to the creamed mixture. Stir with a spoon or with the hand to incorporate the flour.

4. The dough may be rolled out immediately or chilled for a short period and then rolled.

5. Roll out one-sixth of the dough at a time on a lightly floured board to one-quarter-inch thickness. Cut with small, fancy cookie cutters and place on a lightly greased baking sheet. Decorate each cookie with a piece of candied cherry or citron peel.

6. Bake ten minutes, or until lightly browned. Cool on a rack. Store in an airtight tin or jar. The cookies will keep a week to ten days.

Yield: About three hundred and fifty one-half-inch to one-inch cookies.

Note: If the cutting becomes tedious, the dough can be rolled to one-quarter-inch thickness, sprinkled with sugar and cinnamon mixture (one-quarter cup sugar to one tablespoon cinnamon) and cut with a pastry wheel or knife into diamond shapes.

Lizzies

VERMONT

1	pound raisins	½	teaspoon allspice
½	cup whiskey	½	teaspoon nutmeg
¼	cup butter	½	teaspoon cinnamon
¾	cup light brown sugar	1½	tablespoons milk
2	eggs	¾	pound candied cherries
2	cups flour	¾	pound candied pineapple
½	teaspoon baking soda	3	cups pecans, chopped.
½	teaspoon ground cloves		

252

1. Soak the raisins in the whiskey one hour until plump.
2. Preheat the oven to 325 degrees.
3. Cream the butter and gradually beat in the brown sugar. Add the eggs, one at a time, beating well after each addition.
4. Sift the flour with the baking soda and spices. Add to creamed mixture alternately with the milk.
5. Add the plumped raisins, candied cherries, candied pineapple and pecans. Drop by teaspoonsfuls onto buttered baking sheets. Bake fifteen minutes, or until browned and done. Cool on a rack. Store in an air-tight container or freeze.

Yield: About four dozen.

Maple Syrup Wafers

VERMONT

½ cup maple syrup	½ cup flour
¼ cup butter	¼ teaspoon baking powder
⅛ teaspoon baking soda	⅛ teaspoon salt.

1. Preheat the oven to 350 degrees.
2. Combine the syrup and butter in a small pan and bring to a boil. Boil hard, while stirring, thirty seconds.
3. Sift together the remaining ingredients and add all at once, stirring briskly (the batter will be lumpy).
4. Drop by half teaspoonfuls onto a greased baking sheet, about four at a time. Bake six to eight minutes, or until golden.
5. Let set on the baking sheet a second or two and then, while still warm, quickly roll each wafer around the greased handle of a wooden spoon to shape a roll or a cone. Cool on a rack.

Yield: About twenty-eight.

Note: The cooled cones or rolls may be filled with whipped cream if desired.

Molasses Fruit and Nut Bars
NEW HAMPSHIRE

⅓ cup shortening
¼ cup granulated sugar
¼ teaspoon baking soda
1 teaspoon salt
1 teaspoon cinnamon
⅔ cup unsulphured molasses
1 egg

1¼ cups flour
1 cup finely cut dates
½ cup chopped walnuts
¾ cup confectioners' sugar
4 teaspoons water
1 tablespoon grated orange
   rind.

1. Preheat the oven to 375 degrees.

2. Cream together the shortening, granulated sugar, baking soda, salt and cinnamon. Beat in the molasses and then the egg. Stir in the flour, dates and walnuts.

3. Spread in a greased and lightly floured nine-inch square baking pan.

4. Bake twenty-five minutes. Cool. Turn out onto a cutting board.

5. Combine the confectioners' sugar, water and orange rind and spread over all. Cut into bars.

Yield: About forty-two.

St. Nikoloos Cookies
MASSACHUSETTS

½ cup butter
½ cup lard
1 cup sugar
2 cups flour
2 teaspoons cinnamon

¼ teaspoon nutmeg
¼ teaspoon ground cloves
¼ teaspoon baking soda
¼ cup buttermilk
½ cup chopped nuts.

1. Day before, beat the butter, lard and sugar together until creamy. Sift together the flour, cinnamon, nutmeg, cloves and baking soda and add with the buttermilk and nuts to the creamed mixture.

2. With the finger tips, work into a dough. With floured hands, shape the dough into two long rolls, each one inch to one and one-half inches in diameter. Wrap in wax paper and refrigerate overnight.

3. Next day, preheat the oven to 375 degrees.

4. Cut the rolls into one-eighth-inch slices and place on ungreased baking sheet. Bake until light brown, about eight minutes. Cool on a rack.

Yield: About three dozen.

Maple Nut Bars

VERMONT

1 cup shortening	½ teaspoon baking powder
1 cup soft maple sugar	¼ teaspoon salt
2 eggs	1 cup chopped walnuts
¾ cup flour	Confectioners' sugar.

1. Preheat the oven to 350 degrees.

2. Cream the shortening and maple sugar together. Beat in the eggs. Sift together the flour, baking powder and salt and stir into batter.

3. Stir in the walnuts and spoon into a greased eight-inch square baking dish. Bake thirty minutes. Cool in the dish. When cold, cut into bars and coat with confectioners' sugar.

Yield: Sixteen.

Frazer's Cheaters (Nut Squares)

CONNECTICUT

1 cup plus two tablespoons flour	2¼ cups light brown sugar
2 tablespoons granulated sugar	2 eggs
1 teaspoon salt	1 cup coarsely chopped pecans
½ cup butter	1 cup grated coconut.

1. Preheat the oven to 350 degrees.

2. Combine one cup of the flour, the granulated sugar and salt in a mixing bowl. Using a pastry blender, cut in the butter. Mix with the hands and press the dough over the bottom of an eight-inch square baking pan. Bake ten minutes.

3. Increase the oven heat to 375 degrees.

4. Blend the brown sugar, eggs, pecans, coconut and remaining flour. Spread the mixture over the bottom crust. Bake twenty minutes. Cool. Cut into squares and remove from the pan with a narrow spatula.

Yield: Sixty-four one-inch squares.

Orange Oatmeal Cookies

RHODE ISLAND

2 cups sifted flour
2 cups sugar
4 teaspoons baking powder
1 teaspoon salt
1 teaspoon nutmeg
1 cup soft shortening
2 eggs

2 tablespoons freshly squeezed orange juice
3 teaspoons grated orange peel
3 cups quick-cooking rolled oats.

1. Preheat the oven to 375 degrees.
2. Sift together the flour, sugar, baking powder, salt and nutmeg into a large mixing bowl.
3. Add the shortening, eggs and orange juice and beat until smooth. Stir in the orange peel and oats. Drop by teaspoonfuls onto an ungreased baking sheet. Bake twelve to fifteen minutes. Cool on a rack.
Yield: About five dozen.

Refrigerator Cookies

VERMONT

1 cup butter
2 cups light brown sugar
2 eggs, lightly beaten
1 teaspoon vanilla

3½ cups flour
1 teaspoon baking soda
1 teaspoon salt
1 cup finely chopped nuts.

1. Beat the butter and brown sugar together until light and fluffy. Beat in the eggs, one at a time. Beat in the vanilla.
2. Sift together the flour, baking soda and salt and stir into the creamed mixture. Stir in the nuts. Form into a roll two inches in diameter, wrap in wax paper and chill until firm enough to cut, about six hours.
3. Preheat the oven to 350 degrees.
4. Cut the roll into one-quarter-inch thick slices and place on an ungreased cookie sheet. Bake about eight minutes, or until lightly browned.
Yield: About five dozen.

Rocks

NEW HAMPSHIRE

1	cup light brown sugar	¾	cup chopped dates
¾	cup shortening	2	cups raisins
2	eggs, lightly beaten	2	cups chopped pecans or
2	cups flour		walnuts
1	teaspoon allspice	1	teaspoon baking soda
¼	teaspoon salt	1	tablespoon boiling water.

1. Preheat the oven to 350 degrees.
2. Cream the brown sugar and shortening together until light and fluffly. Beat in the eggs.
3. Sift the flour, allspice and salt into a bowl. Add the fruits and nuts and toss to coat. Stir into the batter.
4. Dissolve the baking soda in the boiling water and stir into the mixture. Drop by teaspoonfuls onto a lightly greased baking sheet and bake about fifteen minutes, or until lightly browned.

Yield: About four dozen.

Shortbread

MASSACHUSETTS

2	cups flour		Pinch salt
1	cup cornstarch	1	cup butter.
1	cup confectioners' sugar		

1. Preheat the oven to 250 degrees.
2. Sift the flour, cornstarch, sugar and salt into a bowl. Add the butter and, using the fingers or a pastry blender, work the butter into the dry ingredients very well. Flatten to about one-inch thickness in a circle or oblong shape.
3. Place on an ungreased baking sheet and mark into cookies by cutting about halfway through the thickness of the dough. Bake on the top shelf of the oven thirty minutes, turning the baking sheet after twenty minutes for even baking.
4. Cool the shortbread and cut into indicated shapes.

Yield: Eighteen to twenty-four cookies depending on size.

Crisp Sugar Cones

NEW HAMPSHIRE

¼	cup butter	¾	cup flour
½	cup sugar	1	cup heavy cream
2	eggs		Strawberry jam.

1. Preheat the oven to 300 degrees.

2. Melt the butter and stir in the sugar. Beat in the eggs, one at a time, and then the flour. Drop spoonfuls of the batter about four inches apart onto a well-buttered baking sheet. Smooth the batter into ovals. Bake about six minutes.

3. Remove the cookies with a spatula and quickly roll into cone shapes while the cookies are still hot and flexible. (Gloves may be handy for doing this.) Let the cones cool. Rebutter the baking sheet before each addition.

4. At serving time, whip the cream and fill the cones with it. Add a little strawberry jam to the center of the cream.

Yield: About fifteen.

Miscellaneous

Pickles, Relishes and Preserves

Easy Bread and Butter Pickles
VERMONT

25 cucumbers, each measuring
one inch to one and one-
half inches in diameter
(about four quarts),
scrubbed and thinly sliced
8 onions, thinly sliced
½ cup salt

5 cups cider vinegar
5 cups sugar
2 tablespoons mustard seeds
2 tablespoons celery seeds
2 teaspoons turmeric
½ teaspoon ground cloves.

1. Combine the cucumbers and onions. Sprinkle with the salt and let stand three hours. Drain well.

2. Add the remaining ingredients, bring to a boil and ladle immediately into hot sterilized canning jars. Seal immediately. Process in a boiling water bath ten minutes. Cool. Test seal. Store in a cool, dark, dry place.

Yield: About six pints.

Winchester Center Bread and Butter Pickles

CONNECTICUT

1	gallon cucumbers (about twenty-five)	4	cups sugar
8	small onions, chopped	3½	cups cider vinegar
1	green pepper, seeded and chopped	1½	cups water
½	cup coarse salt	1½	teaspoons turmeric
2	quarts ice cubes	1	tablespoon celery seeds
		½	teaspoon ground cloves
		2	tablespoons mustard seeds.

1. Wash the cucumbers and slice thinly into a large bowl or crock. Add the onions, green pepper and salt. Mix. Top with the ice cubes. Let stand at room temperature eight hours. Drain. Rinse lightly.

2. Combine the remaining ingredients in a kettle and add the cucumber mixture. Heat, stirring to dissolve the sugar, until the mixture comes to just below the boiling point. Pack into hot sterilized jars. Seal. Process in a boiling water bath ten minutes. Cool. Check seals. Store in cool, dry, dark place.

Yield: About five quarts.

Ernie's Mustard Pickles

CONNECTICUT

1½	quarts one-inch chunks halved, peeled cucumbers	1½	cups sugar
		¼	cup flour
2	large onions, chopped (about six cups)	1½	teaspoons celery seeds
		1½	teaspoons dry mustard
3	tablespoons salt	½	teaspoon turmeric
1	quart water	2	cups white vinegar.

1. Combine the cucumbers, onions, salt and water in a crock or earthenware bowl. Let stand at room temperature three hours.

2. Mix together the sugar, flour, celery seeds, mustard and turmeric in a saucepan. Gradually stir in the vinegar. Heat, stirring, until the mixture thickens and is smooth.

3. Drain the cucumbers and onions, rinse briefly and add to the boiling mustard sauce. Bring to a boil again. Pour into hot sterilized jars. Seal. Process in a boiling water bath fifteen minutes for pints, thirty minutes for quarts. Cool and store in a cool, dark, dry place.

Yield: About two quarts.

Green Tomato Mincemeat

MAINE

6	cups chopped peeled apples	1	teaspoon ground cloves
6	cups chopped peeled green	¾	teaspoon ground allspice
	tomatoes	¾	teaspoon mace
4	cups light brown sugar	2	teaspoons salt
1⅓	cups cider vinegar	¾	teaspoon freshly ground
3	cups raisins		black pepper
3	teaspoons cinnamon	½	cup butter.

1. Mix the apples and tomatoes together and drain well. Add the remaining ingredients except the butter. Bring gradually to the boiling point and let simmer three hours, stirring often.

2. Add the butter and mix well. Spoon into hot sterilized canning jars and seal the covers. Process in a boiling water bath twenty minutes. Cool and store in a cool, dark, dry place.

Yield: About five pints.

Venison Mincemeat

MAINE

5	pounds tough cuts venison, very finely cut or diced	2	cups cider, scalded
		1	cup unsulphured molasses
1	tablespoon plus one-quarter teaspoon salt	2	cups honey
		2	cups sugar
¼	teaspoon freshly ground black pepper	1	teaspoon ground cloves
		1	teaspoon cinnamon
4	pounds Northern Spy apples, peeled, cored and chopped	1	teaspoon ground allspice
		½	pound raisins
		1	pint blackberry brandy.

1. Cover the venison with cold water. Add one tablespoon of the salt. Let stand at room temperature two hours. Drain and place in a kettle.

2. Cover with fresh water. Add the remaining salt and the pepper and cook, covered, until the meat is very tender.

3. Add the remaining ingredients except the brandy. Bring to a boil and simmer until the apples are tender. Cool.

4. Add the brandy, reheat almost to the boiling point and pack into

hot sterilized jars. Seal. Process in a pressure canner at ten pounds pressure for forty-five minutes. Cool and store in a cool, dry, dark place for at least one month before using.

Yield: About eight quarts.

Vermont Mincemeat

2 pounds cooked roast beef or venison, ground
4 pounds apples, peeled, cored and ground
1 pound beef suet, ground
2 pounds currants
2 pounds raisins, ground
6 cups light brown sugar or granulated sugar
4 cups cider, vinegar or grape juice

2 teaspoons nutmeg
1 tablespoon ground allspice
1 tablespoon cinnamon
½ teaspoon ground ginger
1 teaspoon ground cloves
1 tablespoon salt
1 pound mixed diced candied fruit peels.

1. Mix all the ingredients in a large heavy kettle. Simmer, stirring, thirty minutes, or until mixture is the correct consistency.

2. Pack into hot sterilized jars and seal the caps. Process in a pressure cooker for one hour at ten pounds pressure. Store in a cool, dark, dry place.

Yield: Six to eight quarts.

Chow Chow Pickles
NEW HAMPSHIRE

2 sweet red peppers, cored, seeded and chopped
2 green peppers, cored, seeded and chopped
4 cups green tomatoes, chopped
1 cup chopped celery
2 large onions, chopped

1 small head cabbage, chopped
½ cup salt
3 cups cider vinegar
1 teaspoon dry mustard
1 pound light brown sugar
1 teaspoon turmeric.

1. Day before, arrange the peppers, tomatoes, celery, onions and cabbage in alternate layers, sprinkling each layer with salt, and let stand at room temperature overnight.

2. Next day, drain well and add the remaining ingredients. Bring to a boil and cook twenty minutes, stirring frequently. Turn into hot sterilized jars. Seal. Process in a boiling water bath fifteen minutes for pints, thirty minutes for quarts. Cool and store in a cool, dark, dry place.

Yield: About five pints.

Hancock Shaker Village India Relish

MASSACHUSETTS

8 pounds very small green tomatoes	2 tablespoons ground ginger
8 cups light brown sugar or maple sugar	3 lemons, very thinly cut
	2 cups citron, shredded
2 cups water	3 cups raisins
3 sticks cinnamon	Peel of one small orange, finely chopped.

1. Wash the tomatoes and cut into quarters.

2. Bring the sugar and water to a boil, stirring until the sugar dissolves, and simmer two to three minutes. Add the tomatoes and remaining ingredients. Simmer, stirring, three hours, or until the lemon slices and citron peel look transparent and the tomatoes are very tender. Pour into hot sterilized containers and seal. Process in a boiling water bath fifteen minutes for pints, thirty minutes for quarts. Cool and store in a cool, dark, dry place. Serve with cold meat.

Yield: About eight to ten pints.

Ruby Relish

NEW HAMPSHIRE

6 cups cooked chopped beets	½ teaspoon freshly ground black pepper
6 cups shredded raw cabbage	
¾ cup freshly grated horseradish	3 cups cider vinegar
3 teaspoons salt	1½ cups sugar.

1. Combine the beets, cabbage, horseradish, salt and pepper. Heat the vinegar, add the sugar and stir to dissolve. Bring to a boil.

2. Add the vegetable mixture and cook twenty minutes. Pour into hot sterilized jars and seal. Process in a boiling water bath fifteen minutes for pints, thirty minutes for quarts. Cool and store in a cool, dark, dry place.

Yield: About five pints.

Uncooked Cranberry Relish
MASSACHUSETTS

4 cups cranberries	2 cups sugar.
2 seedless whole oranges	
Juice of one orange	

Wash the cranberries well and chop them. Chop the oranges and add to the cranberries. Add the orange juice and sugar and mix well. Refrigerate twenty-four hours before serving.

Yield: About four cups.

Fresh Onion and Pepper Relish
MAINE

3 medium-size onions, thinly sliced	Tabasco to taste
1 green pepper, cored, seeded and thinly sliced	3 teaspoons sugar
	Juice of one lemon
1 tomato, peeled and thinly sliced	½ cup wine vinegar
1 cucumber, peeled, seeded and thinly sliced	2 tablespoons oil.

Combine all ingredients and chill until ready to serve.

Yield: Four to six servings.

Chili Sauce
CONNECTICUT

24	large ripe tomatoes, cored		Pinch cayenne pepper
4	large onions	5	cups cider vinegar
4	large green peppers, cored, seeded and chopped	8	tablespoons sugar
		2	tablespoons salt
1	tablespoon ground cloves	1	tablespoon cinnamon.
1	teaspoon ground allspice		

1. Put the tomatoes through the medium-coarse blade of a grinder. Place in a kettle, bring to a boil and simmer briefly. Drain. Return the tomato pulp to the kettle.

2. Put the onions and green peppers through the grinder and add them, along with the remaining ingredients, to the tomatoes. Bring to a boil and simmer one and one-half hours.

3. Put the sauce into sterilized jars and seal. Process in a boiling water bath five minutes for pints, ten minutes for quarts. Cool. Store in a cool, dark, dry place. Serve with pot roast, cold ham or loin of pork.

Yield: Two to two and one-half quarts.

Cranberry Sauce
MASSACHUSETTS

4	cups cranberries	1½	cups sugar.
2	cups water		

1. Place the cranberries in a saucepan and add the water. Cover and cook until berries pop, about ten minutes.

2. Add the sugar and continue cooking fifteen minutes. Mold, if desired, and chill.

Yield: About three cups.

Whole Cranberry Conserve
MASSACHUSETTS

4	cups cranberries	Juice of one lemon
2	cups water	Grated rind of one orange.
2	cups sugar	

265

1. Use a darning needle and run it through each cranberry, piercing the stem end first.

2. Combine the water and sugar and simmer ten minutes to make syrup. Add cranberries, the lemon juice and orange rind and cook over high heat twenty minutes, or until syrup thickens and sheets from spoon in two streams. Pour into hot sterilized jars. Pour two thin layers of melted paraffin over. Cool, cover and store in a cool, dark, dry place.

Yield: Four to five eight-ounce jars.

Apple Chutney
MASSACHUSETTS

40	good-size tart, hard cooking apples, peeled and cored	¼	cup finely chopped garlic
1½	pounds seeded muscat raisins	4	large onions, quartered
		½	cup preserved ginger
1½	pounds currants	6	pounds sugar
¾	pound chopped citron peel	3	quarts cider vinegar
½	cup dried hot chili peppers, crumbled	1	tablespoon nutmeg
		1	tablespoon ground ginger
½	cup chopped fresh ginger-root	1	tablespoon cumin seeds.

1. Put the apples, raisins, currants, citron peel, peppers, gingerroot, garlic, onions and preserved ginger through the fine blade of a meat chopper.

2. Place the sugar and vinegar in a large kettle and bring to a boil.

3. Add the nutmeg, ground ginger, cumin seeds and the ground ingredients. Bring to a boil, stirring, and then cook, stirring frequently, until very thick, about six to eight hours. Pour into hot sterilized jars. Seal. Process in a boiling water bath ten minutes. Cool and store in cool, dark, dry place. Serve with curries, cold meats and poultry.

Yield: About twenty pints.

Bourbon Peaches
CONNECTICUT

9 pounds ripe peaches (about eighty good size)	4 sticks cinnamon, broken
	2 tablespoons whole cloves
9 pounds sugar	2 fifths bourbon.
4 cups water	

1. Scald the peaches, a few at a time, and peel.

2. Dissolve the sugar in the water. Tie the cinnamon sticks and cloves in a muslin bag and add. Bring to a boil. When the syrup is clear, add the peaches, a few at a time, and simmer until barely tender. Do not overcook.

3. Drain the fruit on a platter, returning the excess syrup to pan, and repeat until all the fruit is cooked. Boil the syrup until it is slightly thickened (222 degrees on a candy thermometer). Cool slightly.

4. Stir in the bourbon. Place the fuit as it drains in hot sterilized jars. Cover with bourbon syrup. Seal. Store in cool, dark, dry place.

Yield: Nine to one dozen quarts, depending on size of fruit.

Peach Preserves
CONNECTICUT

1 large lemon or two small lemons, finely chopped	5 cups sugar
	½ teaspoon ground ginger or one-quarter cup chopped crystallized ginger
1 small orange, finely chopped	
7 cups scalded, peeled and chopped firm ripe peaches, with all bruised spots removed	½ cup blanched slivered almonds.

1. Combine the lemons, orange and peaches in a stainless steel or enameled kettle and simmer gently fifteen to twenty minutes, until the orange and lemon skins are tender.

2. Add the sugar and ginger and bring to a boil, stirring until the sugar is dissolved. Boil rapidly until the mixture sheets off a spoon or registers 220 degrees on a candy thermometer. Add the almonds during the last five minutes of cooking.

267

3. Pour into hot sterilized jelly glasses. Pour two thin layers of melted paraffin over or pour into sterilized half-pint canning jars. Adjust caps and process in a boiling water bath ten minutes. Cool. Cover paraffin-topped jars. Store in a cool, dark, dry place.

Yield: About eight and one-half pints.

Apple-Blueberry Conserve
MAINE

4	cups chopped, cored, peeled tart apples (about four medium-size apples)	6	cups sugar
		½	cup raisins
		¼	cup lemon juice
4	cups blueberries, stemmed and washed	½	cup chopped pecans.

1. Combine all the ingredients except the pecans in a large saucepan. Bring to a boil slowly, stirring occasionally until the sugar is dissolved.

2. Cook rapidly until thick, about twenty minutes, stirring frequently to prevent sticking. Add the pecans during the last few minutes of cooking. Pour the boiling hot conserve into hot sterilized half-pint canning jars. Adjust the caps. Process in a boiling water bath ten minutes. Cool and store in a cool, dark, dry place.

Yield: About six half-pint jars.

New England Carrot Marmalade
NEW HAMPSHIRE

4	cups cooked (slightly underdone) carrots	2	oranges, seeded
		6½	cups sugar.
2	lemons, seeded		

1. Coarsely grind the carrots, lemons and oranges, reserving any liquid or juice that comes from them. Place carrots, lemons, oranges and any reserved liquid or juice in a large kettle and bring to a simmer.

2. Add the sugar and stir to dissolve. Cook slowly, stirring occasionally, until mixture is thick.

3. Pour into hot sterilized jelly glasses. Pour two thin layers of melted paraffin over or pour into sterilized half-pint canning jars. Adjust caps

and process in a boiling water bath ten minutes. Cool. Cover paraffin-topped jars. Store in a cool, dark, dry place.

Yield: About six eight-ounce jelly glasses.

Cucumber Marmalade
RHODE ISLAND

1½ pounds cucumbers, peeled and chopped finely or ground (two cups)	⅓ cup lemon juice
4 cups sugar	Green food coloring
2 tablespoons grated lemon rind	½ bottle liquid fruit pectin.

1. Place the cucumber pulp in a large saucepan. Stir in the sugar, lemon rind, lemon juice and a few drops of food coloring and mix well.

2. Place over high heat and bring to a full rolling boil. Boil hard one minute, stirring constantly.

3. Remove from the heat and immediately stir in the pectin. With a metal spoon, skim off the foam. Stir and skim for five minutes to cool slightly and prevent floating cucumber.

4. Ladle into hot sterilized jelly glasses and cover with one-eighth inch of hot paraffin wax or pour into sterilized half-pint canning jars. Adjust caps and process in a boiling water bath fifteen minutes. Cool. Cover paraffin-topped jars. Store in a cool, dark, dry place.

Yield: Six six-ounce jelly glasses.

Lime Marmalade
CONNECTICUT

12 large or eighteen medium-size limes, washed	Sugar

1. Two days before, put the limes through a food chopper. Measure the resulting pulp and add three cups water for each cup pulp. Set aside overnight in a pottery or ceramic bowl.

2. Next day, transfer the mixture to a kettle and bring to a boil. Simmer gently twenty minutes. Let stand overnight again in the bowl.

3. Next day, measure the mixture into a large kettle and add one cup

269

sugar for each cup lime mixture. Bring to a boil, stirring until the sugar dissolves. Boil rapidly, stirring to prevent sticking, until the marmalade sheets from the spoon, a drop chilled on a plate leaves a track when pushed by the finger or the mixture registers 220 degrees on a candy thermometer.

4. Let cool in the kettle about twenty minutes and then ladle into hot sterilized jelly jars. Top with two thin layers of melted paraffin or pour into sterilized half-pint canning jars. Adjust caps and process in a boiling water bath ten minutes. Cool. Cover paraffin-topped jars. Store in a cool, dark, dry place.

Yield: About twenty six-ounce jelly jars.

Quince Marmalade

MASSACHUSETTS

4 to six medium-size quince Grated rind and juice of one orange	1 teaspoon finely chopped yellow part of lemon peel Sugar.
2 apples, peeled, cored and sliced	

1. Wash the quince. Place in a pan and add water to three-quarters cover. Bring to a boil and simmer ten minutes.

2. Remove the quince from the cooking liquid. Peel and core the quince, returning the skin and cores to the cooking liquid. Chop the quince and reserve.

3. Cook the skin and cores slowly thirty minutes. Strain and reserve liquid.

4. Place the chopped quince, grated rind and juice of the orange, apples and lemon peel in a heavy pan. Add reserved liquid until pulp is covered by one-half-inch liquid. Bring to a boil and simmer gently until fruit is very tender. Mash the fruit.

5. Measure the pulp into a pan and add three-quarters cup sugar for each cup of pulp. Heat and stir until the sugar dissolves. Boil rapidly until a set is reached, about ten minutes. (To test for set, put a drop of mixture on a saucer, refrigerate and push the finger into the cooled drop. The finger should leave a clean path when the marmalade is done.)

6. Pour the marmalade into hot sterilized jelly glasses, pour a thin layer of paraffin over or pour into sterilized half-pint canning jars. Adjust caps and process in a boiling water bath ten minutes. Cool. Cover paraffin-topped jars. Store in a cool, dark, dry place.

Yield: About six six-ounce jelly glasses.

Tomato Marmalade

RHODE ISLAND

8 pounds ripe plum tomatoes, approximately	3 lemons
Boiling water	8 sticks cinnamon
3 oranges	1 tablespoon whole cloves
	Sugar.

1. Dip the tomatoes, a few at a time, into a kettle of boiling water. Remove skin, chop the tomatoes roughly and measure four quarts. Let stand while preparing the oranges and lemons.

2. Finely chop the skin and pulp of the oranges and lemons.

3. Place in a large kettle. Add the cinnamon sticks and cloves.

4. Pour off and discard most of the tomato liquid that has accumulated in the tomatoes. Measure the tomatoes and add to the kettle. Add one cup of sugar for each cup of tomatoes.

5. Bring to a boil, stirring until the sugar is dissolved. Boil, stirring to prevent sticking, until the marmalade sheets off the spoon, registers 220 degrees on a candy thermometer or a drop chilled on a plate leaves a track when pushed by a finger.

6. Remove the cinnamon sticks and most of the cloves. Ladle the marmalade into hot sterilized jelly glasses. Top with two thin layers of melted paraffin or pour into sterilized half-pint canning jars. Adjust caps. Process in a boiling water bath ten minutes. Cool. Cover paraffin-topped jars. Store in a cool, dark, dry place.

Yield: About two dozen six-ounce jars.

Beach Plum Jelly

MASSACHUSETTS

1. Gather as many beach plums as convenient. All jellies should be made in relatively small batches, rarely more than three to four quarts at a time.

2. Assemble enough jelly jars, glasses or canning (screw-top) jars and lids to contain the jelly when it is made. Wash in hot soapy water and rinse. Cover with hot, not boiling, water and bring to a boil. No further boiling is necessary.

3. Pick over the beach plums, rinse well and put them into a six-quart to eight-quart kettle. Add water barely to cover. Simmer just until the fruit is soft. Strain the juice through a jelly bag or cheesecloth bag all night or for several hours. Do not squeeze the bag if you want a totally clear jel-

ly. A faster method, however, and one that gives a greater yield, is to squeeze the bag until most of the juice is extracted and then to restrain the juice through another clean, damp jelly bag without squeezing.

4. When ready to cook, measure the juice, bring it to a boil and cook briskly ten minutes. Add one cup of sugar for each cup of juice and stir just until the sugar is dissolved.

5. Let the mixture boil furiously until it reaches the jellying point. There are two methods to determine this. One is to dip a large metal spoon into the boiling syrup. Tilt the spoon so that the syrup drips from the bottom rim. When the syrup is premature, it will run in a stream from the spoon. When the jellying point is reached, the syrup will not flow in a steady stream. Rather, two distinct drops will form and these will run together on the bottom rim.

The other method for determining the jellying point is to spoon a generous drop of the boiling mixture onto a saucer, to let the mixture cool to lukewarm and then with one finger to push the drop. If the jellying point has been reached, a skin will form in front of the finger and the jelly will not flow back easily and cover the finger track.

Thermometers are helpful when cooking jelly, but the jellying test with a spoon should be used in any event. The jellying point of jellies is 220 to 222 degrees F.

6. When the jelly is finished, skim off the foam and pour the hot syrup into the prepared jelly jars, leaving space one-quarter inch from the top. Cover immediately with a one-eighth-inch layer of hot paraffin. Let cool; then cover with metal lids, if desired. If the screw-top jars are used, pour in the hot jelly to one-eighth inch from the top. Adjust caps and process in a boiling water bath ten minutes. Cool. Store in a cool, dark dry place.

The yield for this recipe will depend on the quantities of beach plums, water and sugar used.

Sauces

Pesto Genovese for Spaghetti
CONNECTICUT

1 cup loosely packed basil leaves	2 cloves garlic
½ cup shelled walnuts or pignoli (pine nuts)	¾ cup freshly grated Parmesan cheese
	½ cup olive oil.

1. Place the basil in the container of an electric blender and add the nuts and garlic. Blend, stirring down carefully with a rubber spatula if necessary. When well blended, add the cheese.

2. Gradually add the oil while blending on low speed.

3. Pass the pesto sauce separately with spaghetti or toss with the pasta before serving.

Yield: Four servings.

Tomato Sauce
CONNECTICUT

¼ cup olive oil	1 six-ounce can tomato paste
1 large onion, finely chopped	Salt and freshly ground black pepper to taste
1 clove garlic, finely chopped	
1 two-pound-thirteen-ounce can Italian plum tomatoes or one quart peeled, seeded and chopped fresh tomatoes	1 bay leaf
	1 teaspoon basil
	½ teaspoon thyme
	½ teaspoon oregano.

1. Heat the oil in a large saucepan. Sauté the onion and garlic in the oil until tender but not browned.

2. Add the tomatoes, tomato paste, salt, pepper, bay leaf and basil. Bring to a boil and let simmer twenty minutes.

3. Add the thyme and oregano and let simmer five minutes longer.

Yield: About one quart.

Sandra's Tomato Sauce

CONNECTICUT

½ cup olive oil
1 large onion, finely chopped
2 two-pound-three-ounce cans tomatoes in tomato puree
1 tablespoon sugar

1 teaspoon salt
3 leaves fresh basil or one-half teaspoon dried basil
1 sprig fresh oregano or one-quarter teaspoon dried oregano.

1. Heat the oil in a saucepan and sauté the onion in it until tender. Add the tomatoes and cook, uncovered, one hour or until well blended.

2. Add the remaining ingredients and cook five minutes.

Yield: About two quarts.

Marinara Sauce with Sausage

CONNECTICUT

1 carrot, thinly sliced
1 onion, thinly sliced
¼ cup olive oil
1 clove garlic, finely minced
1 two-pound-three-ounce can tomatoes
1 six-ounce can tomato paste
2 leaves fresh basil
3 whole cloves
½ teaspoon oregano
Salt and freshly ground black pepper to taste

6 Italian sweet or hot sausages
¾ cup dry white wine
6 tablespoons butter
6 fresh mushrooms, thinly sliced
6 dried Italian mushrooms (optional)
Boiling water.

1. Cook the carrot and onion in the oil until lightly browned. Add the garlic, cook briefly and add the tomatoes and tomato paste. Stir and add the basil, cloves, oregano, salt and pepper.

2. Meanwhile, in another skillet, cook the sausages, turning occasionally, until brown all over. Pour off the fat from the pan. Add the wine to the skillet and partly cover. Cook until most of the wine is evaporated. Add the sausages and pan liquid to the tomato sauce. Partly cover and simmer forty-five minutes.

3. Meanwhile, heat two tablespoons of the butter and cook the fresh mushrooms in it briefly. Place the dried mushrooms in a mixing bowl and add boiling water to cover. Let stand ten minutes. Remove the dried mushrooms and slice them. Reserve the soaking liquid.

4. Remove the sausages from the sauce and put through a food mill or sieve. Return the sauce to a boil and add the sausage, fresh mushrooms, sliced dried mushrooms and the soaking liquid. Bring to a boil; then remove from the heat. Immediately stir in the remaining butter. Serve immediately, with spaghetti or polenta.

Yield: Four to six servings.

Blender Hollandaise

CONNECTICUT

3	egg yolks	⅛	teaspoon cayenne pepper
1	teaspoon lemon juice	½	cup butter, melted.
¼	teaspoon salt		

1. Warm the blender container.

2. Place the egg yolks, lemon juice, salt and cayenne in container. Cover. Switch the blender on and off.

3. Turn blender to high speed and add the butter in a steady stream. Keep warm by standing container in hot water.

Yield: About one cup.

Tartar Sauce

MAINE

1½	cups mayonnaise	1	teaspoon chopped chives
2	tablespoons chopped sour pickle	1	teaspoon mustard, preferably Dijon or Düsseldorf
1	teaspoon finely minced onion	½	teaspoon finely chopped tarragon
2	tablespoons finely chopped parsley		Lemon juice to taste
2	tablespoons coarsely chopped capers	1	hard-cooked egg, sieved (optional).

Combine all ingredients and chill.
Yield: About two cups.

Anchovy and Caper Sauce

RHODE ISLAND

3	cloves garlic, finely minced	5	anchovy fillets, finely
¼	cup finely chopped parsley		minced
¼	cup olive oil	2	teaspoons chopped capers
2	tablespoons tomato paste		Freshly ground black pep-
¼	cup water		per to taste.

1. Stirring frequently, cook the garlic and parsley five minutes in the oil over low heat. Do not brown. Add the tomato paste and water and simmer about ten minutes longer.

2. Remove the sauce from the heat and stir in the anchovies, capers and pepper. Serve with grilled pork chops.

Yield: About one cup.

Game Sauce

CONNECTICUT

6	large onions, quartered	1	cup sugar
½	cup butter	1	cup Duff Gordon amontil-
2	juice oranges		lado sherry
1	eight-ounce jar black cur-	1	jigger cassis
	rant jelly	1	jigger cognac or armagnac
1	teaspoon salt		Drippings from roasting
2	navel oranges		game or stock.

1. In a heavy casserole or pan, sauté the onions in the butter until transparent and tender. Squeeze the juice oranges and add the juice to the casserole. Add the jelly and salt. Cook slowly, so that the sugar in the jelly does not burn, until the sauce is brown, partially caramelized.

2. Meanwhile, with a vegetable peeler, peel the navel oranges so that only the orange-colored part is removed. Cut the strips into tiny slivers about one-and-one-half-inches long and one-sixteenth-inch wide.

3. Place in a small pan, cover with water, bring to a boil and boil ten minutes. Drain and discard water.

4. Dissolve the sugar in one-third cup water. Boil in another small

pan until syrup registers 230 degrees on a candy thermometer. Remove from the heat and stir in the drained peel. Let stand at least thirty minutes.

5. Remove the browned sauce from the heat and stir in the sherry, cassis and candied orange slivers. Just before serving, stir in the cognac and drippings.

Yield: About two and one-half cups.

Beverages

Fisherman's Swizzle
MAINE

12	lemons	2	cups peach brandy
36	oranges	3	cups Jamaica rum
2	pounds confectioners' sugar	4	quarts club soda
2	cups cognac		Ice.

1. Squeeze juice from the lemons and oranges into a punch bowl. Add the confectioners' sugar and stir until it dissolves.

2. Add the cognac, peach brandy and rum.

3. Just before serving, add the club soda and ice.

Yield: About two gallons.

Wassail Bowl
MASSACHUSETTS

1	gallon cider	¼	teaspoon salt
½	pound dark brown sugar	2	cups dark rum
1	tablespoon whole allspice	2	lemons, cut into thin slices
1	tablespoon whole cloves		and halved
2	sticks cinnamon	3	oranges, cut into thin slices
2	blades mace		and halved.

1. Place the cider and brown sugar in a large kettle. Tie the allspice, cloves, cinnamon and mace in a muslin bag and add with salt. Bring to a boil and simmer fifteen minutes.

2. Remove spice bag and add the rum, lemons and oranges just before serving. Serve hot.

Yield: About three dozen servings.

278

Hot Buttered Rum
CONNECTICUT

1 teaspoon light brown sugar	1 pinch nutmeg
¼ teaspoon minced lemon rind	1 jigger light rum
	Boiling water
3 pinches cinnamon	Sweet butter.

1. Combine the brown sugar, lemon rind, cinnamon, nutmeg and rum in a warmed ten-ounce glass.

2. Fill with boiling water and drop in a generous teaspoon of sweet butter.

Yield: One serving.

Dandelion Wine
VERMONT

4 quarts boiling water	½ cake compressed yeast or
4 quarts dandelion blossoms, washed	one and one-half teaspoons active dry yeast, dissolved
3 lemons	in two tablespoons luke-
3 oranges	warm water.
3½ pounds sugar	

1. Pour the boiling water over the washed blossoms and bring to a boil. Cool and set aside three days. Strain and discard the blossoms.

2. Cut the thin colored part of the rind from the lemons and oranges (avoid including the bitter white pith) and add to the strained liquid. Bring to a boil and boil fifteen minutes. Add the lemon and orange pulp and the sugar; stir well. Cool.

3. Add the yeast and set the brew in a cool place for a week to ten days. Strain and bottle.

Yield: About five quarts.

Candies

Caramel Popcorn
CONNECTICUT

3 tablespoons corn oil
½ cup yellow hull-less popcorn
½ cup butter
1 cup firmly packed light
   brown sugar

¼ cup light corn syrup
½ teaspoon salt
½ teaspoon vanilla
¼ teaspoon baking soda.

1. Preheat the oven to 250 degrees.

2. Pour the oil into a four-quart to five-quart heavy, deep skillet or kettle. Place over medium-high heat and add a kernel of popcorn. When the kernel pops, remove it and add the one-half cup popcorn. Place the cover on the kettle, leaving a small air space at the edge of the cover. Shake the pot frequently until the popping stops. Remove the pot from the heat.

3. Measure two and one-half quarts of the popcorn (the remainder can be eaten plain) and place in a large roasting pan or metal bowl. Place in the oven and keep warm.

4. Melt the butter in a two-quart saucepan. Stir in the sugar, syrup and salt. Bring the mixture to a boil and boil five minutes. Remove from the heat and stir in the vanilla and baking soda. Pour over the warm popcorn, mixing well to coat each piece.

5. Separate the pieces of popcorn and place one layer only on two large baking sheets. Bake one hour. Cool the popcorn completely (it crisps on standing). Store in an airtight container.

Yield: Two and one-half quarts.

Maple Fudge
VERMONT

2 cups maple syrup
1 tablespoon light corn syrup
¾ cup light cream

1 teaspoon vanilla
¾ cup coarsely chopped walnuts or butternuts.

1. Combine the maple syrup, corn syrup and cream in a heavy saucepan.

2. Place over moderate heat and stir until the mixture begins to boil. Continue boiling, without stirring, until a small amount of the mixture forms a soft ball in cold water (234 degrees on a candy thermometer).

3. Remove the pan from the heat and let cool, without stirring, until lukewarm (110 to 120 degrees). Beat the mixture until it thickens and loses its gloss.

4. Add the vanilla and nuts and pour into a buttered 8-by-8-by-2-inch pan. When cool, cut into squares.

Yield: About twenty-five one-and-one-half-inch squares.

Hard Candies
VERMONT

2 cups sugar	Food colorings
⅔ cup light corn syrup	Skewers or ice cream sticks
1 cup water	for lollipops.
½ teaspoon oil of lemon or	
other concentrated flavor	

1. Place the sugar, syrup and water in a pan. Heat, stirring, until the sugar dissolves. Continue to cook, without stirring, until the syrup reaches 310 degrees on a candy thermometer. Keep the pan clear of crystals by washing down the sides once or twice with a brush dipped into water.

2. Remove from the heat, add the flavoring and coloring and spoon quickly, one teaspoon at a time, onto a greased baking sheet. Immediately place a skewer or stick in position before the candy sets. Alternately, the syrup may be poured into lightly greased tiny muffin cups to give round candies.

3. Remove the lollipops or round candies as soon as they are set. Wrap in clear plastic wrap.

Yield: About two dozen.

Peanut Brittle

VERMONT

3 cups sugar	4 teaspoons baking soda
1 cup light corn syrup	1½ tablespoons butter
½ cup water	1½ teaspoons vanilla.
2 cups raw peanuts	

1. Place the sugar, syrup and water in a heavy saucepan and heat, stirring, until sugar dissolves. Continue cooking without stirring until the mixture registers 240 degrees on a candy thermometer.

2. Add the peanuts and continue boiling, stirring, until the mixture registers 300 degrees on the thermometer, the hard-crack stage.

3. Remove from the heat and stir in the baking soda, butter and vanilla. Pour onto a greased marble surface. Let cool. When cold, break the candy into pieces.

Yield: About two pounds.

Dressings (Stuffings)

Cranberry-Corn Bread Stuffing
MASSACHUSETTS

4	cups cranberries	1	small onion, chopped
1	cup water	½	cup diced green pepper
1½	cups sugar	½	teaspoon thyme
1	pound sausage meat, cooked and crumbled, with drippings	½	teaspoon marjoram
		½	teaspoon sage
9	cups crumbled corn bread (page 172).	1	small unpeeled red apple, cored and chopped
1	cup diced celery	¼	cup lemon juice
		1	cup applesauce.

1. Preheat the oven to 350 degrees.

2. In a saucepan, combine the cranberries, water and sugar. Bring to a boil and simmer ten minutes, or until berries are tender. Drain off juice.

3. Combine drained berries with the remaining ingredients. Turn into a greased casserole and bake one hour. Or use to stuff a fourteen-pound turkey.

Yield: Ten servings.

Oyster Stuffing
MASSACHUSETTS

¼	cup butter or goose fat	1	teaspoon salt
1	onion, finely chopped	½	teaspoon freshly ground black pepper
½	cup chopped celery		
1	goose liver, chopped	1	egg, lightly beaten
6	cups stale one-quarter-inch white bread cubes	½	teaspoon thyme
2	cups oysters with liquor	¼	teaspoon marjoram.
2	tablespoons chopped parsley		

283

1. Melt the butter or fat in a skillet and sauté the onion and celery in it until tender but not browned. Add the liver and cook quickly two to three minutes. Put the bread cubes in a bowl and add the liver mixture.

2. Strain the oyster liquor, through cheesecloth if gritty, into a saucepan. Bring to a boil and add the cleaned oysters. Simmer three minutes, or until the edges just curl.

3. Skim out the oysters and quarter them if they are very large, halve them if they are average. Add to the bread mixture.

4. Add the remaining ingredients and enough oyster liquor, usually about one third cup, to moisten the dressing.

Yield: Enough stuffing for a seven-pound to eight-pound goose or turkey.

Fruit Stuffing
CONNECTICUT

¼ cup butter	2 tablespoons chopped parsley
1 large onion, finely chopped	
½ cup chopped celery	Grated rind of one large lemon
6 cups stale firm one-quarter-inch white bread cubes	
⅓ cup currants	1 teaspoon salt
3 firm tart apples, peeled, cored and diced	½ teaspoon freshly ground black pepper
½ tablespoon chopped fresh sage leaves or one teaspoon dried sage	1 tablespoon lemon juice
	Dry white wine.

1. Melt the butter in a skillet and sauté the onion and celery in it until tender but not browned. Put the bread cubes in a large bowl and add the onion mixture.

2. Add the remaining ingredients, including enough wine just to moisten the stuffing.

Yield: Enough stuffing for a seven-pound goose or a six-pound duck.

Cranberry-Sausage Stuffing
MASSACHUSETTS

1	pound (four cups) cranber-ries	1	cup diced celery
1	cup water	1	small onion, chopped
1½	cups sugar	½	cup diced green pepper
1	pound sausage meat, cooked until brown with drippings reserved	½	teaspoon thyme
		½	teaspoon marjoram
		1	tablespoon chopped parsley
8	to nine cups coarsely crum-bled corn bread (page 172)	1	unpeeled small red apple, cored and chopped.

1. Place the cranberries, water and sugar in a saucepan and cook until the cranberries are tender, about ten minutes. Drain off the excess juice.

2. Combine the drained berries, sausage, drippings and remaining ingredients. Use to stuff turkey or capons. Or place the stuffing in a casserole and bake one hour in a preheated 325-degree oven.

Yield: Enough to stuff a twelve-pound turkey or two five-pound capons; as a casserole, about three quarts.

Potato Stuffing
MAINE

5	medium-size potatoes, boiled without salt	½	cup butter
1	onion, finely chopped		Salt and freshly ground black pepper to taste.
3	ribs celery, finely chopped		

Peel and mash the potatoes and add the remaining ingredients.

Use to stuff a duck or a goose.

Yield: Enough to stuff a four- to six-pound duck, or double recipe for a ten-pound goose.

Dumplings

Dumplings for Soup
MASSACHUSETTS

1 cup sifted flour	1 tablespoon butter
¼ teaspoon salt	6 tablespoons milk, approxi-
2 teaspoons baking powder	mately.

1. Sift together the flour, salt and baking powder into a mixing bowl. With the fingers, work in the butter.

2. Add the milk, little by little, while stirring with a fork. Add just enough milk to make a soft dough. Drop tablespoons of the batter into simmering soup, cover tightly and cook fifteen minutes.

Yield: About sixteen.

Potato Dumplings
MAINE

4 cups cold mashed potatoes	1 egg, lightly beaten
3 cups flour	Boiling salted water.
1 teaspoon salt	

1. Combine the potatoes, flour, salt and egg and mix lightly. Form into a roll, cut off two-inch lengths and make into balls.

2. Drip into rapidly boiling salted water, cover and cook fifteen minutes.

Yield: Fifteen servings.

Index

293

296

299